ICONOGRAPHIES OF OCCUPATION

ICONOGRAPHIES OF OCCUPATION

Visual Cultures in Wang Jingwei's China, 1939–1945

Jeremy E. Taylor

University of Hawaiʻi Press
Honolulu

Printed in the United States of America

26 25 24 23 22 21 6 5 4 3 2 1

Library of Congress Cataloging-in-Publication Data

Names: Taylor, Jeremy E., author.
Title: Iconographies of occupation : visual cultures in Wang Jingwei's China, 1939–1945 / Jeremy E. Taylor.
Other titles: Visual cultures in Wang Jingwei's China, 1939–1945
Description: Honolulu : University of Hawai'i Press, 2021. | Includes bibliographical references and index.
Identifiers: LCCN 2020044525 | ISBN 9780824883324 (cloth) | ISBN 9780824887704 (pdf) | ISBN 9780824887711 (epub) | ISBN 9780824887728 (kindle edition)
Subjects: LCSH: 880-01 Wang, Jingwei, 1883–1944. | Collaborationists—China. | Political culture—China—History—20th century. | China—Politics and government—1937-1945.
Classification: LCC DS777.5195.W34 T39 2021 | DDC 951.04/2—dc23
LC record available at https://lccn.loc.gov/2020044525

ISBN 978-0-8248-8799-5 (paperback)

Cover art: Advertising poster for Taiwanese green tea (circa 1941) featuring Manchukuo, RNG Chinese and Japanese women, and the flags of these three countries. Courtesy of the National Museum of Taiwan History, Tainan (Image ID 2013.038.0003).

University of Hawai'i Press books are printed on acid-free paper and meet the guidelines for permanence and durability of the Council on Library Resources.

For my sons

Contents

Acknowledgments

The idea for this book first emerged out of a number of research initiatives pursued from 2012 onward. It would never have been completed, however, had it not been for the support of the European Research Council (ERC), which in 2016 awarded me a Consolidator Grant. With this grant, I was able to launch the Cultures of Occupation in Twentieth Century Asia (COTCA) project and dedicate much-needed time to this book. Research for this book was thus made possible through the ERC under the European Union's Horizon 2020 research and innovation program (Grant Number 682081).

A number of former teachers, peers, friends, and colleagues read earlier drafts of sections of the book and offered valuable advice. The list includes Craig Reynolds, Grace C. Huang, and Tehyun Ma. I am also indebted to numerous scholars who discussed some of the ideas that inspired the book with me, including (among others) Andrea Germer, Barbara Mittler, Sumathi Ramaswamy, Sophia Lee, Hsiao-ting Lin, Zhiyi Yang, Mire Koikari, David Serfass, Parks Coble, Diana Lary, Lu Fang-shang, Kari Shepherdson-Scott, and Ethan Mark. I also thank the anonymous reviewers for their erudite and constructive suggestions for improvements to the manuscript.

In Nanjing, I thank the staff of the Second Historical Archives and the Nanjing Library, all of whom were extremely helpful during my visits to that city. I also thank Zhang Chengyu at the Nanjing University of Science and Technology for her friendship. Staff at the Shanghai Library were also very helpful. In Taipei, I thank the staff at Academia Historica (especially Wen-Shuo Liao) and the Institute of Modern History, Academia Sinica. In the United States, a number of people at the Hoover Institution (especially Lisa Nguyen and Hsiao-ting Lin) and the Stanford East Asia Library (especially Zhaohui Xue) were extremely helpful and encouraging. Staff at the C. V. Starr East Asian Library, University of California, Berkeley (especially Deborah Rudolph), also provided much-needed assistance, as did staff at the Library of Congress' Asian Reading Room. In the United Kingdom, staff at the British Museum, such as Helen Wang and Alfred Haft, were always very kind in answering queries and allowing me access to collections.

Some sections of this book were presented in seminar form or as conference papers. I thank all those who offered suggestions on such occasions, including panel members (or organizers), discussants, and audience members at the following events: the Department of East Asian Studies seminar at the University of Cambridge in 2014; the "Artful Bodies: Charisma and the Aesthetics of Power" workshop at the Heidelberg Centre for Transcultural Studies in 2015; the European Association of Chinese Studies conference in St. Petersburg in 2016; the Chinese Studies seminar series at the University of Nottingham (Ningbo campus) in 2017; the Department of Chinese Studies at the National University of Singapore in 2017; the Association for Asian Studies Conference in Toronto in 2017; the "Visual Histories of Occupation" workshop at the University of Nottingham in 2017; and the Chinese Studies seminar series at the University of Edinburgh in 2018. In 2019, sections were also presented in seminar form at the University of Sydney, the University of Technology Sydney, and the Australian National University.

Finally, I owe a deep debt of gratitude to my wife and children for their love and loyalty, and especially for their patience during my time abroad in pursuing research for this book—and in writing it. This book would never have been completed without their support.

ICONOGRAPHIES OF OCCUPATION

Introduction

The Second Sino-Japanese War (1937–1945) is one of the most the most widely studied periods in modern Chinese history. Indeed, the seventieth anniversary of the war's end in 2015 heralded a veritable industry of monographs, conferences, and exhibitions dedicated to the memory of this conflict throughout the Chinese-speaking world, and throughout the field of Chinese historical studies. The result of such activity was a newly invigorated interest in the war, a range of new studies written from a wide array of methodological, conceptual, and ideological perspectives, and a reconsideration of the war's far-reaching impact on China and the wider region.[1]

In light of the sheer volume of scholarship that was produced in and around 2015, one could be forgiven for thinking that there is little left to learn about Japan's invasion and subsequent occupation of China. However, 2015 came and went with some aspects of this conflict being left untouched by scholars and officials alike. While, as we shall see, the story of Japanese conquest and Chinese suffering is already well documented, there is still much we do not know about the nature of life, culture, and politics in those areas of China that were formally occupied by Japanese forces, despite the best efforts of a growing body of historians who have been focusing on such questions over the last decade or more. Indeed, on both sides of the Taiwan Strait, this conflict was officially depicted in 2015 as a life-and-death struggle between two diametrically opposed sides: Chinese and Japanese.[2] There seems to have been little historiographical space left for the consideration of those caught in between, such as Chinese who worked in the service of Japanese occupation.

The Second Sino-Japanese War began with the Marco Polo Bridge Incident of July 7, 1937. Japanese forces completed their invasion of much of north China within a matter of weeks. As the Japanese advanced inland, they established "client regimes."[3] These client regimes drew on templates developed earlier in other parts of Japanese-occupied Asia, such as the quasi state of Manchukuo, which had been established in 1932 by the

Kwantung Army (Kantōgun) and existed as a nominally independent "empire," with the Manchu emperor Puyi as its head of the state. In occupied Beijing, a Provisional Government of the Republic of China (Zhonghua minguo linshi zhengfu) (PGROC) was inaugurated in December 1937. This regime would nominally rule over large swathes of the north China plain and many of the major cities of the region until 1940.[4] In east China, a Reformed Government of the Republic of China (Zhonghua minguo weixin zhengfu) (RGROC) was established in 1938 along the same lines.[5] Both of these administrations claimed only limited autonomy from the Japanese, and both were shrill in their condemnation of Chiang Kai-shek's Nationalists, international (and Chinese) communism, and Western colonialism.

Over the course of 1939, however, the longevity of both these regimes would be brought into question. With the defection of the former Republican Chinese premier Wang Jingwei from the wartime Chinese capital of Chongqing in late 1938, and the start of negotiations between Wang and the Japanese government, the notion of some new and much larger client regime began to crystallize. The consequent Reorganized National Government (RNG) of the Republic of China was officially inaugurated on March 30, 1940, with the PGROC and the RGROC both being technically subsumed into this new entity.[6] Despite ongoing tensions between Wang Jingwei and the Japanese (which would last until Wang's death in 1944), the RNG would administer much of east and south China for the remainder of the war. It would claim to administer many of the wealthiest areas of the country and would rule over many millions of Chinese people. Wang's regime would become virtually synonymous with "collaboration" and "treason" in many official, academic, and lay interpretations of the occupation, and Wang himself would become one of the most reviled figures in modern Chinese history.[7]

For decades, the period in which Wang ruled over areas of occupied China has been presented in the starkest of shades. Indeed, despite recent scholarly interventions questioning the very notion of collaboration, there has been little room for subtlety or nuance in many depictions of the occupation or of those Chinese who worked under the Japanese during it. Occupied China has commonly been depicted as a dark and colorless place.[8]

Such depictions are, of course, not unique to China. Referencing Brecht, Hannah Arendt wrote figuratively of occupation as "dark times."[9] And both popular and scholarly writing about Vichy France has long condemned this period as "the dark years" of French history.[10] We can also find regular references to the Japanese occupation of other parts of Asia as a "dark period."[11]

In the case of China, the massacres of civilians throughout the country in 1937 and 1938, to say nothing of the corruption, violence, and poverty that typified daily life for many people living under occupation, have all shaped the ways in which this period is thought about and have produced in China's collective memory a vision of occupation that is universally bleak.[12]

What is noteworthy, however, is the extent to which an obsession with darkness and its opposite—light—permeates the descriptions, not only of those who remember this period as figuratively dark, but equally of those who simply sought to "keep calm and carry on" under occupation. This dichotomy of darkness and light—and calls to turn the narrative of "occupation as darkness" on its head—was everywhere in the self-mythologizing of the RNG, just as it was in the narratives propagated by those who resisted the Japanese invasion. On pamphlets manufactured during the occupation, city gates and pagodas were depicted as emitting golden rays that beckoned a war-weary populace to peace.[13] RNG youth groups organized dawn mobilizations (*liming dongyuan*) so that they might swear allegiance to Wang Jingwei's administration as the first light of day spread over Nanjing. And Chinese cadres who were responsible for Rural Pacification (*qingxiang*)—that is, the purging of resistance in the countryside—were instructed to think of themselves as actual sunshine (the peasantry they ministered to being sunflowers).[14]

None of these examples are raised to suggest that the sun actually *did* shine brighter in Japanese-occupied China. Nor does an attention to RNG propaganda negate the very real sense of darkness that many people undoubtedly felt in wartime. Rather, it suggests that the occupation was and still is imagined or remembered in highly visualized ways—not just by those who suffered under it, but also by those Chinese who chose (for reasons we may never know) to work for client regimes. If we acknowledge that crude propaganda pamphlets presented occupation in an overly colorful or bright fashion, then we must also accept that the attachment of adjectives such as "dark" to scholarly assessments of the occupation are part of a wider discursive practice that dates back to the war itself. Both interpretations deserve to be seriously analyzed, not because one is more accurate than the other, but because both represent constructs that reflect differing but equally "colorized" perspectives on the occupation.

One point of this book is to prompt us to move beyond the recycling of tropes about darkness and light that have been perpetuated since 1937. In order to do this, we must analyze what occupation was made to look like—and how it was represented and imagined—by those who supported, accepted, or simply made do with it.[15] For this to be achieved, we need to separate the moral objections that we hold about the behavior of some agents of client regimes under occupation from our study of the mythologies that these client regimes themselves sought to create. We also need to acknowledge that the occupation was no more of an actual dark time than it was one long, bright summer's day.[16]

This book represents what is perhaps the first attempt to assess the iconographies that were created and developed under Wang Jingwei's RNG. I will explore how this administration sought to present itself to the people over which it ruled at different points between 1939 (when this administration was first being formulated) and August 1945, when it chose to fold itself out of existence. What sorts of visual tropes were used in regime iconography, for example, and *how* were these used? What can the intertextual movement of visual tropes and motifs tell us about how RNG artists and intellectuals (and, indeed, artists and intellectuals who worked under—if not always *for*—the RNG) made sense of the war? How did such groups visually represent Wang Jingwei, the people of China, and China itself?

For Chinese engaged in various forms of visual production, the activities that are frequently labeled "collaborationist" involved complex decisions about how to present oneself to others (including those engaged in overt acts of resistance); how to balance the limitations placed on one by a belligerent occupant with a personal desire for self-expression; and even what sorts of cultural production were appropriate in the context of a wartime regime that sought to project itself as patriotic, despite its alliance with a foreign invader. To be sure, some cultural workers, including even those who became most active in the creation or distribution of occupation iconographies, may well have worked for the RNG against their will. Others may have done so out of a genuine sense of loyalty to Wang Jingwei or the ideas he espoused. The central point, however, is not *why* hundreds of Chinese individuals continued to draw, paint, and take photographs in the period between 1939 and 1945. Rather, it is *what* drawings, paintings, and photographs they produced and distributed. There is no doubting that the RNG existed at the whim of a belligerent occupant and that the iconographies that evolved under it reflected Japanese, as well as Chinese, aims. Nonetheless, the visual and archival record shows us that even the most loyal of Chinese cadres or artists could express themselves in ways that were at odds with both the Japanese military *and* the resistance. By considering the visual realm, then, we can bring questions about the autonomy (or otherwise) of this regime into far clearer focus.

"Collaboration" and Its Histories

The patriotism that had been demanded of the Chinese people by Chiang Kai-shek's Nationalists, the Chinese Communist Party (CCP), and other resistance groups in response to the Japanese invasion of 1937 meant that all Chinese were expected to be *seen* to resist. As a rich body of scholarship on cultural expression produced in the name of resistance has demonstrated, it was through image rather than word that this message was often spread.[17] Contrarily, public expression of support for (or acceptance of) the occupation—or merely for peace—would result not simply in an individual's name being sullied but also in rhetorical and visual attacks on those assumed to be "traitors to the Chinese race" (*hanjian*). This might occur through the performance of "living newspaper" plays (*huobaoju*), in which actors were dressed as traitors and publicly vilified by audiences.[18] Alternatively, the likenesses of traitors might be reproduced as statues upon which patriots could ritually spit.[19] Resistance manuals even instructed artists on how best to draw *hanjian* so as to discourage others from collaborating.[20]

The visual realm was never a monopoly of the resistance, however. Visual expression mattered to all of the client regimes, but especially to the RNG, for a number of key reasons. First, the production of propaganda, culture, and political ritual would remain one area in which Wang Jingwei's administration was allowed some measure of autonomy. In the production of visual propaganda, it relied mainly—though by no means exclusively—on Chinese intellectuals and artists, some of whom had followed Wang for many years prior to the war or who had worked for pre-1939 client regimes such as the PGROC, the RGROC, or Manchukuo. It was the task of these individuals (who will be examined in chapter 2) to craft a set of visual icons, and to recycle older ones, in support of the RNG cause. It was also the task of such individuals—by allowing the continuation of a quasi-independent commercial media and print culture—to convince the people of occupied China that life was better under Wang Jingwei.

Public spectacle also took on an inflated importance under occupation precisely because, as one observant American of the day sarcastically noted, "the government [of Wang Jingwei] has nothing to do."[21] Lacking in financial capital (Wang's government relied heavily on Japanese loans) and political capital (legitimacy always being in question), the RNG fell back upon symbolic capital as its main currency. The celebration of national holidays, official visits to *lieux de mémoires,* and all the blazonry of patriotism that we associate with modern nation-states certainly mattered to

Chiang Kai-shek's regime, both before and after its relocation to Chongqing at the end of 1938. All of this mattered far more to the RNG, however, because Wang's administration had so little else it could lay claim to. The energy that might otherwise have been directed to the prosecution of military campaigns, for example, was diverted to march-pasts (*yuebing*) and mass rallies.

Finally, we need to take into account the roles of individual leaders within the upper echelons of the RNG. While many of Gerald Bunker's observations of the Wang Jingwei regime (written over four decades ago) have been qualified by more recent findings, Bunker's belief that "Wang, a brilliant ceremonialist, had always put a lot of faith in ceremonies and trappings" still seems entirely plausible when we examine the visual record of the RNG today.[22] Wang was himself a seasoned propagandist, and he appears to have welcomed the ceremonial role that occupation thrust upon him. The creation of a pervasive Wang Jingwei personality cult during the war years (examined at length in chapter 3), was one of the primary tasks undertaken by the RNG propaganda apparatus from 1939 until Wang's death in 1944.

Despite all this, RNG propaganda, to say nothing of non-regime-affiliated visual cultures developed in the RNG realm, has not been granted a prominent position in the now extensive academic literature on Sino-Japanese "collaboration." Barak Kushner's suggestion that the RNG should "be considered a fourth propaganda center" during the war (alongside the Imperial Japanese Army, the Nationalists in Chongqing, and the communists in the northwest) has not yet been taken up in any scholarship on this regime, and little has been done to explore just how this "often neglected player in the propaganda war" attempted to win Chinese "hearts and minds."[23]

In China today, and despite the "new remembering" of the war that has seen remarkably nuanced interpretations of the period start to emerge,[24] collaboration remains either a taboo topic or else one that merits only limited serious analysis. Such an approach is perhaps best summed up in the title of a seminal monograph on the topic by the late historian Cai Dejin—*Freak of History* (*Lishi de guaitai*)—which posited that the RNG represented an aberration in the teleological narrative of Chinese political history and the march toward 1949.[25] Such an approach influenced later scholarship, such as Zhang Xianwen's multivolume and oft-cited study of Republican China, which detailed the enslaving education (*nuhua jiaoyu*) system enforced by pro-Japanese surrenderors (*qin-Ri toudi fenzi*) and which acknowledged resistance as the only development of note to arise out of this chapter of the recent past.[26] A similar approach is adopted in studies of cultural expression in occupied China, which assumes that the only activities of significance were clandestine expressions of resistance.[27] As Wang Ke-wen notes, many of these studies were informed by a desire to pass judgment on Wang Jingwei's actions, rather than to consider this regime in the context of its time.[28]

Nonetheless, a new generation of scholars is starting to challenge such interpretations. Liu Jie, for example, suggests that recent PRC scholarship is now granting the RNG far greater agency and is beginning to reconceptualize the RNG in terms of its place on a continuum of "cooperation and conflict."[29] The extensive work of historians such as Huang Meizhen and Pan Min is also evidence of a move away from condemnation and toward a more detached study of the RNG that seeks to understand the institutional framework of this regime in light of its Republican heritage.[30]

In other instances, however, scholars have chosen to couch their studies of client regimes like the RNG in highly empirical detail. Indeed, an entire genre of edited collections of archival documents about the RNG developed in the 1980s.[31] Within this genre sits one of the few collections that have made use of the RNG's own visual output—that is, the two-volume set of occupation-era photographs published by the Second Historical Archives (Zhongguo di'er lishi dang'anguan).[32] There has also been a tendency toward biographical studies of Wang and those around him that seeks to find the roots of wartime collaboration in prewar political or personal careers.[33]

As a result, there remains a good deal we are yet to understand about the RNG. As Yingying Gao notes of the field as a whole:

> A large portion of these [scholarly] achievements remain on the level of uncovering and criticism, and conclusions usually still try to prove the aggression of the Japanese and puppet governments while lacking in-depth analysis. Reasons for this include the lack of problem awareness in our research process, the scarcity of holistic and theoretical frameworks of interpretation, and the diversity of research methods. Some scholars are aware of this and are trying new approaches. But so far, we have not seen any fully developed results of these efforts.[34]

If PRC-published studies lack "theoretical frameworks of interpretation," the same cannot be said of some of the research emerging outside China in recent years. Building on questions about the "impossible dilemma of wartime collaboration" that were first asked by John Hunter Boyle in the

1970s,[35] scholars such as Timothy Brook have done much to deconstruct the very notion of collaboration.[36] Taking as his focus the often unremarkable local elites who first engaged with the Japanese, Brook has been central in granting agency to those once denounced as collaborators, reminding us that the creation of client regimes was "a process of negotiation, misrepresentation, and subterfuge in which Chinese were involved as more than passive puppets."[37] As I hope this book will demonstrate, this went as much for those involved in the iconographies produced in client regimes as it did for the local elites who are Brook's quarry.

A central element in much of this "revisionist" scholarship has been the concept of "collaborationist nationalism." This is defined by Brook as "a historically specific form of late colonial ideology that is always bound to declare independence under a condition of dependence."[38] Based, in many cases, on testimonies provided by convicted "traitors" after the end of the war, this scholarship has demonstrated how the RNG might be defined as a patriotic Chinese regime, even while it accepted the reality of Japanese rule in China. It also suggests that the RNG maintained a fundamentally different position from Chiang Kai-shek's Nationalists in terms of its interpretation of the "nation" in wartime. Dongyoun Hwang, for example, has argued that RNG collaborationist nationalism placed far greater emphasis on the people (*min*) than on state institutions, overtly rejecting Chiang Kai-shek's approach of trading space for time when responding to Japanese imperialism.[39] Similarly, Margherita Zanasi suggests that Wang Jingwei's wartime nationalism was more concerned with the preservation of "national vitality" and the protection of China's eastern heartlands than with the survival of the Republican Chinese state per se.[40] The concept of collaborationist nationalism remains an important part of the burgeoning literature on the RNG, and we shall revisit it at different points throughout this book.

Such work has been crucially important in justifying the entire study of collaboration. It has also provided a much-needed counterweight to the emotional scholarship that still pervades so much of the historiography in China. However, it has also tended to limit the story to one of sociopolitical machinations in the lead-up to the moment of collaboration or to one of the motivations of collaborators themselves. Historians have expressed an interest in the consequences of the decisions that many Chinese made in the late 1930s, for instance, but it is how people arrived at such decisions that remains the primary interest in a good deal of recent work. In contrast, cultural life under occupation *after* 1940 still tends to be marginalized.[41] Such an approach is exemplified in Rana Mitter's recent study of the war, in which the story of the RNG is more about the process leading to this administration's creation over the course of 1939 and early 1940, and in which the regime itself is described as having been viewed by those who worked within it as a "historical dead end."[42]

This is not to suggest that no significant studies of cultural developments in occupied China have been undertaken. On the contrary, some of the most innovative work on occupied China is that based on specific fields of cultural production. Poshek Fu has done much to shed light on the role of "cultural collaborators" (*wenhua hanjian*) in fields such as literature and filmmaking in occupied Shanghai, for instance, examining how those employed in the creative industries adopted a range of strategies either for dealing with the Japanese or for reverting to various forms of nationalism or nostalgia to cope with the realities of occupation.[43] Zhiyi Yang has analyzed the poetry that Wang Jingwei himself produced during his time as head of the RNG and has shown how literature could be deployed to sustain a powerful public persona for Wang among the educated classes.[44] Studies like these have helped overcome a tendency to view the occupation as a time—in Nicole Huang's words—"conventionally characterized by themes of chaos, instability, insecurity, destruction, and transience."[45]

Such scholarship builds on an earlier generation of research that first explored the literary and dramatic arts of occupation and was best represented in a seminal and still highly influential monograph by Edward Gunn Jr.—*Unwelcome Muse*. Gunn was one of the first scholars to highlight the growth of entire fields of cultural endeavor under occupation, as well as the sheer diversity of literary styles produced in this context. His argument that "the experience of occupation resulted in particularly important literary achievements" remains a contentious yet convincing one.[46] And his suggestion that we study cultural production in the occupied zones with an eye on the social and cultural practices encouraged in areas beyond Japanese or RNG control has influenced more recent interventions.[47]

Nonetheless, despite the contributions made by Gunn and others, there have been fewer attempts to look in detail at the visual cultures or iconographies produced under occupation. Many scholars *have* used images of Wang Jingwei drawn from Japanese and Chinese media sources to illustrate their narratives.[48] With the notable exceptions of Nicole Huang, Andrew Cheung, and Shaoqian Zhang, however, few scholars have sought to rigorously analyze such images, and even fewer have considered why such images exist in the first place.[49]

This is all the more surprising given the significant visual archive that the RNG left to posterity. Thanks partly to the race for intelligence-worthy materials among the Allies following 1945, occupation-era propaganda and cultural products can be found in a number of institutions all over the world. Much of the material that I have drawn on for this book can be accessed in archives and libraries in the United States, Japan, the United Kingdom, and Taiwan—as well as, of course, the PRC. With the recent (and partial) reopening of the Second Historical Archives in Nanjing, and with the availability of photographic collections of direct relevance to the RNG in libraries and institutions elsewhere, scholars have been able to achieve a far clearer view of cultural production under occupation, as well as the role of various arms of Wang's administration in encouraging, sponsoring, censoring, or tolerating different types of visual expression.

In considering how the RNG attempted to assemble and distribute an ever-changing set of visual icons to fit its needs at any given time, I will be focusing on print culture, graphic art, photography, cinema, painting, public art, and pictorial ephemera produced in occupied China itself. I will also be considering the performative aspects of RNG political culture, ranging from the dramatic arts to political spectacle. In doing this, I am not discounting Carolyn FitzGerald's entirely valid point that ideas, people, and images moved across the porous borders between different regions of China in wartime.[50] Nor am I belittling the various forms of expression undertaken by individuals or groups who chose to resist the Japanese. I fully acknowledge that anti-Japanese graffiti was scrawled across walls in occupied Nanjing,[51] just as Nanjing's city walls were occupied by sprawling messages of support for the Japanese. Nonetheless, only by putting occupation visual culture and iconography at the center of analysis—by resisting the temptation to retell the story of the war, yet again, through the lens of overtly resistance-inspired culture in the communist base areas or the "great hinterland" (*da houfang*)[52]—will we be able to properly grasp how various groups within the RNG saw themselves and the land over which they claimed dominion. By combining such analysis with a survey of the archival records left by this regime, we will be able to obtain a clearer sense of the shifting ideologies, imaginaries, and contradictions that typified the RNG until its disappearance in 1945.

Visual History

In observing the shift toward both the increasing use of visual sources and the attention given to the "visuality of history and the historicity of the visual," the German theorist Gerhard Paul has spoken of an approach that he calls "visual history." For Paul, visual history is not necessarily a new discipline. It is, rather, an overarching sensitivity to the need to take "the visual" seriously when studying the past. It is also "transdisciplinary" in its perspective and is open to the use of methods developed in fields such as "art history, media and communication science."[53] Indeed, Paul's approach is clearly influenced by the theoretical advances of the art historian Horst Bredekamp, who, through his notion of *Bildwissenschaft* (science of the image), has stressed the need for historians to consider not just how images are created but also how images themselves have the power to shape events.[54]

Modern Chinese history has been slow to respond to the "visual turn" of which Paul has written. Nevertheless, in recent years an increasing awareness of the need to put visual texts at the center of historical analysis has become more apparent. Chang-tai Hung's work on the popular culture of wartime resistance and Henrietta Harrison's study of the iconography of early Republican China have both set a high standard for the use of visual sources, for example.[55] Since the publication of these monographs, an increasing number of scholars have started to "engage in critical analysis of *image-making* as a force in shaping historical dynamics" in China.[56] Historians of China are now accepting that, as Sumathi Ramaswamy puts it, "pictures, too, have stories to tell and arguments to manifest" and that "images are not just illustrative and reflective but also constitutive and world-making rather than world-mirroring."[57] As a result, there are now more frequent attempts by historians of China "to probe further into the relationship between the visual, the spoken, and the textual."[58] Such an approach has started to complement, if not necessarily challenge, the "archive-based empiricism" that has been a hallmark of the field for some years now.[59]

We can see the fruits of such an approach in a lively body of scholarship on Mao-era political culture, encompassing everything from performative arts in Yan'an to public expressions of fealty for Mao in the mid-1960s. Such work is helping to fundamentally challenge long-held views derived from scholarship that once shunned visual sources. Commendable examples include the work of Chang-tai Hung on the political culture of the early PRC and that of Barbara Mittler on the Cultural Revolution, both of which have fundamentally altered the study of these respective periods by adopting something closer to a "visual history" approach.[60]

However, Japanese-occupied east and south China have rarely been approached in such a manner. Indeed, occupied China has often been conspicuously absent from many edited collections that engage directly with Chinese visual cultures more generally,[61] while some studies of cultural expression in wartime China simply dismiss visual forms of expression produced under RNG sponsorship as irrelevant.[62] When such studies have been attempted, the results have usually focused on Japan's "colonial gaze" in China—that is, the visual relationship through which Japanese occupiers created a Chinese "Other" under occupation, while simultaneously rendering entire areas, people, and events in China invisible.[63]

This silence may reflect a long-held reluctance—first expressed by Western sympathizers with the Chinese resistance in the 1930s and 1940s[64]—to acknowledge the validity of the RNG or to merit any cultural production that occurred under it. In any case, it makes wartime China unusual, for certain approaches that Paul considers central to visual history, such as the consideration of visual cultures that develop under occupation, have been important threads in the study of occupation in many other contexts. Some of the most important contributions to the study of visual culture as a field have, in fact, emerged from the study of foreign occupation, while it has been visual culture theorists who have been most persuasive in stressing the links between foreign occupation and what John Berger once called "ways of seeing."[65]

Take the American invasion of Iraq in 2003 and the subsequent occupation of that country, for example. Theorists such as Nicholas Mirzoeff have suggested that this conflict marked a fundamental turning point in the realm of visuality at multiple levels, with entirely new theoretical notions that are now prevalent in the field of visual cultures—"image weapons," for instance—being developed through the study of this conflict.[66] This ranged from the extensive use of the American news media for the circulation and control of images pertaining to US military might, to the controversy surrounding the images of Iraqi prisoners produced by American military personnel in Abu Ghraib prison, which emerged in 2004 (and which subsequently generated an entire subfield of critical inquiry in their own right).[67] For Mirzoeff, the concealment and eventual release of these images laid bare the inherent visuality of occupation, empire, and war in the twenty-first century.[68] Yet such theoretical advances have prompted historians to revisit historical cases of occupation and consider such cases anew from the perspective of their visuality.[69]

Since the invasion of Iraq, other theorists have considered the links between occupation and visual history in new and stimulating ways, often by turning their attention to the longest "occupation" in modern history. In *Visual Occupations,* for instance, Gil Hochberg demonstrates how we can usefully explore the "making of the [Israel / Palestine] conflict . . . by focusing on the distribution of the visual." Noting that occupation, by its very nature, leads to acts of concealment, as well as the proscription of certain "ways of seeing," Hochberg suggests that new questions need to be asked about occupation itself by starting with the visual. These include "what or who can be seen, what or who remains visible, who can see and whose vision is compromised" in the occupation context.[70] Such questions build on Mirzoeff's argument that "visuality is a specific technique of colonial and imperial practice . . . by which power visualizes History to itself."[71] Yet they also demonstrate how a focus on visuality can help us understand more broadly the power relations that develop under occupation.

Japanese-occupied China is not directly comparable with the twenty-first-century Middle East. Nonetheless, the notion that study of the visuality engendered through occupation in the West Bank or Iraq can help us better understand wartime China is well worth contemplating. If we apply some of Hochberg's questions to Wang Jingwei's Nanjing, for example, then the vast range of visual representations of China that were produced in that context (coupled with the concealment of many other types of representation) begin to take on new complexities.

When it comes to the scholarship on the Second Sino-Japanese War, however, the question of "what or who can be seen" takes on an additional meaning. Successive Chinese governments have long sought to obfuscate, dismiss, or render invisible the visual cultures that were sustained by Chinese living under occupation and by the organs of the RNG state. In studying wartime China, therefore, we need to be aware of not just the ways of seeing that were proscribed by a foreign power and its local clients but also the politically motivated attempts since 1945 to render the legacy of those client regimes unseeable.

For methodological frameworks that might help overcome such enforced invisibility, I have looked to the academic literature on Vichy France. In the research on the Pétain personality cult, the "poster war" in occupied Paris, and the use of the landscape in Vichy political culture, we find examples of how a close analysis of visual texts can shed light on the nature of a cognate regime that, like the RNG, existed at the whim of a foreign occupier.[72] Most importantly, the Vichy historiography reminds us that, under foreign occupation, there is more than just a "colonial gaze"/"resistance visual culture" dichotomy to consider. Client regimes like Vichy and the RNG inhabited a unique cultural space in which the occupied tried to carve out distinct visualities. To be sure, such visualities were always conditioned by the demands of the occupier. Nonetheless, they were equally reactive to resistance rhetoric, as well as to the exigencies of war (in which the vanquished had very little say). As Laurence Bertrand Dorléac argues, for example, many artists who were feted under Vichy sought to "run with the hare and hunt with the hounds, to support both France and Germany, national pride and Nazi pretensions."[73] At the same time, the work of these same artists might include coded messages of resistance, for even the use of particular color schemes under Vichy "could easily be understood as a declaration of war against the foreign presence."[74]

The literature on Vichy also demonstrates how the context of occupation not only gives rise to new icons and archetypes but also endows existing visual symbols, tropes, and images with entirely new significance. The extensive work on the reinvention by Vichy of existing French icons such as Joan of Arc, for example, has done much to explain the processes by which old symbols can be recycled and re-signified in the extraordinary context of occupation.[75] Similarly, gender historians have shown how client regimes like Vichy can give rise to new visual archetypes that long outlive the regimes from which they arose.[76] I will return to such scholarship at various points throughout this book.

Iconographies of Occupation

As such examples suggest, historians of Vichy have usefully applied an approach that is sometimes referred to as "iconology" or "iconography."[77] Owing much to the pioneering work of Aby Warburg, whose initial research was undertaken in response to the explosion of visual media experienced in Europe during World War I,[78] iconography is an approach that enables scholars to investigate how "images of widely different materiality and shape have an impact on individuals and social groups."[79] While some scholars have limited their studies of iconography to particular forms of visual media,[80] most have tended to cast a wide net in an attempt to capture a more holistic sense of a particular regime, period, or moment. Indeed, when Warburg first developed his approach, he stressed the need to give equal weight to high art and mass-produced propaganda when coming to terms with the wider visuality of wartime Europe.[81] The approach that Warburg developed, however, "is not content with the deciphering of motifs or the description of their migration" across these different forms of media. Rather, it "analyses the intention and reception of pictures, buildings, symbols, or ceremonies, and displays the visual signs of invisible conceptions like justice, democracy, or virtue."[82]

Scholars most closely associated with this approach, such as Martin Warnke, have shown how "political iconographies" are not limited even to visual media but can also include the natural and built environments. In *Political Landscape,* for example, Warnke traces not just the ways in which representations of landscape can be made to serve a multitude of political ends but also how human intervention in the physical landscape can interact with such depictions to form part of wider iconographies.[83] Others have looked at specific moments and explored the various visual media that were created around these, seeking to analyze how modes of representation reflected the aims of these images' creators and how these, in turn, altered interpretation of historical events. Thus, while the study of iconographies involves tracing the trajectory of particular images across a range of media (and in the physical world) and across time—the writing of "cultural biographies" of specific images, for example[84]—it also seeks to understand how these images work together in a wider scheme unique to their historical context. In other words, "iconography is not to be interpreted as a chain of motifs but as a field of energy that extends beyond the simple format of the image."[85]

In adopting such an approach in this book, my aim is therefore not simply to document images created or re-signified under Wang Jingwei's regime. Instead, I am hoping to provide a broader understanding of how various groups within the RNG sought to reimagine and visualize occupied China. Part of this endeavor involves the analysis of how institutions and individuals working under the RNG responded in visual ways both to the "compromised sovereignty" that they experienced[86] and to the visual attacks—"image weapons," to reference Mirzoeff—that were launched against them by other Chinese. More importantly, however, it seeks to gain a clearer understanding of how cultural workers under the RNG visualized China itself in the light of occupation. My aim, in other words, is to better understand the "fields of energy" that linked together the visual images created or recycled by the agents of this regime.

At the same time, I am conscious of the important lessons that can be learned from the field of visual culture and its emphasis on ways of seeing under occupation. For this reason, I will also be considering how the iconographies of occupation operated within particular modes of visuality—and in the context of a set of visual cultures that developed in a state of compromised sovereignty. Such visual cultures were shaped by both Japanese and RNG control of the means to represent wartime China. However, they were also shaped by what I shall refer to throughout this book as the "occupied gaze"—that is, a "way of seeing" adopted by the RNG state that set it apart from Japanese agents (including military bodies, government institutions, and news agencies) and from the Chinese resistance.[87] To be sure, this occupied gaze existed at the whim of the Japanese military. Yet it also adopted recognizably Republican Chinese modes of visuality that could align with expressions of Chinese nationalism without directly contradicting imperial Japanese ideologies (e.g., Pan-Asianism). At the same time, it attempted to view China in ways that would not attract overt censorship from the Japanese or Chinese ire about supposed RNG treason.

To be sure, the realm of the visual was always contested in occupied China, even when it came to actors who were supposedly on the same side. The occupied gaze existed even while the occupied Chinese were themselves gazed upon by Japanese occupiers. For instance, the RNG put great store in ensuring that its leaders were *seen* to visit the Sun Yat-sen Mausoleum (Zhongshan ling)—the most symbolically important architectural site in China's capital during the war—and that pictorial representations of that site were appropriately solemn. Yet contemporary accounts suggest that most visitors to this site were in fact Japanese and that it was standard practice for such visitors to instruct Chinese armed guards at the mausoleum's entrance to stand in just such a way as to make for pleasing holiday snapshots.[88] Even the most hallowed of RNG icons, in other words, could be visually trivialized by Japanese tourists.

Nevertheless, by considering the RNG's visualization of China, we can start to discern things about this regime that earlier studies have overlooked. For example, by looking at what RNG cultural workers drew, photographed, or painted under occupation—rather than what RNG leaders *said* during or after the war—we can test some of the paradigms that have shaped discussion of this regime in recent years. Do the iconographies adopted by this regime support or disrupt the now widely accepted notion of collaborationist nationalism, for example? And how does the much older (but still common) accusation that the RNG was little more than a puppet of the Japanese empire stand up to scrutiny when the visual record is analyzed? If we accept Hochberg's suggestion that the contestation of the visual realm lies at the very heart of occupation as a politico-cultural milieu, then we can come to terms with the RNG itself only by considering it from a "visual history" perspective.

A focus on the iconographies of occupation might also highlight just how much this regime had in common with those Chinese entities against which it defined itself. The written rhetoric of this regime, with its focus on Pan-Asianism, may seems at odds with the "salvationist" language adopted by the resistance. As I hope to show, however, the visual record complicates this distinction. If anything, it suggests that this supposed "freak of history" shared the visual space with those regimes that it apparently opposed. An analysis of how these very different visions of China interacted with each other can thus provide a more comprehensive picture of China's broader wartime experience. There is no denying that occupation led to all manner of visual concealment in what would become the RNG realm, not least because the RNG capital had also been the site of some of the worst atrocities of the war in December 1937. Yet, cultural workers demonstrated remarkable ingenuity in carving out a decidedly *Chinese* visual space within the strict parameters placed upon them by a belligerent occupant.

Of course there is a good deal that this approach, when applied to the RNG, does *not* tell us. This is especially so when it comes to reception. A significant body of memoir literature has been produced over the decades since 1945 on both sides of the Taiwan Strait. Some of this work provides insights into the manner in which residents of wartime China responded to iconographies of occupation, though much of it is shaped by retrospection. For this reason, while I have used some such accounts at different points throughout this book, I have sought to do so critically. I have also made use of examples in the secondary literature that have been based on oral histories or diary entries of the war in appropriate sections.

Such sources are scant, however. This scarcity exists because few Chinese institutions have, until recently, shown any inclination in allowing, let alone preserving, contemporary accounts of public reactions to RNG propaganda that do not correspond to official condemnation of Wang Jingwei or to the narrative of mass Chinese revulsion against the RNG. Nonetheless, where possible, I have in this book included references to even the most fleeting accounts of public responses to the iconographies of occupation where these exist. These include reports of everything from iconoclasm to official anxiety about public indifference.[89] While such accounts are only partial, they are perhaps the best sources we have for understanding what this regime expected of its people in terms of reception.

I have structured this book thematically. After considering how we might best define the RNG in chapter 1, I lay out in chapter 2 the cultural, artistic, and political context in which iconographies of occupation were developed. Thereafter, I will examine how specific themes and tropes emerged in visual cultures developed under the RNG. When looking at depictions of Wang Jingwei himself in chapter 3, for instance, we will see how this regime struggled to maintain a coherent vision of its leader right through until the moment when Wang was rendered "invisible" in 1944. In chapter 4, we will see how competing archetypes of Chinese womanhood and manhood reflected wider debates within the regime about how Chinese people should behave, and be *seen* to behave, under occupation. And in chapter 5, I trace how sections of the RNG state (and non-state agents operating within its jurisdiction) imagined—or, indeed, obscured—the land of China itself. This was perhaps one of the most contentious fields of iconography for a regime that was always sensitive to its lack of territorial integrity.

If there is one element that brings all these themes together, it is a lack of coherence when it came to visual cultures across the life of the RNG—hence my use of the plural word "iconographies" in this book's title. Different representations of Wang Jingwei, of Chinese men and women, and of China itself reflected two overarching truisms about this regime. The first was the existence of a diverse range of Chinese cultural actors who were active under occupation and who had quite different perspectives on a range of issues relating to the war. Such different perspectives influenced what they chose to render in images and how they did so.

The second was the changing circumstances of the war itself. This resulted in a constantly evolving relationship between Wang Jingwei's administration and its Japanese protectors, between the RNG and those areas of China beyond Japanese control, and (though this is often overlooked) Nanjing's relationship with other parts of the "Axis world." The RNG was hostage to Japanese military fortunes, and its changing place within a world at war was reflected in a rapidly shifting set of icons across a period of little more than four years. A visual history of this regime thus brings into sharp relief the fragmentation and tensions that lay at its very heart.

Just as a greater focus on visuality has helped unsettle received understandings of other periods of the Chinese past (e.g., the Cultural Revolution), it is my hope that this focus on the iconographies of occupation will contribute to a better understanding of wartime China more generally. Such an endeavor is important not simply because it fills a large gap in our understanding of the Second Sino-Japanese War. By bringing the RNG back into wider conversations about political culture, visual culture, and iconography in modern China—from the study of Chinese personality cults to the emergence of the "modern girl"—we will have a better ability to understand developments since 1945 more broadly. And by bringing China itself into discussions about the visuality of occupation, we can test the utility of ideas and approaches that have rarely been deployed in the Chinese context before.

CHAPTER 1

Contextualizing the Wang Jingwei Regime

Some of the existing scholarship on Wang Jingwei's wartime government that was touched upon in the introduction is useful for considering the very nature of the RNG at various points in this regime's short life. Rather than revisiting the internal intrigues of this regime or assess its political economy—topics that have been thoroughly addressed before[1]—this chapter demonstrates how individuals and institutions within the RNG sought to define and justify their administration in the context of occupation. How sections of the RNG presented their regime in the broader sweep of the modern Chinese Republic, and what they hoped China might become, are also considered. The broader picture that results will allow us to contextualize, in later chapters, the eclectic iconographies that developed in Wang Jingwei's China. Indeed, without a sense of what the RNG was, we cannot properly appreciate the messages that various arms of this administration (and its non-state allies) sought to visualize.

The RNG's "Return"

The RNG has always been inextricably linked to the figure of Wang Jingwei—the former premier of Nationalist China who led this wartime regime from March 1940 until his death in November 1944. Wang's regime was presaged, however, by a more nebulous campaign that both overlapped and diverged from it—the Peace Movement (*heping yundong*). This movement included members of the Chinese Nationalist Party, or Kuomintang (KMT), who had chosen to split with Chiang Kai-shek (following the fall of Wuhan in October 1938 and Chiang's subsequent flight westward to Chongqing) and lobby for a cessation of hostilities with the Japanese.[2] The Peace Movement included within its ranks some of the same individuals who had displayed political loyalty to Wang in earlier years. Most would come to take up important posts in Wang's wartime administration. These included former communists and staunch critics of Chiang Kai-shek such as Chen Gongbo (who would serve as mayor of Shanghai under the RNG), Zhou Fohai (who would emerge as one of the main negotiators with the Japanese and would later serve as finance minister), and Li Shiqun (who would become head of intelligence); the Soviet-trained newspaper editor and long-term ally of Wang, Lin Baisheng (who would serve as the RNG's minister of publicity);[3] Wang's brother-in-law, the French-educated KMT cadre Chu Minyi (who would later serve as the RNG foreign minister); and Wang Jingwei's wife and long-term revolutionary comrade, the Malaya-born Chen Bijun (who would exert considerable influence in Guangdong Province during the occupation). Almost all of these same individuals would go on to develop factional cliques under the RNG, and all would hold quite different ideas about the regime itself.[4] Indeed, factionalism was inherent even in this regime's self-definition, for the "reorganized" element of its name was not a sign of wartime innovation but a reference to the reorganization faction (*gaizupai*), an anti–Chiang Kai-shek clique within the KMT that dated to the 1920s.[5]

Given the Kuomintang heritage of virtually all of its main protagonists, it is unsurprising that the RNG looked, sounded, and acted remarkably like the prewar Republican state. Indeed, Wang's regime claimed to be the only legitimate Republican Chinese government when it came into existence on March 30, 1940—an event that, significantly, was referred to not as the founding of a new political entity but as the "return [of the Republican state] to the capital" (*huandu*) of Nanjing. Despite all the emphasis on "new China" in occupation-era propaganda then, this regime never officially described itself as "new." It was, rather, the natural and legitimate heir to the Republic that had been founded following the 1911 Revolution.

Accordingly, the RNG resurrected the institutions of the moribund Republican state. It celebrated October 10 (the anniversary of the Xinhai Revolution) as its national day. And it swore allegiance to "one party, one ideology, and one leader" (*yige dang, yige zhuyi, yige lingxiu*), while justifying all of its policy decisions on the ideological basis of Sun Yat-sen's Three Principles of the People (*Sanmin zhuyi*)—that is, nationalism (*minzu*), the people's rights (*minquan*), and the people's livelihood (*minsheng*).[6] Indeed, veneration of Sun was central to the RNG and to the legitimacy of Wang's power. As Mara Yue Du has recently explained, for example, the very notion of Sun as the "father of the nation" (*guofu*) emerged out of the struggle between the RNG and the Chongqing Nationalists over Sun Yat-sen's legacy at the time of Wang Jingwei's "return" in 1940.[7] The siting of Sun statuary in Nanjing today is, likewise, a result of RNG attempts to reorganize the streetscape to emphasize the regime's supposed fealty to Sun: a bronze statue of Sun, commissioned by Sun's late Japanese benefactor Umeya Shōkichi in 1928 and sculpted by the artist Makita Shōya, was relocated to central Nanjing's Xin Jiekou intersection on the seventy-sixth anniversary of Sun's birth in November 1942.[8]

As such contestation suggests, the RNG's main point of difference with the prewar Republican state was that it maintained a Chinese "Other." The initial raison d'être of the RNG was to restore a version of Republican Chinese orthodoxy that had been forfeited by Chiang Kai-shek. Chiang's apparent capitulation to communism, his corruption, and his lust for personal power—to say nothing of his willingness to abandon China in the face of Japanese expansion—were all betrayals of the ideals of the 1911 Revolution. If, in the RNG worldview, Chiang Kai-shek and his government of resistance in Chongqing now represented dictatorship, corruption, and subservience to Soviet (or, later in the war, British and American) masters, then Wang would become the true defender of Republican institutions, and his government—as Andrew Cheung puts it—a bastion of "constitutionalism."[9] This distinction would remain a central part of RNG thinking for the remainder of its existence and would ensure that this regime oscillated between emulation of the Chongqing Nationalists and a contradictory impulse to distinguish itself from them.

The RNG also underlined anticommunism as a main tenet of its ideology, outdoing even Chiang Kai-shek in the vitriol of its attacks on the Chinese Communist Party (CCP) (Zhongguo gongchandang) and its supposed Soviet backers. For Wang Jingwei, international communism represented a fundamental betrayal of Sun Yat-sen ideals, and Chiang Kai-shek's willingness to work with the CCP in opposing the Japanese was tantamount to a betrayal of Sun's legacy.

There was another key difference between the RNG and its Chongqing rivals, however. This was that Wang's regime existed at the whim of a foreign occupier, not simply sharing power with an overwhelming and belligerent force but also coexisting alongside other client regimes that had been put in place by the Japanese prior to 1940. In this regard, we might see the RNG as inhabiting what David Serfass (referring to Timothy Brook) has recently defined as an "occupation state." For Serfass, this occupation state was never a single coherent body. Rather, it can be conceptualized as an ever-evolving project in which competing centers of power vied for greater levels of control.[10] These centers included, of course, the Japanese. It was ultimately the Japanese who held, for instance, the purse strings of occupation. It was Japanese advisers who were seconded to key RNG government ministries. And it was Japan's China Expeditionary Army (Shina hakengun) that acted as Wang's ultimate protector. Yet the occupation state also included other groups who aided in its maintenance and operations. Among these were conservative elites in east and south China who had filled the vacuum left by the fleeing Nationalists in 1937 and had been enthusiasts for earlier client regimes, such as the RGROC in Nanjing. In 1940, such groups still held considerable power at the local level while others were subsumed into RNG institutions at the behest of the Japanese.

Within this fluid occupation state, the RNG—including Chinese government institutions, the Kuomintang, and the armed forces—represented a third center of power, and one that served initially (as Serfass puts it) as a facade for the occupation itself.[11] However, as with the other prongs of the occupation state, it could never claim complete power. It was always reliant on its Japanese and local elite partners to administer an occupied China and hence had to adhere to imperial Japanese policies, regardless of how humiliating they might be. That the RNG recognized and subsequently shared talent and staff with the Japanese-backed state of Manchukuo was perhaps the clearest example of this. In other ways also, however, the RNG was forced to accept humiliating conditions for its own existence. Wang's administration was not even officially acknowledged as a legitimate government by Tokyo until the signing in November 1940 of the Treaty concerning Basic Relations (between the RNG and Japan) (Hua-Ri jiben guanxi tiaoyue)—some eight months after the *huandu*.[12]

Nonetheless, and as Serfass and others have shown, the balance of power within the occupation state was constantly shifting. Indeed, if in 1940 it had been the Japanese holding the reins of economic, military, and diplomatic power, the war ended with Wang's administration exerting a far greater influence over fiscal policy and enjoying a far greater reach into the counties and towns of occupied China beyond Nanjing. The RNG also deployed trusted, prewar modes of mobilization that would enable it to exert significant levels of control over the lives of its Chinese citizens. One example of this was the Scouts (*tongzijun*). Dating back to the 1910s, the Scouts had represented a vehicle of youth mobilization for the Republican Chinese state prior to the war. The Scouts had become a "key component of civic training in secondary schools by the early 1920s,"[13] and during the Nanjing decade the Nationalist state had centralized their management under the KMT. In the spring of 1941, however, the RNG minister of education Zhao Zhengping revived this reliably Republican institution to help "develop [children's] personalities" (*gexing zhi fazhan*) and encourage "positive habits" (*lianghao xiguan*) among China's youth—and to populate mass demonstrations of support for Wang's administration when necessary.[14]

The RNG also established its own armed forces, thereby enabling it to exert far greater influence on specific areas of policy, such as counterinsurgency, and to shape the lives of conscripted men. Some of these armed forces were composed of units that had defected from Chiang Kai-shek's Nationalists or served earlier client states. Many others, however, were conscripted through the *baojia* (local-level civil defense and law enforcement) system that was resurrected under the RNG as a means of extending state control at the local level.[15] The RNG armed forces included a navy, a small (and largely symbolic) air force, and a Peace National Salvation Army (Heping jiuguo jun).[16] By 1945, the RNG could claim up to 900,000 soldiers.[17] These forces were nominally administered under a Military Affairs Commission (Junshi weiyuanhui).

Military forces could not, however, disguise that this regime exerted only limited control over entire areas of China to which it laid claim. This state of affairs reflected the ultimate failure of Wang and his Peace Movement in the prolonged negotiations that they had engaged in with Tokyo over the course of 1939. Indeed, while Wang had originally envisaged his RNG "peace area" (*heping diqu*) as representing a single region of China beyond Japanese control (such as the southwest), he emerged in 1940 as the nominal head of a patchwork of occupied areas centered on the Yangtze and Pearl River deltas, the boundaries of which ebbed and flowed with Japanese military fortunes.[18] Entire areas of south China, such as the island of Hainan, remained directly occupied by the Japanese throughout the war.[19] The cities of Shanghai and Xiamen were initially granted "special status" as a result of their proximity to Japan and colonial Taiwan, respectively. Most importantly, vast areas of north China previously claimed by the PGROC were granted effective autonomy under a North China Political Affairs Commission (Huabei zhengwu weiyuanhui) in 1940. This was headed by the very same PGROC officials who had been in power there since the end of 1938, a group that operated almost entirely independently of Wang's Nanjing-based administration.[20] All the same, the areas over which Wang did claim dominion were not insignificant. In 1940, Wang's regime administered parts of Jiangxi, Jiangsu, Zhejiang, Guangdong, and Fujian. In 1941, as a result of Japanese successes, its reach extended into areas of modern-day Hunan and Hubei.[21] And later in the war, the administration even experimented with the creation of new provinces that would better reflect its control of areas in what is today northern Jiangsu.[22]

In light of such territorial fluidity, it is hardly surprising that RNG obloquies directed at Chongqing were often articulated in expressions of provincialism. References to Chiang Kai-shek's Nationalists as being simply the Chongqing side (*Yu fang*) suggested, more than anything else, a sense of territorial inadequacy on the part of Wang Jingwei's followers. And if the records left to posterity by leading RNG statesmen such as Zhou Fohai are to be believed, then Wang's regime spent much of its energy arguing with Japanese advisers—sometimes unsuccessfully—about the need to return lands conquered by the Japanese military to RNG control.[23] These frustrations about a lack of territorial control would plague this regime for the rest of the war, despite what Brian Martin has referred to as the RNG's "pretensions to nationwide rule."[24] They also help explain why even the most modest of geographic enlargements mattered so much in wartime Nanjing.

The "return" (*tuihuan;* sometimes given as "*jiaohuan*") of the International Settlement (Gonggong zujie) in Shanghai (as well as foreign concessions in other cities) to nominal RNG control in the summer of 1943 was the most significant symbolic triumph for the regime in its short existence. While the foreign concessions represented little more than dots on the larger map of wartime China, the ability to claim ownership of spaces denied to Wang's administration in earlier years—and so closely associated with imperialism—cannot be overstated.

If the RNG excelled at reclaiming cities, the same cannot be said of its record in the countryside. Indeed, the introduction from the summer of 1941 of the Rural Pacification campaigns—described by Brian Martin as "the most important politico-military policy of the Nanjing government"[25]—represented a tacit admission of a lack of power beyond urban China. It was also indicative of Nanjing's frustration about the continuing power of local elites in the countryside. Rural Pacification was a set of Japanese-initiated campaigns aimed at wiping out resistance in areas of Jiangsu and Zhejiang. Indeed, it was introduced with the purpose of ridding those areas of the New Fourth Army (Xin si jun), which had been leading resistance efforts there since prior to the *huandu*.[26] These were not purely Japanese campaigns, however. Much like the occupation state itself, Rural Pacification was characterized by a Sino-Japanese division of labor, with Japanese forces managing military matters (though RNG troops would also come to play a key role) and RNG cadres managing political and cultural matters in the "pacified" areas.[27]

The political side of Rural Pacification was directed by the RNG chief of intelligence, Li Shiqun, from the city of Suzhou. Lasting until late in the war, these campaigns were designed along many of the same lines as the anticommunist campaigns that Chiang Kai-shek had directed in the prewar years.[28] They were as much a cultural project as a military purge, however. Rural Pacification involved RNG cadres traveling alongside Japanese and Chinese troops as they cleared villages of suspected communists, while selling the RNG brand to a restive peasantry and reluctant local elites. Indeed, visual and performative expressions of loyalty to the regime remained a central part of these campaigns, with RNG organizations establishing Rural Pacification drama troupes (*qingxiang jutuan*) and "movable propaganda units" (*liudong xuanchuandui*).[29] Such work was overseen by a Rural Pacification Publicity Team (Qingxiang xuanchuan zongdui), a group managed by a dramatist and propagandist called Lei Yimin.[30]

Republican Iconography and the Theater State

The RNG may have looked very much like the prewar Republican state. However, the context of foreign occupation endowed certain aspects of existing Chinese political culture with new significance in Wang Jingwei's China. This can be seen most clearly in the selective RNG deployment of Republican Chinese iconography. As recent scholarship has revealed, for example, the RNG agreed to "return to the capital" only on the condition that key prewar symbols of Chinese statehood could be restored—a condition extracted from the Japanese by Wang's primary negotiator, Zhou Fohai.[31] This included one icon that would become central to the RNG's claims to legitimacy and a constant feature of its state-sponsored visual culture—the Republic of China (ROC) flag (figure 1.1).

Much has been made of the fact that the flag that initially flew over Wang's China was a compromised version of the original version. Under Wang Jingwei, a yellow pennant that included the phrase "*heping, fangong, jianguo*" (peace, anticommunism, nation-building) would be attached to the flag so as to distinguish it from the ensign used in Chongqing.[32] Even at the *huandu,* however, Wang's Ministry of Publicity confidently predicted that the pennant would be removed "with the disappearance of the Chungking [Chongqing] regime."[33]

The RNG use of (a version of) the ROC flag was more than simply a return to prewar iconography, however. It spoke also to the fetishization of Republican icons that had occurred since the Japanese invasion of 1937 almost always, prior to 1940, in the name of resistance. The story of the "lone battalion" (*gujun*)—in which "China's national colours were flown from a mast above

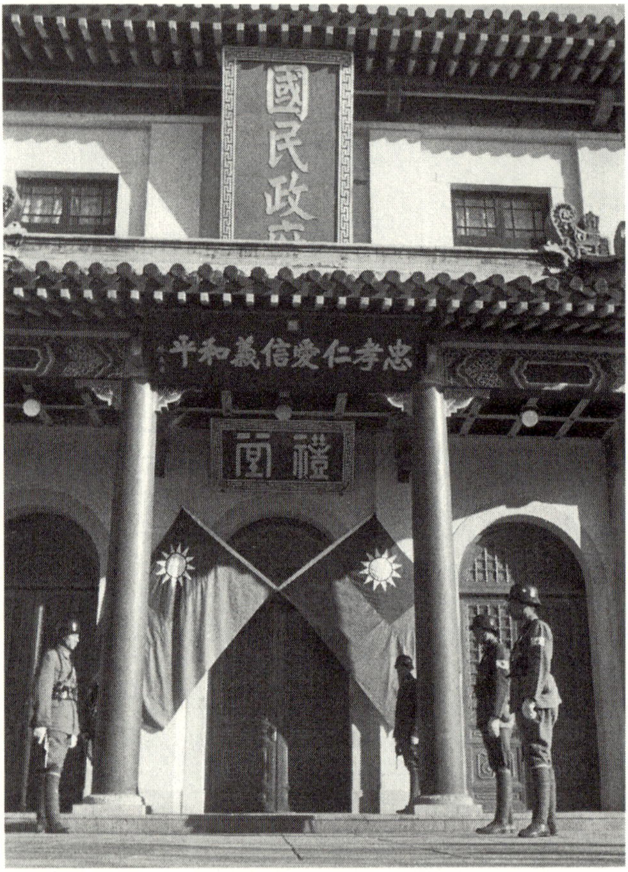

Figure 1.1. The ROC flag (without its pennant) is hung at the entrance to RNG headquarters in late 1940. Courtesy of the National Archives (London), CN 11/11.

a sea of Japanese flags" by soldiers resisting Japanese attacks on Shanghai in 1937[34]—would have been well known to Wang Jingwei and his followers. It had been recounted in Chinese visual art and media in the early war years, with the hoisting of the ROC flag in the midst of shelling during the Battle of Shanghai depicted as one of the great symbolic acts of Chinese heroism.[35] That RNG cadres were able to raise this same flag of the "blue sky, white sun, and a wholly red earth" (*qing tian, bai ri, man di hong*) above Nanjing in spring 1940—even as rank-and-file Japanese soldiers publicly defiled it[36]—suggested, then, not a return to prewar normalcy but an attempt to harness the symbolic significance that resistance lore had given to this icon in the months prior to the *huandu*. Importantly, RNG administrators continued to lobby the Japanese for the removal of the yellow pennant and often used the flag without it. In February 1943, their endeavors would prove successful, when the full, unadulterated ROC flag was hoisted again in Nanjing and Shanghai, just as it was in Chongqing.[37]

The RNG embellished other Republican Chinese icons as well. Take, for example, the figure of Sun Yat-sen. While existing scholarship is correct in stressing the continuities between RNG worship of Sun and the prewar apotheosis of Sun that had been attempted under Chiang Kai-shek,[38] I would argue that the RNG went to even greater lengths than the prewar Nationalists in placing Sun at the center of its political culture. Indeed, veneration of Sun was tied inextricably to deference for Wang Jingwei himself—a man (RNG propagandists never tired of reminding the world) who had been personally and politically closer to Sun than any other living statesman.[39] Wang also seems to have taken great interest in the physical legacies of Sun. He showed a particular concern, for example, in recovering ephemera associated with Sun from Japan during wartime.[40] And in March 1942, the RNG deposited, amid great solemnity, Sun Yat-sen's "remaining entrails" (*yi zang*)—a slice of Sun's intestines that had been preserved in a Beijing hospital after Sun's death in 1925—in the Sun Yat-sen Mausoleum in Nanjing.[41]

In founding its capital in Nanjing, the RNG also took stewardship of Sun Yat-sen's physical remains. The possession of Sun's body represented an important component of RNG claims to legitimacy.[42] Accordingly, the Sun Mausoleum—itself a product of the Nanjing decade and described by Delin Lai as "one of the most sacred sites in modern Chinese history"[43]—became the RNG's most hallowed landmark. Annual commemoration of Sun's birth and death at the mausoleum sat alongside the October 10 anniversary as some of the most important dates on occupied China's calendar. Official visits to pay respects at the mausoleum (*ye ling*) became a staple part of RNG political ritual.[44]

If worship of Sun's body in the mausoleum that housed it emerged as an important practice in the RNG, then so too did worship of prewar Chinese martyrs, for this regime inherited the most important cemeteries of the Republican movement, including the Huanghuagang (Yellow Flower Mound) site in Guangzhou, where the "seventy-two martyrs" (*qishi'er lieshi*) of a failed 1911 uprising against the Qing dynasty had been commemorated since the 1910s.[45] Huanghuagang became a major ritual center for this regime, with the memory of Republican martyrs there conflated with the celebration of Pan-Asian unity.[46] To this prewar pantheon of Republican revolutionaries, however, the RNG added its own Peace Movement martyrs (*heyun xianlie*)—that is, individuals who had died in defense of the RNG or of Sino-Japanese collaboration more generally.[47] These martyrs were granted their own annual memorial day (September 1), placing them symbolically alongside heroes who had died pursuing earlier revolutionary activities.[48]

Martyrdom also became part of the mythology built around Wang Jingwei himself. As Zhiyi Yang has convincingly argued, "Wang consistently portray[ed] himself as a martyr and a romantic figure who was ready to sacrifice not just his life, but even his posthumous reputation, for the salvation of the nation."[49] In wartime hagiography, great emphasis would also be placed on Wang's early career and his own brush with martyrdom during a failed bid to assassinate the Manchu prince regent Zaifeng in 1910. Attempts on Wang's life in Beijing in 1935 and in Hanoi in 1939 were also worked into this narrative.

In other respects, however, the RNG was markedly different from the Nationalist government it replaced. This was especially so in one important element of its self-image—its imagined riparian geography. By this, I am referring at one level to the fact that many of the regime's main centers of power (e.g., Nanjing, Guangzhou, and Wuhan) were river ports. At another level, however, a reliance on rivers and on control of ports along them shaped how the RNG defined itself, as well as the political culture it adopted, and even the ways in which it envisaged China itself. One example of this was in the watered landscapes of Jiangnan that became so common a feature of visual cultures in occupied China, especially beyond Nanjing, in the first two years following the *huandu*. In the eyes of occupation artists and photographers, for example, real and imagined canals, lakes, and rivers dominated artistic representations of rural China, while the bunds of port cities were favored as vistas for landscape photography.[50]

Another example of this riparian imaginary, however, was the symbolic importance given to the RNG navy. Founded at the same time as the *huandu* (but including what had formerly been the RGROC's coast guard), the navy emerged as the most eulogized of this regime's armed forces. Headquartered on Nanjing's Yangtze docks, the navy took pride of place in RNG political culture, though much of its work was, tellingly, restricted to anti-smuggling patrols and ceremonial duties. The very establishment of a navy under Wang Jingwei had been opposed by sections of the Japanese military.[51] This did not stop RNG propagandists from borrowing extensively from Japanese precedents when it came to promoting this force, however. In fact, it may very well explain Wang Jingwei's own obsession with it. As we shall see in later chapters, the flattering images of RNG sailors (and RNG leaders in naval uniform) in photojournalism looked a little too reminiscent of those found in Japanese wartime pictorials.

It is in the ceremonial nature of the navy, however, that we find an indication of the more general nature of the RNG itself. Just as the navy represented more of a symbolic than a military force, so too was the RNG a regime of pomp, in the absence (until late in the war) of any significant power in many areas of public policy. Indeed, in its attention to ritual, its extensive media and propaganda apparatus, and its almost fanatical obsession with historical anniversaries, the RNG might be said to have fulfilled many of the criteria of the Geertzian model of the "theater state."[52]

While recognizing the significant differences between the RNG and the precolonial Balinese polities that inspired Clifford Geertz' coining of this phrase, I follow the lead of other comparative historians in finding the deployment of the "theater state" useful well beyond its original context. Heonik Kwon and Byung-Ho Chung, for example, have shown how the notion of the theater state was initially formulated by Geertz in the context of the "politics of spectacle" and "charismatic rule" in Sukarno's Indonesia (even though it was applied to the study of precolonial Bali).[53] The issue for these two scholars, then, is not whether this paradigm has a place in modern political systems but, rather, "how to come to terms with the state's forceful politics of display (and politics as display) as a fundamentally modern political practice." For Kwon and Chung, the notion of a (rather than "the") theater state can help explain the prominence given to display and ritual in the society that is their topic of study—that is, North Korea. They use this paradigm to explain how narratives from the past—which, in the North Korean case, include the foundational myths that are so central to the Korean Workers' Party's claims to legitimacy—can be transformed into key elements of the political present. By continually reenacting past glories through state-led spectacles, the North Korean regime ensures that the "old heroism" of the revolutionary struggle against Japanese rule can be transformed into "an ever-new glory of the polity's contemporary life."[54]

We can find parallels with such dynamics in the RNG, while acknowledging the fundamental structural differences between pre- or postcolonial Indonesia, North Korea, and Wang's China. The RNG was a regime that based its entire legitimacy on its supposed provenance in the Republican Chinese past and went to extreme lengths to underline such provenance through ritual commemoration, especially of the republic's nominal founder, Sun Yat-sen. In Geertz' original definition, the "expressive nature" of the state was pointed "toward spectacle, toward ceremony, toward the public dramatization of the ruling obsessions of . . . culture."[55] In Geertz' thesis, such ritual was itself a source of power. This was not the case for the RNG. But if one of the major criticisms of Geertz' *Negara* paradigm is that it places culture before politics, it is perhaps logical that the idea of the theater state can also make sense when applied to a regime that held little autonomy *except* in fields such as culture and propaganda. In other words, while the RNG was unable to achieve much in terms of political autonomy, it did manage to carve out a ritual space for itself when it came to commemorating events and individuals from the Chinese past. Indeed, it invented an entire state apparatus—from drama troupes to propaganda colleges—to train the occupied Chinese intelligentsia in the art of state theater.

In this regard, I would argue that the RNG was fundamentally different from most twentieth-century Chinese governments. The source of that difference lay in the reality of an administration that was so reliant on a belligerent occupant for its very existence but was granted extensive autonomy in the realm of culture. If the RNG struggled to force its Japanese guarantors to live up to the economic and political assurances it had been promised in 1939 (ranging from control of finances to the right to establish diplomatic relations with foreign powers), and if its lack of territorial integrity was too significant a fact to properly conceal, then at least the RNG could find solace in the realm of iconography.

This RNG focus on theater extended not just to secular, political events but even to the embellishment of traditional festivals and celebrations, as Nanjing was transformed into a community of flag-waving students, Scouts, and servicemen. As Mark Eykholt has argued, public attendance at such events did not necessarily equate to support for occupation or for Wang's regime. Rather, it may well have reflected the sheer boredom experienced by many residents of Nanjing at the time, or perhaps was even a form of escapism.[56] Nonetheless, public celebrations were an important part of life in occupied Nanjing. In 1942, the Taiwanese writer Wu Zhuoliu, who worked in Nanjing at the time as a journalist for the newspaper *Tairiku shinpō,* described this tendency toward theatrics candidly, hinting as he did so at the reasons behind what he interpreted as the widespread public participation in such events:

> Every time there is some commemoration in Nanjing, a big procession [*youxing*] is held. Needless to say, all the commercial guilds and associations become involved. But as well as that, each county,

> *baojia* unit, and district competes with each other to come up with something new, making all sorts of things that they can use in such processions. When I was in Nanjing, the biggest procession was one held on the fifteenth day of the first month [i.e., the Lantern Festival]. All kinds of organizations, student groups, and the municipal police formed long, winding lines of marchers, so long that they would take a number of hours to pass. The crowds on the streets would watch as these lines of marchers went by, and in the area around Fuzimiao, events would go on well into the night. It was enough to make you imagine that there was no war going on somewhere else on the mainland.[57]

Pacifism, Pan-Asianism, and Fascism

At its "return," the RNG sided with Japan, yet maintained a position of neutrality. It justified such a decision by referring to Japan's commitment to wiping out communism in China. However, at the same time, and as Wai Chor So has explained, the RNG maintained an attitude toward the Western powers, especially the United States, that vacillated between ambivalence and amity.[58] In 1940, the RNG's professed enemy was not "the West" but the "subversive and peace-disturbing activities" of international communism.[59] The RNG sought to taint the Chinese communists, and more importantly Chiang Kai-shek's Nationalists, by association with this malevolent force.

However, while Nanjing's official line was that resistance as espoused by Chongqing was harmful to the Chinese people, it also declared that it would not fight Chiang Kai-shek's armies. It continued to honor this commitment up until the end of the war.[60] This is not to suggest that it maintained official relations with Chongqing or that it sympathized with Chiang's resistance. On the contrary, the RNG promoted itself as an administration associated with "peace and collaboration" and thus as the direct opposite of a Chongqing government "associated with war and resistance."[61] This tendency toward defining itself by what it was not—by presenting itself as the antithesis of Chongqing—dominated a good deal of RNG rhetoric in the pre–Pearl Harbor era. It would also define how the RNG presented itself to China and to the world.

This initial emphasis on peace had a number of implications beyond differentiation from Chongqing, however. For example, the regime's professed commitment to pacifism resulted in an admiration for Buddhism, even as the RNG inherited the claims to secularism that had been a hallmark of the prewar Republican state.[62] Buddhism in its various forms not only represented a fittingly "Pan-Asian" religion that could be called upon to underline cultural affinity between China and Japan—something already emphasized in other client regimes in Japanese-occupied Asia[63]—but could also be used to emphasize RNG claims to self-sacrifice. Wang Jingwei invoked Buddhist allusions in his speeches.[64] Hagiographers likened Wang Jingwei himself to a Bodhisattva who was "giving up not only his life but also his reputation" for the nation.[65] And the RNG sought to preserve or rebuild sites within occupied China that held significance in Buddhist history.[66]

If the RNG had started the 1940s true to its Peace Movement credentials, however, it ended the war as a militantly nationalist regime that looked remarkably like a Chinese pretender to Axis power status.[67] In some regards, this was the result of internal struggles over the fate of this regime; in others, however, it reflected the RNG's need to react to continually shifting geopolitical trends over which it had little control. The signing of the Soviet-Japanese Non-aggression Pact in April 1941, for example, put the RNG in a difficult rhetorical position. Under a flag that still announced anticommunism as a core tenet of this regime, RNG cadres were forced to turn their attention away from the Soviet menace in China and instead curse more nebulous notions of resistance. It was this subtle shift that energized the Rural Pacification campaigns—with their emphasis on Chinese resistance rather than international Bolshevism—from the summer of 1941 onward. Diplomatically, however, this period was also characterized by a series of successes for Nanjing, culminating in the formal recognition of Wang's China by Italy and the Third Reich. Given that Wang's administration had not been recognized even by Tokyo until late 1940, this represented a considerable achievement.[68]

Following the transformation of the "China Incident" into the Greater East Asia War (Dai Tōa Sensō) in December 1941, however, the wider geopolitical context changed once more for the RNG. Now, despite remaining officially neutral, the RNG was forced to adopt an increasingly anti-British and anti-American line in keeping with Japan's war against the Allies. It was also in this period that the RNG began to take on more authoritarian tendencies, with the adoption of the New Citizens Movement (NCM) (Xin guomin yundong). Officially launched by Wang Jingwei himself on New Year's Day 1942, this movement has been characterized as little more than a copy of prewar mobilization efforts by Chiang Kai-shek's Nationalists.[69] The NCM went far beyond earlier efforts, however, and its aims were not entirely the same. The NCM certainly did combine elements of prewar Republican nationalism and mobilizational strategies with a strong dose of anti-imperialist sentiment. Indeed, its promoters openly cited the May Fourth Movement as a source of inspiration,[70] while handbooks on its implementation demanded the propagation of Sun Yat-sen's Three Principles; the implementation (*guanche*) of the Peace Movement; the eradication of corrupt thinking; the mobilization of the people; an emphasis on material production; and respect for the supreme leader (*zuigao lingxiu*) Wang Jingwei.[71] Without doubt, however, the NCM also borrowed rhetoric and performative practices directly from wartime Japanese models, the movement's motto being "to fulfill the Chinese Revolution and realize the liberation of East Asia."[72]

Under the NCM, a quasi-military Youth Corps (Qingnian tuan), members of which were expected to publicly profess complete allegiance to Wang, was established for people aged between sixteen and twenty-five. Founded by Lin Baisheng in 1942, the Youth Corps maintained chapters at municipal, county, and school levels and was originally designed to challenge the monopoly on youth mobilization that Chiang Kai-shek's Nationalists were claiming through Chongqing-based groups such as the San Min Chu I Youth Corps (Sanmin zhuyi qingnian tuan).[73] Members of NCM Youth Corps adopted the same emphasis on May Fourth nationalism that their peers in Chongqing did. Indeed, as oral histories of Chinese students who had taken part in such groups have shown, the Youth Corps' activities were seen as a means of expressing a distinctly Chinese patriotism when few other outlets for such sentiments existed.[74]

In early 1943, however, the Youth Corps was combined with the Scouts to form a new Youth League (Qingshaonian tuan). This league operated under its own logo—a KMT white sun superimposed over a bundle of three intersecting arrows. Members were trained in behaviors that looked remarkably similar to those undertaken by the young members of fascist movements in Europe and Asia yet also emulated practices common during the Nanjing decade. At specially designed summer camps, Youth League members were trained in public speaking, the production of propaganda, and the writing of critical "self-assessments" (*zishu*).[75] They also regularly engaged in quasi-military parades and rallies to celebrate RNG rule.

Through the NCM, the RNG thus came to adopt the language, aesthetics, and many of the accoutrements of the Axis states. Crucially, however, it combined these with the language of May Fourth anti-imperialism. As the Greater East Asia War raged on, the RNG dedicated itself—despite still adhering to the rhetoric of peace—to encouraging anti-Western sentiment, while concurrently establishing links with youth groups in other parts of the Axis world. Foreign incursions against China over the former century now became the focus of RNG vitriol, as the war against the Allies was conflated with China's own struggle for "liberation" (*jiefang*).

The adoption of the New China Policy by the Japanese government in late 1942, in response to changing fortunes in the wider war, marked an important moment of change when it came to the balance of power within the occupation state. As Margherita Zanasi has argued, the new relationship between Tokyo and Nanjing that developed as a result of this policy—and that would eventually culminate in the signing of the Sino-Japanese Pact of Alliance (Zhong-Ri tongmeng tiaoyue) in October 1943—led to a greater stake for RNG rule in various fields that had previously been dominated by the Japanese.[76] This policy turn also contained an important visual element, however, for it entailed making the markers of Japanese military power less visible in occupied China, and replacing these with "the police, the soldiers, the office-holders, of the Nanking regime."[77]

This goes some way to explain the seemingly counterintuitive militarization of the RNG that occurred after this administration was granted extensive new levels of autonomy by the Japanese. Autonomy, in other words, would culminate, not in a move back toward the neutrality of 1940, but toward increasingly frequent expressions of belligerent Chinese nativism. The RNG eventually became a combatant in World War II on January 9, 1943—the day Wang Jingwei declared war on the Allies. In the very same month, the RNG initiated a "general mobilization of the national spirit" (*guomin jingshen zong dongyuan*), through which youth activists called for the overthrow of Anglo-American imperialism.[78] A regime based on "peace, anticommunism, and nation-building" now presented itself as an integral part of the Greater East Asia Co-Prosperity Sphere (Dai Tōa Kyōeiken), or GEACPS.

The self-congratulatory reverie surrounding the return of the foreign concessions in the summer of 1943—and especially the International Settlement in Shanghai—marked the high point of the RNG's war and was a supposed victory for Chinese nationalism under occupation. If Wang's administration had always aspired to regaining Chinese sovereignty, then direct rule over cities that had once been marked out by their extraterritoriality was a concrete achievement that could be celebrated. Yet such celebrations also paved the way for more public expressions of Chinese nationalism under occupation. These included physical attacks on "decadent" opium dens and dance halls[79] and criticism of residual treaty port culture. In such a context, the RNG even went so far as to redefine Chongqing as a regime inhabited by compatriots (*tongbao*) rather than rivals, instructing its cadres that "the main objectives of our propaganda attacks should now be Britain and America."[80] In other words, while the RNG had started in 1940 by defining itself against Chongqing, by 1943 it was emphasizing all that it shared with Chiang Kai-shek's administration (and, contrarily, everything that set it apart from the Allies). In the context of the radical expressions of nationalism that were also being articulated in Chongqing via Chiang's magnum opus, *China's Destiny,* at precisely the same time, the late-war RNG began to look far more like the regime from which it had split.[81]

By the time Wang Jingwei attended the Greater East Asia Conference (Dai Tōa kaigi) in Tokyo in November 1943, the RNG looked almost unrecognizable from the pacifist, civilian administration that had returned triumphantly to Nanjing in the spring of 1940. Despite the "emptiness" of the Greater East Asia Conference,[82] this event marked the fulfillment of the RNG's transformation into a pretender to Axis status and the transformation of Wang Jingwei into an icon of Pan-Asian "liberation."[83] Observers of the RNG are correct in pointing out that RNG armed forces never fired a shot in anger at the Allies.[84] The point, however, is that being a combatant was, for this theater state, more about adopting the aesthetics and performative strategies of the Axis powers than engaging in combat. The RNG had bought into the "look" of what Madeleine Herren has referred to as "fascist internationalism."[85]

Herein lies one of the great ironies of the RNG, for throughout the period during which this regime lacked any genuine political autonomy, it cleaved to pacifism. Over the course of 1942 and early 1943, however, this regime underwent a complete transformation. While the RNG may never have succumbed to the racism that inspired fascism elsewhere,[86] it took on many of the "hyper-militaristic" affectations that Louise Young has noted were central to what she has called "Asian-style fascism."[87] Indeed, superficially, the late-war RNG fitted perfectly within Young's typology of "fascist imperialism," under which "fascist ideas interacted with anti-colonial nationalisms and gave rise to new forms of sovereignty" throughout Japanese-occupied Asia.[88] This was even reflected in visual culture. The RNG introduced far more stringent rules on cultural expression and on the control of Chinese cultural workers in the aftermath of its declaration of war on the Allies. A new Basic Outline on Policy for Wartime Culture and Propaganda (Zhanshi wenhua xuanchuan zhengce jiben gangyao) was introduced by Wang's regime in June 1943. This set out a cultural policy that would thereafter be highly controlled, rationalized, and centralized from Nanjing. It also included nativist calls for the purging of foreign influence and ideas from all Chinese visual expression.[89]

It would be a mistake, however, to see the RNG's "fascist turn" as purely the result of Japanese influence, for fascism was nothing new to Republican China. The language and aesthetics of fascism had been adopted by a variety of groups in prewar China, often as a means of countering imperialist (including Japanese) influence, as well as the rise of communism. As Maggie Clinton has argued, none of this necessarily contradicted a professed loyalty to Sun Yat-sen's 1911 Revolution. It did, however, represent an often violent rejection of communism, as well as a distinctly "nativist turn" away from the anti-Confucian sentiments of May Fourth activism on the Left. In the iconoclasm of flag-waving RNG youths we find not so much an ideological capitulation to Japanese imperialism, therefore, but rather a return to prewar forms of Chinese fascist mobilization—a revival of the "cultural revolution from the Right" that Clinton has observed as having been adopted by many sections of the KMT in the 1930s.[90] In the context of occupation (during which international communism was blamed for many of China's ills, but in which a more assertive RNG sought ways in which to stake a claim to autonomy from the Japanese), fascism could be used as means of nationalist (i.e., Chinese) agitation against both communist resistance and belligerent occupation.

In examining this unsubtle shift from pacifism to the aesthetics and ritual of fascism, however, we might also consider RNG commitments to a number of ideologies with which it has often been associated. Pan-Asianism, for example, was a common feature of RNG rhetoric, with Wang's government "emphasizing the pan-Asian elements," as Timothy Brook puts it, "when it relaunched Sun Yatsen's thought."[91] Indeed, the extrapolation of Pan-Asian ideas as articulated by Sun in two speeches delivered in Kobe in 1924 was frequently highlighted as one of the fundamental justifications for Wang's decision to work with the Japanese in the first place.[92]

Torsten Weber, however, argues that the RNG adoption of this ideology was "neither a mere invention for propaganda reasons nor a wholesale and uncritical adoption of Japanese wartime rhetoric."[93] Instead, Wang and his courtiers celebrated notions of Pan-Asianism that invariably linked the idea of "Asian liberation" to Chinese nationalism—a fact that saw writings on the topic by Wang significantly edited when they were published in Japan.[94] When the RNG head of overseas propaganda, T'ang Leang-li, published a new collection of Sun Yat-sen's work's on Pan-Asianism in 1941, the emphasis was on Sino-Japanese friendship and cooperation couched in the language of the Chinese Revolution.[95] The RNG might agree with Japanese advisers on the need to put a distinctly Pan-Asianist spin on events like the centenary of the end the First Opium War in 1842 (which, serendipitously, fell in August 1942). The significance of such commemorations, however, could be viewed quite differently in Nanjing and Tokyo. In other words, RNG interpretations of "Pan-Asianism," while sounding remarkably similar to militaristic Japanese claims that had emerged out of the Shōwa Research Association (Shōwa Kenkyōkai) and calls for a Japanese-led "new order" (*shinchitsujo*),[96] were often deployed in pursuit of distinctly Chinese aims. This ranged from the defense of Chinese forms of cultural expression to calls for the fulfillment of Sun Yat-sen's revolution. In the hands of RNG propagandists, including even those associated with organizations founded by the Japanese—such as the East Asia League (Dong Ya Lianmeng)[97]—a woolly phrase like "Greater East Asia" (Da Dong Ya) might well be spoken in attacks on the "Anglo-American" presence in China. However, it might just as easily be deployed to imagine a postwar and post-occupation China free of *all* foreign interference.

The RNG claimed dominion over the wealthiest and most cosmopolitan of China's regions—the urban east and southeast. This regime was led by an elite that could make significant claims (though it seldom did so) to an internationalist outlook. Its leadership included individuals who had been educated in Europe, the Soviet Union, colonial Southeast Asia, Japan, and China's treaty ports. The occupation state, of which the RNG was but a part, also inherited a vibrant commercial media and culture industry that was home to a vast array of opinions and voices, many of which tested the boundaries of occupation cultural expression.

The fate of the RNG, however, was inextricably linked to Japan's fortunes in the wider war. Denied any significant political or economic sovereignty until late in the war, lacking stable borders, and struggling to keep abreast of changes to Japanese imperial policy, RNG leaders retreated into a world of spectacle and ritual, clinging to the symbolism of Republican Chinese nationalism while selectively adopting Japanese and Axis aesthetics. This highly factionalized regime also bred very different ideas about what China should look like. All these factors contributed to the emergence of an eclectic set of iconographies that sometimes sat at odds with the RNG's verbal rhetoric.

None of this suggests, however, that the RNG is not worthy of study. Nor is the RNG's lack of genuine military or economic autonomy a reason to dismiss this regime as inconsequential. The RNG's relevance lies precisely in the extent to which it can illustrate the resilience—and limits—of the ideologies that first developed in the prewar Chinese Republic and, indeed, in the Japanese empire. Its significance lies not in its apparent treason—though almost all of the scholarship on this regime thus far has focused on the extent to which the label "collaborationist" can be aptly applied to it—but in the fact that it represented a set of short-lived and continually shifting visions of Chinese nationalism adapted to the exigencies of foreign occupation. Chinese icons, ideas, and modes of visuality that had been developed prior to the Japanese invasion (and sometimes in response to the threat of Japanese invasion) could be given new significance under occupation by inventive RNG propagandists, and by Wang Jingwei himself. Equally, however, the RNG could use the technologies, talent, and icons of the Japanese empire (and the wider Axis world) to serve distinctly Chinese goals. In the chapters that follow, we will see just how this was done.

CHAPTER 2

Visual Cultures under Occupation

Pictorial traces of the RNG are not difficult to find today. Calligraphy by Wang Jingwei dating from the war years and earlier has sold for significant sums at auction.[1] The wartime oil paintings of one of occupied China's best-known artists, Fan Tchunpi, have been the subject of a number of exhibitions abroad.[2] At the same time, a quite different trade in RNG imagery has developed on the Internet. Photographs of occupation provenance abound online, many lifted directly from the pages of wartime newspapers. These are copied and pasted from one site to another (rarely being dated or attributed in the process) and are frequently used to make political judgments about the RNG. For example, one of the most regularly reproduced images on blogs is a photograph of Wang Jingwei raising a toast with Heinrich Georg Stahmer (the German ambassador to China) in front of a Nazi swastika—*Wang and Nazis,* as it is called on Wikimedia Commons (figure 2.1).[3]

Taken out of context (as they often are), these quite different sorts of ephemera present an image of the RNG that is reductionist or simply misleading. Calligraphy or paintings produced by Wang and his acolytes can be held up as evidence of the apparently urbane character of the regime's leaders. Contrarily, photographs of Wang standing beside symbols of the Third Reich can be called upon whenever an implied association between the RNG and Nazism is desired. Such interventions, however, rarely explain the background to, or origins of, these pictorial traces. They tell us little about the specific context in which a portrait may have been painted, or even the date or original purpose of a now infamous photograph. Removed from any temporal specificity, the moment in which such images were produced can be presented as indicative of the entire regime: the RNG was led by either literati or Nazi sympathizers—or both.

In reality, the production and circulation of visual media—painting, photography, graphic art, cinema—comprised a complex and continually shifting set of processes in Japanese-occupied China. For the RNG, the development of such forms of expression were crucial precisely because they

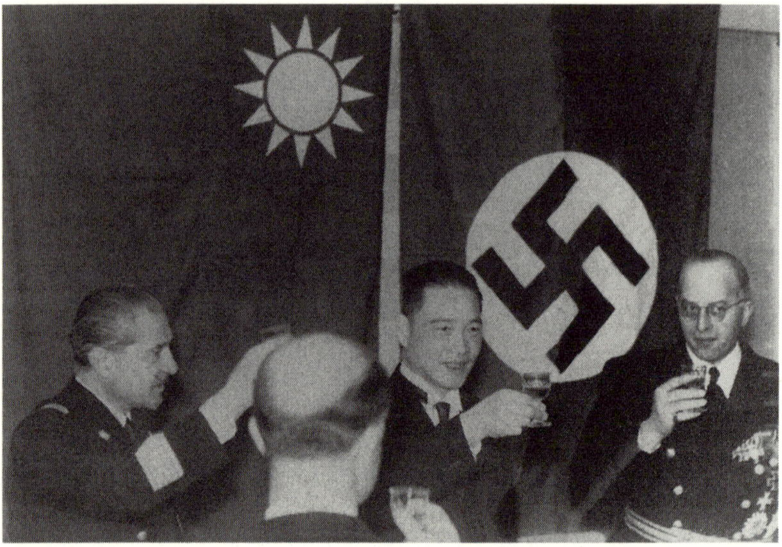

Figure 2.1. Wang Jingwei toasting Georg Heinrich Stahmer, German ambassador to China (*right*), and Francesco Maria Taliani de Marchio, Italian ambassador to China (*left*), in January 1942. Courtesy of Academia Historica.

enabled sections of this regime to develop and express their own specific views about what an occupied China should look like. An "occupied gaze" would be possible only if Chinese cultural workers had access to techniques and technologies that would allow that gaze to be reproduced in a diverse range of media; that same occupied gaze would survive, however, only while the RNG was able to control, censor, or entirely eradicate alternative "ways of seeing" under occupation. The fostering of the RNG's iconographies of occupation therefore needs to be appreciated in a wider context in which various Chinese and Japanese-sponsored administrations (and individuals) were competing for control of the visual in occupied China.

Just as importantly, this occupied gaze, and the iconographies of occupation that were fostered under it, were never static or monolithic. They were, rather, both eclectic and inconsistent. They reflected the highly factionalized nature of this regime and the fact that it was continually responding to changes in Japanese military fortunes over which it had no control—to say nothing of more mundane variables that shaped visual and artistic practice, such as access to paper, ink, or film stock. In the RNG realm, therefore, the appreciation of oil paintings by French-trained artists took place alongside the drawing of bawdy cartoons and the creation of extravagant propaganda murals. All had their place in certain contexts and at specific moments throughout the short life of the RNG. This is precisely why a visual history of the RNG can provide us with a unique insight into this regime. One of the points I wish to make in this book, for example, is not that Wang Jingwei was *not* a fascist but, rather, that the adoption of Axis-inspired aesthetics gathered pace well after *that* photograph was taken (almost certainly by a Japanese newsman on January 19, 1942).[4] It is the visual record that allows us to trace such subtle changes.

One aim of this chapter, therefore, is to move beyond misconceptions that both the art trade and the blogosphere have, perhaps unwittingly, sustained about visual practices developed under occupation. Artwork was created, photographs taken, and thoroughfares festooned by a vast array of groups and individuals during the occupation. More specifically, however, this chapter is designed to contextualize the wider sphere of cultural production—particularly in terms of visual cultures—in RNG China, so that we can make sense of the diverse iconographies that developed under occupation. Who was tasked with building visual cultures in occupied China between 1939 and 1945? What institutions were created or restructured to foster, mediate, or censor visual expression? And how did Chinese cadres and cultural workers manage their relationship with the Japanese (or, for that matter, with each other)? An overview of the media and cultural infrastructure that was developed under occupation, as well as an institutional history of various types of artistic practice that informed a wide set of visual cultures, will address these questions. While such an analysis is worthwhile in its own right, it is provided here to set the scene for later chapters, in which the evolution of particular visual narratives are explored along thematic lines. This chapter, however, also seeks to do something that has been attempted far too rarely in scholarship on wartime China—that is, to take seriously the work of Chinese institutions and individuals who operated under occupation.

Occupation Precedents

As the research of a number of scholars working on the imperial Japanese presence in Asia has already shown, the creation of client regimes under Japanese tutelage was frequently accompanied by the development of distinctive visual cultures. Barak Kushner, Kari Shepherdson-Scott, and others have demonstrated how visual propaganda was utilized by the Japanese and their allies among local elites to promote Sino-Japanese cooperation.[5] So important was this pictorial side of the Japanese advance that it constituted what I have elsewhere called a "visual invasion."[6]

The development of visual cultures under the RNG needs to be understood in light of such antecedents. The RNG inherited some of its most recurrent visual narratives from client regimes in China that predated it, as well as directly from the Japanese military. This is hardly surprising, as Japanese advisers sat alongside Chinese cadres in some of the key institutions tasked with producing or censoring pictorial media.[7] RNG archival files are full of references to high-ranking members of the Propaganda Corps (Hōdōbu) attached to Japan's China Expeditionary Army, for this body also assisted the RNG in distributing the propaganda it produced. For example, the Propaganda Corps' Mabuchi Itsuo, a "key figure in the link between military and civilian propaganda operations in China and Japan,"[8] worked directly with the Ministry of Publicity (MoP) to coordinate propaganda policy. Under the guidance of Mabuchi, the Japanese continued to employ dozens of Japanese artists to produce visual propaganda for distribution in rural areas and in regions on the front line.[9] Artists attached to the Japanese military, such as Kawashima Riichiro and Ōta Tenkyō, produced vast amounts of printed propaganda, some of which celebrated the "return" of the RNG—despite never actually serving Wang's regime.[10] And regional newspapers edited by Chinese within the RNG realm habitually republished pictorial propaganda produced by Japanese news agencies.[11]

We should not, however, assume that this meant a complete lack of agency on the part of Chinese cultural producers or a wholesale adoption of discursive practices from Japanese military or media organizations on the part of the RNG. To be sure, the RNG "returned" at a moment when visual practices, developed elsewhere in Japanese-occupied Asia, were already available as a set of prêt-à-porter precedents. In addition to these, however, the RNG inherited Chinese political, cultural, and media institutions, as well as cultural workers themselves. The agencies of the RNG drew on all of these—sometimes selectively but often because it had no other choice.

The wellspring of much of the imagery initially adopted by the RNG, as well as institutional modes of putting such imagery into practice, was Manchukuo. While the "empire" of Manchukuo was ideologically and structurally far removed from the RNG, it cast a long shadow over virtually all client regimes that followed it, especially in terms of cultural production. The RNG was not immune to such influence. It is for this reason that a consideration of Manchukuo visual culture and the cultural institutions through which this was fostered is important for any study of iconographies of occupation under Wang Jingwei.

Manchukuo fostered an entire visual culture aimed at celebrating and sustaining the life of this state until its disappearance in 1945. Institutions such as the South Manchuria Railway Company's (Mantestu) Film Unit and, later, the Manchukuo Film Association (Man'ei)—the "dream factory" of Japanese imperialism, as Michael Baskett has described it[12]—were instrumental in producing what Jie Li has characterized as a "phantasmagoria that had enchanted various utopian fantasies" in this outpost of Japanese imperialism.[13] Perhaps the most celebrated living icon of Manchukuo in the wider region was the Man'ei star Li Xianglan (Ri Ko Ran), that "enduring symbol of the Chinese culture produced within Japanese-occupied Manchuria."[14] Li Xianglan not only became the most marketable celebrity associated with Man'ei. Her extra-diegetic face also emerged as one of the most recurrent symbols of occupation visual cultures more broadly, appearing regularly on the covers of pictorials and in print advertising produced in, and in support of, this new state in the northeast.

Institutionally, Manchukuo also provided a model of how best to mobilize cultural producers in the service of Japanese rule. It was here, for example, that the Kwantung Army founded the Kyōwakai (Concordia Association), originally as a "propaganda and information-gathering agency . . . [that] concentrated on promoting and publicizing the new regime."[15] The Kyōwakai also fostered pro-regime artistic expression in Manchukuo, thereby establishing a template through which a state-sponsored mass organization could bring local cultural workers together with Japanese agents to produce visual (and other) propaganda.

In terms of aesthetics, as well as the processes through which such aesthetics were reproduced, Manchukuo set the standard for other, post-1937 client regimes in China. As I have described elsewhere, for example, many of the "institutional models of mobilization" put in place by the PGROC in north China were derived directly from Manchukuo templates.[16] This included the Xinminhui (New People's Association), a north China–based propaganda and political body founded by the Japanese but staffed by Chinese and modeled directly on the Kyōwakai. Tasked with mobilizing local citizens to support Japanese war aims, the Xinminhui published its own newspapers and pictorials and fostered a cohort of artists, writers, and musicians. Its cultural influence in north China remained potent until the end of the war.[17]

In east China, a similar pattern emerged. Here, the analog of the Concordia Association was an organization called the Daminhui (Great People's

Association). Organized by the Japanese special service in Shanghai[18] but directed by the veteran KMT member Wen Zongyao and affiliated with the RGROC,[19] the Daminhui has been described as the "flagship enterprise of the Reformed Government [i.e., the RGROC]."[20] It learned its trade, however, directly from the Xinminhui; indeed, propagandists associated with the north China body, such as Miao Bin,[21] served as advisers to the Daminhui, as did the aforementioned Mabuchi Itsuo. It was such individuals who guided the Daminhui's Propaganda Department (Xuanchuanbu), within which were employed all manner of Chinese cultural workers. The Daminhui made a particular name for itself in rousing local communities at pro-occupation celebrations.[22]

Despite this very clear Manchukuo influence, much of the propaganda work undertaken by the Daminhui looked remarkably similar to the "salvationist" (*jiuguo*) propaganda that had been developed by the Chinese resistance in Wuhan in 1938.[23] This resemblance was due to a number of the Daminhui's affiliated agencies having been specifically designed to emulate what the Japanese saw as effective methods of persuasion developed by the Chinese resistance early in the war.[24] Nonetheless, the Daminhui developed its own "brand." It operated under a logo composed of a five-pointed star and a crescent moon. This logo became so prominent in the RGROC that, at one stage, it adorned Nanjing's city walls.[25]

As well as crafting an institutional framework for propaganda production that drew on Manchukuo precedents, the Japanese also initiated projects in the late 1930s that would have a lasting impact on visual cultures in occupied China, including the establishment of Chinese-language and bilingual (Japanese-Chinese) pictorials.[26] Japanese news agencies and their proxies on the Asian continent began producing such publications within months of the 1937 invasion. In time, these became one of the key forms of media through which occupation iconographies would come to be nurtured and circulated. Some of these publications were modeled on commercial Chinese pictorials that had survived the Japanese onslaught of 1937 by relocating to Shanghai's International Settlement. The *New China Pictorial* (*Xin Zhonghua huabao*) was one such example. Financed by the Japanese military and edited by a Peace Movement journalist called Wu Linzhi, this pictorial looked almost identical to the glossy magazines produced by commercial Chinese publishers when it first appeared on Shanghai newsstands in June 1939.[27] Others were associated with specific groups that the Japanese had established in occupied China. These included the East Asia League (EAL) (Dong Ya Lianmeng), established in February 1940 to foster Pan-Asian sentiment,[28] and the Sino-Japanese Cultural Association (SJCA) (Zhong-Ri wenhua xiehui), established in the summer of 1940 with the support of Chu Minyi (the RNG foreign minister). Both of these organizations have been dismissed as inconsequential in some of the literature on the occupation.[29] Nevertheless, they played an important role in providing space for the production of highly politicized Chinese artistic expression under occupation. In Guangzhou, the local chapter of the East Asia League published *Dong Ya Lianmeng huabao* (Toa pictorial), a periodical that would develop into one of the primary vehicles for the dissemination of occupation iconographies in that city. The *Changjiang huakan* (Yangtze pictorial) was established by the local chapter of the SJCA in Wuhan and, under the editorship of local dramatist and author Xie Xiping, promoted the work of Wuhan-based artists, writers, and photographers.[30] The similarities that such publications could claim with the colorful magazines of Republican Shanghai were more than coincidence. Wang Jingwei's Peace Movement had lamented the lack of a pictorial it could call its own in 1939 and subsequently co-opted *Liangyou* (Young companion) into its stable of media products.[31] Wu Liande, the founder of this most commercially successful of prewar pictorials, was later listed as a member of the RNG's Special Propaganda Unit (Tezhong xuanchuanzu),[32] meaning that the skills involved in producing glossy pictorials in Shanghai could be made directly available to Wang's regime.

By far the most influential of occupation magazines, however, was the *Huawen Daban meiri* (*Kabun Ōsaka mainichi*)—a publication I shall refer to hereafter as the *Kabun*. This bimonthly periodical, edited originally in Osaka but specifically for a literate Chinese audience in China itself, was first published in November 1938. Initially, the *Kabun* adopted a north China perspective, reporting on developments in the PGROC and Manchukuo. Its distribution was aided by the Japanese military as the latter pushed through China in the pre-RNG period, and by early 1941, the *Kabun* claimed a circulation of over 600,000 in China.[33] While such self-published figures should be viewed with some skepticism, they nonetheless give some indication of the importance of this periodical to occupation authorities.

Despite being created at the time of Japanese conquest, this was not a purely dogmatic publication, however. Indeed, as Norman Smith has noted, the *Kabun* maintained a measure of editorial autonomy, which meant that Chinese intellectuals could publish within its pages material that might otherwise have been censored in Manchukuo or occupied China.[34] In the *Kabun*, partisan features on leading figures in early client regimes sat alongside illustrated essays about painting or interviews with Chinese film celebrities.

This magazine also provided a forum for Chinese cultural workers who had "stayed behind" after the Japanese invasion. A significant number of individuals who populate subsequent chapters of this book were featured in the *Kabun,* and many of the visual tropes that would come to be used most frequently by the employees of RNG institutions were first explored on its pages by Chinese illustrators.

Rebuilding a Visual Infrastructure

The RNG thus "returned" to an occupied China that was already brimming with what might be termed distinct "occupation visual cultures" championed in Japanese-sponsored pictorials, organized by Japanese-initiated organizations, and promoted by Pan-Asian celebrities such as Li Xianglan. All of these would continue to play a role, to varying degrees, for the remainder of the war.

At a practical level, this existing cultural infrastructure represented a boon for Wang's Peace Movement. In east China, in particular, existing cultural organizations could be appropriated as the nebulous Peace Movement was rapidly transformed from an idea-cum-clique into a "living and breathing" regime. The need to create entirely new cultural institutions from scratch could thus be avoided. Sections of the Daminhui, for example, were absorbed into Wang Jingwei's reorganized KMT, even though the Daminhui itself was officially folded in 1940.[35] RGROC propaganda bureaucrats were kept in post at the local level at the insistence of the Japanese.[36] And the pictorials that Japanese news agencies had established in 1938 and 1939 could continue to be published but could turn their praise away from earlier client regimes and focus it instead on Wang Jingwei. The *Kabun* was a case in point. It shifted its adulation firmly onto Wang in late 1939, while continuing to publish the less overtly political content that had become its staple. In August 1941, in a move that symbolized this magazine's support for the RNG cause, the *Kabun* opened an office in Nanjing.[37]

It was not just institutions that could be brought into the RNG orbit, however. Chinese individuals who had carved out careers in the pre-1940 occupation media could just as easily be put to work for the new regime. Many of the figures who emerged as the main names in RNG cartooning, for example, had started their careers in the employ of RGROC and/or PGROC publications or in the Daminhui. One example was Chen Xiaozuo. A graduate of the Shanghai School of Fine Arts (Shanghai meishu zhuanke xuexiao), Chen came into occupation cartooning thanks to his father, an

RGROC official and well-established writer named Chen Liaoshi. Chen *fils* contributed sketches to Daminhui publications (although he had also contributed artwork to anti-Japanese pictorials prior to the war).[38] Under the *nom d'art* "Ma Wu," Chen was producing cartoons for RGROC pictorials and the newspaper *Nanjing xinbao* from early 1939.[39] He continued to do this until the end of the war, later via an official affiliation with the RNG army Propaganda Corps.[40]

Others artists came to occupation cartooning with different pedigrees. Dong Tianye and Cao Hanmei had both led distinguished careers prior to 1937, often in Chinese pictorials that took a decidedly anti-Japanese line. At different points after 1940, however, both worked for state-sponsored media outlets. From 1942 onward, Dong Tianye produced caricatures of occupation-compliant starlets for the commercial press, increasingly producing overt regime propaganda over the course of the war. Cao Hanmei—the brother of famed Republican-era (and resistance) cartoonists Zhang Guangyu and Zhang Zhengyu—emerged (through the pages of the *Kabun*) as a creator of cartoons and other forms of visual art in RNG-sponsored periodicals like *Guoyi,* while training RNG cultural cadres in propaganda arts. His cartoons and *lianhuanhua* (comics) were published through the Li Shiqun–affiliated newspaper *Guomin xinwen* and various other outlets during the occupation.[41]

The RNG's partial reliance on preexisting talent, as well as its attempts to graft such talent onto its own media apparatus, was not without controversy. The client regimes that predated the RNG had been tasked with denigrating Republican Chinese icons and ideologies.[42] The return of an administration that took pride in its Republican heritage and even revived the ROC flag thus represented a challenge. The residua of earlier occupation tropes, some of which sought to disown or undermine prewar Republican iconography, would linger after 1940, ultimately undermining the coherence of the message that the regime sought to promote.

It was also the RNG's insistence on its Nationalist credentials, however, that would lead to the creation of new institutions tasked specifically with managing Nanjing's message(s). This is best illustrated by the MoP.[43] The MoP predated the return of the RNG to Nanjing by some months, having developed out of the China News Service (Zhonghua tongxunshe)—a Shanghai-based organization that had been established in November 1939 and that maintained close ties to the pro-Wang newspaper *Zhonghua ribao* (Central China Daily News).[44] The process of establishing a new regime under Wang Jingwei needed to be sold to the Chinese people (and others) and hence required management. The return itself was a highly visual affair and demanded the resources of a quasi-governmental ministry to oversee its choreography, though the MoP had little choice but to leave the organization of the day's processions to the Daminhui (a body that specialized in such skills).[45]

The management of the MoP provides us with clues about the ways in which the RNG viewed propaganda and censorship. The MoP's minister was Lin Baisheng. Lin was a Soviet-trained, Cantonese newspaper editor who had followed Wang Jingwei for many years (both in China and in Europe). In 1939, he had operated a de facto Peace Movement propaganda organization from the offices of his *Nanhua ribao* (South China Daily News) on the aptly named Hollywood Road in Hong Kong.[46] He was assisted in his work by intellectuals, such as Hu Lancheng, who had established names for themselves in pro-Wang newspapers prior to the *huandu*.[47] In 1940, however, Lin's MoP was forced by the Japanese to accept into its ranks many members of the Daminhui; and at the local level, its propaganda was initially overseen by Chinese who had worked within the RGROC in 1938 and 1939.[48] This would have major implications for the messages that the MoP sought to impart, especially in the first years or more of the RNG's return.

In Nanjing, the MoP managed virtually all matters relating to the control and censorship of the media, as well as both domestic and international distribution of overt and covert regime propaganda. It was the MoP, for instance, that oversaw regulations, introduced in April 1941, for the banning of photographs and paintings that were deemed undesirable by the regime. These were a broad set of rules that reflected the MoP's attempt to balance the desire for cultural innovation with anxieties about accusations that this was anything but a distinctly Chinese regime. Unsurprisingly, then, these looked remarkably like rules that had been implemented during the Nanjing decade. Photographs and paintings that undermined "respect for the Republic of China" (*Zhonghua minguo zunyan*), went against the Three Principles of the People and national policies, were harmful to "good behavior and public order" (*shanlang fengsu gonggong zhixu*), or depicted areas of significance to national defense were all outlawed.[49] In reality, the breadth of such definitions allowed the MoP and its workers to maintain a wide degree of leeway in deciding what could and could not be seen in occupied China.

So as to train people in making such decisions—and, of course, in producing alternative work that would fit with regime norms—the MoP also established its own Central Propaganda Institute (CPI) (Zhongyang xuanchuan jiangxisuo), attached to the Central University (Zhongyang daxue) in

Nanjing. Here it trained cadres, journalists, and artists in a broad curriculum but also in specialized fields such as propaganda art. The CPI employed the artist Cao Hanmei, the well-established dramatist Chen Dabei, and various other intellectuals to train the next generation of occupation cultural workers.[50] Graduates of this institute were employed in newspapers and publicity bureaus (*xuanchuanchu*) throughout occupied China (as the RNG sought to dilute residual RGROC influence beyond Nanjing).[51] Curricula vitae that still exist for staff in the RNG's Guangzhou Bureau of Publicity provide an insight into the sorts of individuals these were. Almost all high-ranking staff at this office were university graduates;[52] most had held positions in the KMT or the Chinese armed forces prior to 1937; and all had been exposed to a vast array of media work prior to their RNG tenure.[53]

The MoP also created the RNG's only official Chinese purveyor of news. This was the Central News Agency (CNA) (Zhongyang dianxunshe), which was established in May 1941 as a replica of a Nationalist (i.e., Chiang Kai-shek) organization of the same name.[54] Jointly managed by MoP personnel and Japanese media managers such as Yoshino Inosuke of Dōmei, the CNA was responsible for generating content for newspapers (including both copy and images).[55] It also published periodicals, books, and special collections to celebrate important events.

In terms of pictorial content, the CNA was initially reliant on Japanese news agencies, especially Dōmei. One of the main tasks of the CNA's Photographic Unit (Sheyingshe), for example, was to distribute photographs from Japanese sources to Chinese newspapers in the regime's hinterland.[56] In light of the sheer dominance of photojournalism in occupied China by Japanese firms that specialized in the form,[57] there was little opportunity for the CNA to produce it own pictorial content in the early years of its existence.[58] From mid-1941 onward, however, the CNA emerged as the main vehicle of the occupied gaze, especially in terms of documentary and propaganda photography in support of Rural Pacification. It even opened its own regional offices in Suzhou and Wuxi to aid such efforts in the following year.[59] In May 1942, the CNA also embarked on a policy of strengthening its capacity to produce news photography. This program was inspired by the new realities of a post–Pearl Harbor world, in which rival Chinese administrations such as the Chongqing Nationalists were seen to be benefiting from direct interaction with American news media.[60] As a result of all this, the CNA evolved into a producer of its own photography, with individuals such as Xue Diwei and Chen Guoqi playing leading roles in crafting new visions of occupied China that aligned with regime policies.[61] Xue may have been related to a journalist called Xue Huizi (with whom he almost always worked while at the CNA),[62] while Chen was related by marriage to Wang Jingwei himself. Both would produce a significant body of photography for RNG news media and publications. In light of such contributions, the CNA was arguing by 1944 about the need to recognize photography as being "more practical than written propaganda" and a form that was "more popular [*tongsu*] and easy to understand, but [that] can also leave readers with an extremely deep impression."[63]

Mobilizing Cultural Workers

The MoP, its offshoots such as the CNA, and other government and party bodies all produced visual propaganda. These institutions did not, however, represent the full extent of visual expression in Wang Jingwei's China. On the contrary, the development of cultural production beyond government control was not only allowed but encouraged, at least up until 1943. A number of art colleges reopened and organized their own exhibitions,[64] while individual artists continued to sketch, paint, and sculpt—often simply as a means to survive what were, after all, financially trying times.[65] However, both the RNG and the Japanese would seek to consolidate and exact increasing levels of control over such groups, especially as the International Settlement (where significant numbers of non-RNG-affiliated cultural workers had resided) was brought under direct Japanese control in December 1941 and as the RNG put new regulations governing "wartime culture and propaganda" in place in 1943.[66] In other words, as the neutral rhetoric and aesthetics of the *huandu* period gave way to the nativist nationalism and "Axis turn" of the New Citizens Movement, so too did the Japanese and the RNG seek to exert far greater control over cultural production in occupied China more generally.

The approach taken to such cultural consolidation was uniform. It involved the coaxing by the Japanese of artists who had remained in occupied areas to reprise their crafts in the service of occupation. At the same time, and in the spirit of Pan-Asian brotherhood, Japanese artists would be "invited" to work with their Chinese peers, so as to train a new generation of occupation-era Chinese cultural workers. It was this approach that led, for example, to the founding of the Chinese Cartoon Association (CCA) (Zhongguo manhua xiehui) in late 1942. This organization brought together Chinese cartoonists like Ma Wu, Cao Hanmei, and Dong Tianye with cartoonists from the Propaganda Corps and Japanese newspapers like

Tairiku shinpō, including Katō Minosuke and Miura Noa.[67] The CCA produced its own magazine, *Zhongguo manhua* (Chinese cartoons), and organized exhibitions of Chinese cartoons.[68] By 1943, the CCA was the primary institution promoting the art of cartooning in Wang's China.

A lesser-known example was an organization founded to support a field of visual culture that has been almost entirely overlooked in the academic literature on the RNG—*muke*, or woodcuts. Much has been made of the centrality of the woodcut form to the visual cultures of resistance in wartime Yan'an.[69] However, some artists who had long been associated with this form, such as the Beijing-based Wang Qingfang, took to promoting a revival of woodcuts through the pages of occupation magazines such as the *Kabun* from 1939 onward.[70] Organizations such as the Daminhui also employed their own woodcut specialists, with individuals such as Wang Chuan being particularly prolific.

From December 1942 onward, however, a periodical entitled *Zhongguo muke* (Chinese woodcuts) was published in Shanghai. This promoted woodcuts as a legitimate Pan-Asian art form and even went so far as to enlist figures such as Uchiyama Kanzō—a friend of the form's most vocal promoter in prewar China, Lu Xun—to argue for a renaissance of this form under occupation.[71] *Chinese woodcuts* was edited by a Chinese artist called Wang Yingxiao, who appears to have come to the form only after the Japanese invasion. Wang not only went on to publish collections of highly politicized woodcuts but was also, alongside Japanese woodblock artists such as Tagawa Ken, a founding member of the RNG state-backed Zhongguo muke zuozhe xiehui (Association of Chinese Woodcut Artists, or ACWA) in October 1943.[72] The ACWA would take the lead in training CPI graduates and others in woodcut production for the remainder of the war.

Other groups of Chinese artists were also co-opted into regime-backed cultural programs. The China Arts Society (Zhongguo wenyi xiehui) had been founded in the RGROC period by the writer Chen Liaoshi (father of the aforementioned Chen Xiaozuo/Ma Wu) but included prominent visual artists such as Cao Hanmei within its ranks. Its flagship periodical, *Guoyi*, in which various forms of traditional painting, calligraphy, and other visual arts were celebrated, predated the return of the RNG by some months. Nevertheless, it would come to represent an important forum in which acquiescent artists could ply their trade under occupation.[73]

In practice, however, the RNG was anything but purist when it came to the arts. Some of the most active Chinese artists under occupation were those who had been trained in Europe and who undertook what was referred to as "European-style painting" (*yanghua*)—usually meaning they worked in oils. Well-known artists who came under such a definition included Liu Haisu and Yan Wenliang, both of whom exhibited their work in occupied Shanghai.[74] As Michael Sullivan notes, such work continued for largely mundane reasons. Oil paintings were just as important as middle-class status symbols during the occupation as they had been before it.[75]

There were also more political reasons, however, to tolerate such work. Consider, for example, the paintings of one of the most celebrated of Chinese artists to have been trained in Europe—Fan Tchunpi.[76] Described by Craig Clunas as "the first Chinese student of significant artistic experience to study in France,"[77] Fan had been a prominent exponent of modernist oil painting in the pre-RNG era.[78] Due to her direct connections to the Peace Movement—she was the widow of the Peace Movement martyr Zeng Zhongming—Fan was elevated to an unprecedented level of cultural prominence during the occupation (despite being a purveyor of art that was decidedly European in its provenance). She continued to exhibit her work—portraits of her late husband, for example—right up until the final months of the occupation.[79] And by painting an "autumn morning at Zijinshan [Purple Mountain]" in 1944—that is, at almost the exact time that Wang Jingwei was being buried on the slopes of that very mountain—she proved that European styles of painting were, in fact, entirely acceptable to a vehemently nativist regime, providing they were produced by a member of Wang's inner circle.[80]

The Occupation Culture Industry

Bringing cultural workers of prewar pedigree into the fold represented one way in which to seek visual legitimacy. It also provided a pool of talent that could be drawn upon for the purposes of visual propaganda beyond the RNG itself. In many spheres of cultural production, however, the RNG was reliant upon an existing commercial media sector and entertainment industry, either for providing a ready-made source of talent or simply for ensuring that cultural pabulum could continue to be produced for a war-weary populace. In the 1939–1940 period, this in fact represented official Peace Movement policy. Wang's courtiers chose to deliberately conflate political messaging and commercial advertising so that the unwanted attention of censors in colonial Hong Kong, as well as in Shanghai's International Settlement—still administered by a predominantly Western-dominated municipal council—could be avoided.[81]

The problem, however, was that such commercial interests did not always cooperate with RNG (or Japanese) policy makers. Take, for example, cinema. Poshek Fu describes commercial cinema under occupation as an "ambiguous space in which boundaries between heroic and villainous, political and apolitical, private and public were rarely clear and constantly transgressed."[82] Early in the occupation, Shanghai had served as a producer of commercial cinema in spite of the Japanese invasion. Indeed, the Japanese had initially encouraged commercial film exhibition in occupied China, as they would later do in other parts of occupied Asia.[83] Under what Fu has characterized as an "ambivalent partnership," commercial filmmakers and distributors in Shanghai were permitted by Japanese censors to continue their work—making new films but also showing foreign (including Hollywood) films—providing these did not undermine Japanese rule.[84]

Within this context, some in this industry did maintain links with the Peace Movement and, later, the MoP. The director Wong Hing-sue not only made period dramas (*guzhuangpian*) in Shanghai, for example, but also edited graphic pictorials in praise of Wang Jingwei.[85] Lin Baisheng even coopted commercial film stars into state rituals in Nanjing, while celebrities such as Li Lihua provided both copy and photography for the occupation media in accounts of interaction between the MoP and the film industry.[86] And some of the biggest stars of Chinese commercial cinema in the 1939–1940 period would even be cast as "brand ambassadors" for occupation itself.

In the spring of 1942, the Japanese forced Chinese filmmakers to unite under China United Productions (CUP) (Zhonghua lianhe zhipian gufen youxian gongsi) as they sought to encourage a shift toward more overtly Pan-Asian movies in China. Nevertheless, despite ongoing Japanese efforts—including the creation in May 1943 of the China United Motion Picture Company (CUMP) (Zhonghua dianying lianhe gongsi), which came under the direct management of the RNG—the commercial film industry continued to maintain an "entertainment orientation" for its urban clientele. The occupation state—that is, both the RNG and the Japanese—thus found itself balancing a desire to exploit the glamour associated with film celebrities, with an equally urgent anxiety about the potential for this industry to undermine Pan-Asian unity. This tension was never entirely resolved and led to competing ideas about what an occupied Chinese populace should aspire to as the war dragged on.

Other creative industries proved more obedient. Some of the private photographic studios that had proliferated in Chinese cities during the 1920s and 1930s, for example, continued to operate under occupation, producing everything from photographs of celebrities to wedding photography. On the one hand, this industry could be a thorn in the side of censors, especially when it reproduced popular "glamour portraits" of Hollywood celebrities at a time when the RNG was nominally at war with the United States.[87] On the other hand, photographic studios could be employed to craft occupation iconographies. One such example was the Shanghai-based Bann's Studio (Guangyi zhaoxiangguan). Like many of its competitors, Bann's had made a name for itself photographing the rich and famous of Republican China before the war, and its work had even been featured on the cover of the above-mentioned *Young companion*. It took its English trading name from the Anglicization of the surname of its founder, Peng Wangshi, who had emerged as an innovative photographer of landscapes in the 1920s. More importantly, Bann's had produced portraits for cultural and political celebrities in the 1930s.[88] From 1941 onward, however, it would be responsible for producing some of the most frequently reproduced photographic portraits of Wang Jingwei, all while advertising itself as representing "the highest standard in artistic photography" (*yishu zhaoxiang de zuigao shuizhun*).[89] Bann's was proof that a balance could be struck between the commercial media and RNG state aspirations.

The private sector played a role in the creation of visual cultures in other ways too. This was especially the case for specific industries that sought to make the most out of the commercial opportunities that occupation presented. Chief among these was pharmaceuticals. As Sherman Cochran has shown, Japanese pharmaceutical brands such as Jintan were already household names in China by the time of the *huandu*, having long seen in China an important market. Using its "full arsenal of advertising weapons," such as its trademark, Jintan was able to "occupy a prominent place in China's landscape" both before and after the occupation.[90]

Contemporary accounts suggest that the new realities of occupation were fully exploited by such companies when it came to advertising art. In the first year of the *huandu*, the cities of occupied China brimmed with advertisements for Japanese pharmaceutical products (ranging from newspaper adverts to billboards) that conflated commercial messages with highly politicized statements about the need to support the RNG and the notion of a Japanese-led Asia. Describing a train journey from Shanghai to Nanjing in 1941, the Chinese writer (and leading member of the SJCA) Zhang Ziping wrote with surprising candor about the nature of pharmaceutical advertising and visual propaganda that he witnessed along his route:

> All the way along, on both sides of the tracks, was blue hoarding covered in white slogans and advertisements. "Jintan . . . build the

> New Order in East Asia"; "Rohto eyedrops . . . won't tingle or cause pain . . . peace and anticommunism"; "Rebail brand . . . gonorrhea pills . . . only by eradicating communism can we save China"; "Wakamoto enriches the blood and strengthens the body, reverses aging and restores youth . . . save the nation through peace"; "Establish a strong central government"; "China, Japan, and Manchukuo must unite . . . world-famous Daigaku eyedrops." The number of such slogans were seemingly endless. There were so many that I grew dizzy and dozed off.[91]

This overlap between political and commercial (and particularly medicinal) messaging was not unique to occupied areas of China.[92] The expansion of commercial opportunities for Japanese pharmaceutical firms would, however, have significant consequences for the iconographies of occupation. And it is perhaps more than coincidence that—as Zhang Ziping had noticed—Japanese producers of eye care products were particularly prominent in such efforts. The notion that occupation produced new ways of seeing was, in fact, exploited by such companies, as they mixed messages about the supposed clarity that their products could bring to users' eyes and the clarity that Japanese domination could bring to the people of China themselves.[93]

Imagined Audiences

The RNG imagined a diverse range of constituencies. It is important, therefore, to grasp just how this regime tried to prioritize its needs when it came to producing or controlling visual cultures across those parts of China to which it laid claim. Disagreements about the regime's aims often manifested themselves in debates over contradictory though contemporary icons and symbols, as quite different modes of visuality were deployed to different audiences.

In an interview at the end of 1940, the head of an MoP delegation to Japan confided that the main target of RNG propaganda, at least at this early stage of the regime's existence, was almost exclusively Chinese people living outside the RNG realm.[94] The archival record left by the MoP confirms this. We know, for instance, that the MoP assessed the efficacy of its propaganda in "Free China."[95] We also know that RNG cadres collected communist propaganda that they captured during military campaigns, and openly expressed admiration for the skill of communist propagandists at different points throughout the war.[96]

It is equally clear, however, that the nature and content of propaganda being distributed toward Nanjing's rivals differed markedly from that circulating in occupied China itself. And despite claims in 1940 to be primarily concerned with the conversion of residents in Free China to the RNG cause, new markets for visual propaganda opened up at times throughout the war.

Rural Pacification, for example, led to entirely new avenues for the use of various forms of visual culture throughout the Lower Yangtze delta. Indeed, the very nature of these campaigns, in which the RNG sought to root out resistance and rebuild villages in the service of the regime, were visual. MoP cadres painted murals and slogans on the walls of rural compounds, calling on people to "defend Chairman Wang" (*yonghu Wang zhuxi*) and "revitalize the villages" (*fuxing nongcun*). Rural Pacification drama teams performed skits that underlined the futility of resistance. And "Rural Pacification pictorials" (*qingxiang huabao*) spread regime messages via photographs, cartoons, and woodcuts.[97] We have few means of assessing the reception of the visual depictions that were circulated through such media in "pacified" areas themselves. In some contemporary accounts, however, we learn that such efforts were but part of a wider struggle for control of the visual in the occupied countryside. Rural Pacification slogans shared village walls with the propaganda of resistance groups, and local residents were not always able to readily distinguish one from the other in the context of the rapidly shifting borders of the RNG state.[98] This may well have reflected deliberate attempts to emulate modes of visuality already tried and tested in the prewar years.

In the cities of east and south China, students, merchants, and "petty urbanites" (*xiao shimin*) represented the MoP's primary clientele, and one that continued to grow as people returned to the cities in search of stability.[99] The priorities of the RNG in this setting initially focused more on the tolerance of commercial culture that was apolitical in content. It was for the residents of towns and cities that the established forms of visual entertainment, from fine arts to cinema and cartooning, were encouraged.

Nonetheless, the archives left to posterity by the MoP suggest ongoing frustrations about the extent to which these underlying messages were getting through to such imagined audiences. At the first nationwide meeting of propaganda cadres in the summer of 1941, for example, Lin Baisheng singled out the effects of colonialism as one of the main reasons for China's lack of a proper propaganda infrastructure. At the same time, he called for the influence of "compradors and slaves to foreigners" (*maiban yangnu*)—those he deemed to have sold China out to the West—to be purged from China.[100]

Irritation about the lack of enthusiasm for the occupation is a regular theme in MoP reports throughout the war. With the Japanese attack on Pearl Harbor, for instance, local cadres were told to "rouse the Shanghainese to grasp this opportunity of returning to peace and working together to revitalize China and revitalize East Asia under the direction of the supreme leader Wang Jingwei."[101] Clearly, no amount of top-down visual media was enthusing this city's residents in ways that Lin Baisheng may have liked.

There can be little doubt that Japanese military and government institutions played a crucial role in advising on, overseeing, controlling, and molding the visual cultures that were produced and circulated in occupied China. The influx of Japanese pictorials, the dominance of Japanese news agencies, and even the billboards filled with brash advertisements for Japanese pharmaceutical goods all dominated what could be seen—and *how* it was seen—in the cities of the RNG realm. It is also true that the various organs of the RNG state, to say nothing of the culture industry, would simply not have been able to operate without the permission of the Japanese military.

Such support did not, however, equate with complete control over cultural expression. Nor does the fact of Japanese power negate the very real agency that the RNG itself established in building its own cultural infrastructure (or the work that those who operated outside of state control managed to continue to pursue in spite of occupation). In the realm of visual media, RNG agencies found a space in which they could exercise control partially independent of Japanese military rule. They emulated Japanese techniques as well as prewar and early-occupation-era Chinese methods to force (often conflicting) visions upon the occupied people they governed. Using terms that presage the theoretical contributions of scholars such as Nicholas Mirzoeff, one RNG cadre went so far as to argue in 1943 that "pictures [*tuhua*] are the sharpest cultural weapons we have, and have a close connection to politics."[102]

The RNG was, of course, not the only Chinese administration to hold such views. Indeed, RNG discussion of images as weapons sounds remarkably similar to the "paper bullet"–laden language of resistance that was emerging from various parts of Free China at the same time.[103] Such similarities hint that visual cultures in Wang Jingwei's China were not just reactive to Japanese policies but were also designed to respond to various alternative visions of China that were being imagined by rival Chinese regimes and cultural workers. These included those envisaged (until December 1941) by the commercial print media of Shanghai's International Settlement, by cadres and intellectuals in the "great interior," by communist cultural workers in Yan'an and the base areas, and by New Fourth Army guerrillas in the Lower Yangtze delta. The RNG was fully aware of all of these. Indeed, it borrowed ideas and techniques from these alternative visions as it sought to assemble its own iconographies.

Nonetheless, in the sheer breadth of agency that was exercised under occupation by Chinese cultural workers, we can see the emergence of what I call an occupied gaze—a specific mode of seeing and visually representing China that was distinct from that exercised by both the Japanese and the resistance. This gaze sought autonomy from Japanese power by deploying recognizably Chinese modes of visuality, even while it relied on the Japanese presence for its very existence. At the same time, it denied a place to those who questioned Wang's right to rule.

In relying on a foreign power with whom it was constantly negotiating for further autonomy, and in drawing on an eclectic range of Chinese cultural workers, the RNG was never able to achieve visual uniformity in its messages. It may well be that such uniformity was never necessarily desirable for a regime that sought to promote itself as more liberal than its rivals in Chongqing and Yan'an. There were no "talks at the Nanjing forum" under Wang Jingwei.[104] Nor was there ever a single style of artistic expression proscribed under occupation. As a result, the iconographies of occupation that Chinese painters, photographers, cartoonists, and filmmakers created or recycled in support of the RNG, and sometimes in spite of it, were as eclectic as the hastily assembled community of Peace Movement fellow travelers, Daminhui propagandists, and refugee artists itself.

The consequences of such inconsistency were an ever-changing set of iconographies that sometimes competed, not just with those favored by resistance forces, but also against each other. Given all this, the recycling today of photographs of Wang Jingwei with German diplomats or the appreciation of Fan Tchunpi oil paintings at European exhibitions need not be seen as contradictory. They serve, rather, to remind us just how visually disparate the iconographies of occupation would ultimately become.

CHAPTER 3

Visualizing the Occupied Leader

The RNG was, and remains today, inexorably associated with the figure of Wang Jingwei.[1] Wang's name, face, writings, and voice were seen, reproduced, and heard everywhere under occupation (at least up until 1944), and the very idea of the RNG itself was linked to Wang's personal claims to political legitimacy. Despite this, few scholars have looked critically at the ways in which Wang was visualized during the war, or at the use of various forms of visual media in both the promotion and the denigration of him. This is unusual, because so much of the RNG's iconographies of occupation revolved around Wang's figure and face—these being constant objects of official veneration. It also puts the scholarship on the RNG at odds with research on cognate administrations, much of which has demonstrated how the visual veneration of the "collaborationist" leader is so central to understanding client regimes.[2]

This chapter examines the origins, development, and fate of the Wang Jingwei personality cult under Japanese occupation. In keeping with the overall themes of this book, the chapter demonstrates how a focus on the visual realm can produce a quite different perspective from the biographical accounts that have dominated research on Wang thus far, many of which interrogate his decision in 1939 to seek a negotiated peace. A closer reading of the visual texts manufactured as part of the Wang cult—and the responses to these—can shed light on the very nature of the RNG in ways we might not expect.

Various groups—including Japanese news agencies, the Peace Movement, and sections of the RNG bureaucracy—sought to promote and embellish Wang's image for specific purposes and through a variety of visual media. This is not, therefore, a simple story of the celebration of a leader by an authoritarian regime. Rather, it is an account of the manipulation of Wang's image by an array of agents, as well as the place of Wang's image within a wider set of wartime visual cultures. Like the broader iconographies that were generated in occupied China, the Wang personality cult drew on various prewar and early wartime precedents, while responding to wartime changes both in China and abroad. This led to the emergence of a number of different Wangs, each of which could be called upon to promote quite different messages at specific points between 1939 and the end of the war.

Reinventing Wang Jingwei

The Japanese invasion of China in 1937 did not "make" Wang Jingwei. Nor did the *huandu*. As a long-serving Chinese statesman and a veteran of the early revolutionary movement, Wang had been in the public eye for decades. Indeed, the sheer longevity of his public image equaled and perhaps even surpassed that of his main rivals, including Chiang Kai-shek. A standard narrative of Wang's life and career had circulated among the Chinese reading public for well over a decade prior to 1937, especially in those parts of urban China in which Wang enjoyed political support at various periods, such as Guangzhou and Wuhan. This narrative was manufactured by courtiers such as T'ang Leang-li, by the KMT's reorganization faction, and by Wang himself.[3]

The story that all of these groups presented was remarkably consistent. It stressed Wang's credentials as a revolutionary, as witnessed in his arrest and his subsequent "almost martyrdom"—for Wang escaped execution by the Qing authorities—following his attempt to assassinate the Manchu prince regent Zaifeng with explosives in 1910.[4] In such accounts, Wang's personal and ideological proximity to Sun Yat-sen were always highlighted: Wang had, after all, been at Sun's deathbed, had helped pen Sun's testament, and had been a prominent figure in the public expressions of mourning for Sun in 1925.[5] Photography of Wang from before the Northern Expedition (Bei fa) regularly showed an active Wang, dressed in a Zhongshan tunic (*Zhongshan zhuang*), in the throes of oratory (figure 3.1).[6] At a more informal level, Wang is also said to have developed a following among educated women in China in the 1920s as a sex symbol.[7] He was certainly depicted by his followers within the KMT as a man of "consummate elegance and taste."[8]

Concurrently, negative comparisons were often made between Wang and Chiang Kai-shek, the latter presented by Wang's supporters as a dictator.[9] This dichotomy would be intensified in 1927 and again in 1931 when Wang headed short-lived Nationalist administrations that challenged the authority of Chiang. At such times, Wang was presented by his followers as being from the true "revolutionary faction" (*gemingpai*), and Chiang as from the "counterrevolutionary faction" (*fan gemingpai*).[10] This image of Wang as a "romantic revolutionary," as Howard Boorman described it, was also promoted

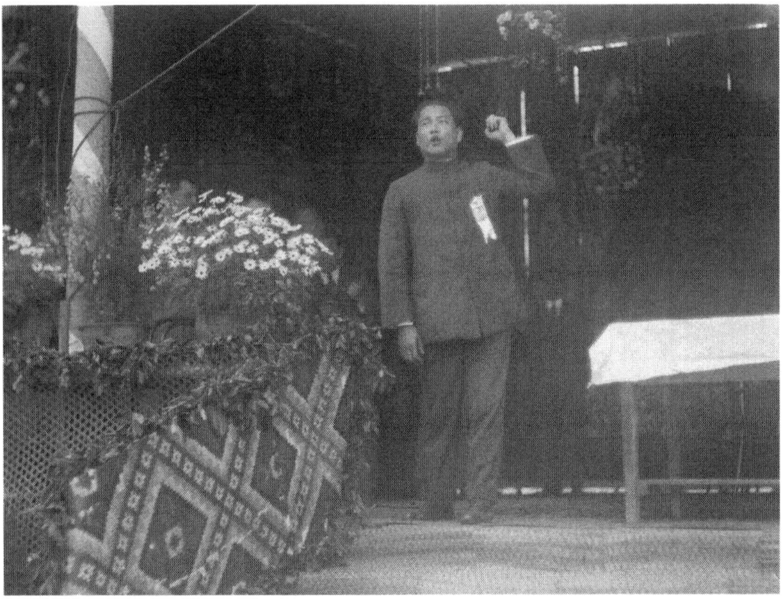

Figure 3.1. Wang Jingwei making a speech at the Second National Congress of the Kuomintang, Guangzhou, January 1926. Photograph by Fu Bingchang. Image courtesy of C. H. Foo, Y. W. Foo, and Historical Photographs of China, University of Bristol (www.hpcbristol.net).

abroad.[11] An illustrated portrait by Samuel Johnson Woolf of "Premier Wang"—looking remarkably like socialist realist imaginings of Mao Zedong in the 1960s—graced the cover of *Time* magazine in March 1935.[12]

A less revolutionary image of Wang also emerged in partisan publications in the 1930s. This development owed much to the burgeoning industry of studio photography in cities such as Shanghai and to the practice of using studio portraits as objects of political veneration, or simply as political gifts, in Republican China.[13] One of the most regularly reproduced photographic portraits of Wang from the time was a 1935 portrait produced by Kwong Hwa Photographic Studio (Guanghua zhaoxiangguan)—a privately run, Nanjing-based studio that was often patronized by KMT politicians.[14] This image, reprinted in hagiographies and in collections of Wang's writings, presented Wang as a man of letters.[15] He wore a contemplative expression, his eyebrows raised toward the center of his forehead so as to give him a slightly "distressed countenance" (*chourong manmian*),[16] his lips pursed, and his cheeks and jowls immaculately shaven (figure 3.2).

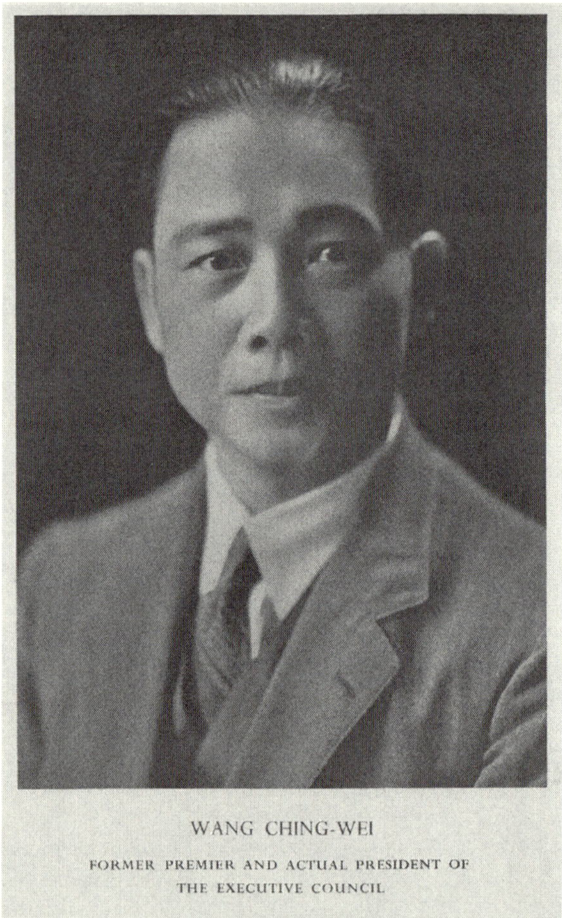

Figure 3.2. Studio portrait of Wang Jingwei (photographer unknown), circa 1935, featured as the frontispiece in Se-yuan Shu, ed., *Poems of Wang Ching-wei* (London: George Allen and Unwin, 1938). © The British Library Board (11110.b.32, frontispiece).

There were also newsworthy events in the 1930s that generated a significant number of images of Wang, though in a far different guise. The attempted assassination of Wang in November 1935 at a meeting of the KMT in Beijing, supposedly by agents affiliated with Chiang Kai-shek, resulted in a series of graphic pictures of an injured Wang in the Chinese press.[17] Photographs produced by international news agencies such as TASS and showing Wang lying on a hospital bed with his left temple bandaged were printed on the front page of major newspapers in China.[18] Such images would be widely circulated for the rest of Wang's career, conveniently deployed by his supporters whenever it was necessary to present Wang as a victim of political violence.[19]

As with other politicians of this era, however, Wang was never able to fully control his own image. He was subject to pictorial satire in the burgeoning print culture developing in Shanghai in the 1930s, just as his contemporaries were. In magazines and newspapers, portraiture of Wang was abstracted and reinvented in diverse ways.[20] Wang's physical traits and facial features proved particularly malleable in the hands of cartoonists such as Zhang Guangyu and Zhang Zhengyu (figure 3.3). These and numerous other artists accentuated Wang's drooping eyebrows, square jaw, and brilliantined hair (in contrast to the cropped and shaven heads of Wang's military opponents), thereby establishing a set of visual and physical markers that would later come to be recycled by Wang's critics, *and* his supporters, during the occupation.[21]

Be it in news photographs or satirical cartoons, the single most important element in imagery of Wang emerging prior to the war was a visual association with civilianism. Images of Wang from the 1930s regularly showed him dressed in a scholar's robe (*changpao*) or a Western lounge suit, for example—that is, clothing that was associated at this time with "worldliness, progress, action, and financial success" rather than with revolution.[22] This was in contrast to depictions of Wang's rivals (such as Chiang Kai-shek), for whom a visual association with martial prowess (via uniforms, capes, and military headwear) was de rigueur. Yet it also set Wang apart from his late mentor, the tunic-clad or (in generalissimo mode) epauletted Sun Yat-sen. Images of Wang circulating in the immediate prewar years thus placed him, not alongside other pretenders to national power, but next to civilian politicians such as Hu Shih and T. V. Soong.

In light of such antecedents, it would be tempting *not* to read Wang Jingwei's defection from Chongqing as marking a new point of departure in the crafting of his public image. The visual record suggests a more complicated story, however. For a start, Wang's disappearance from Free China in December 1938 was precisely that. While Wang did little initially to hide his whereabouts upon arrival in colonial Hanoi, he also did little to publicize his presence there, and few photographs were taken during his early phase of negotiations with the Japanese. Indeed, even news outlets that professed an affiliation with Wang, such as Lin Baisheng's Hong Kong-based *Nanhua ribao*, rarely printed photographs of Wang in this period, while Japanese

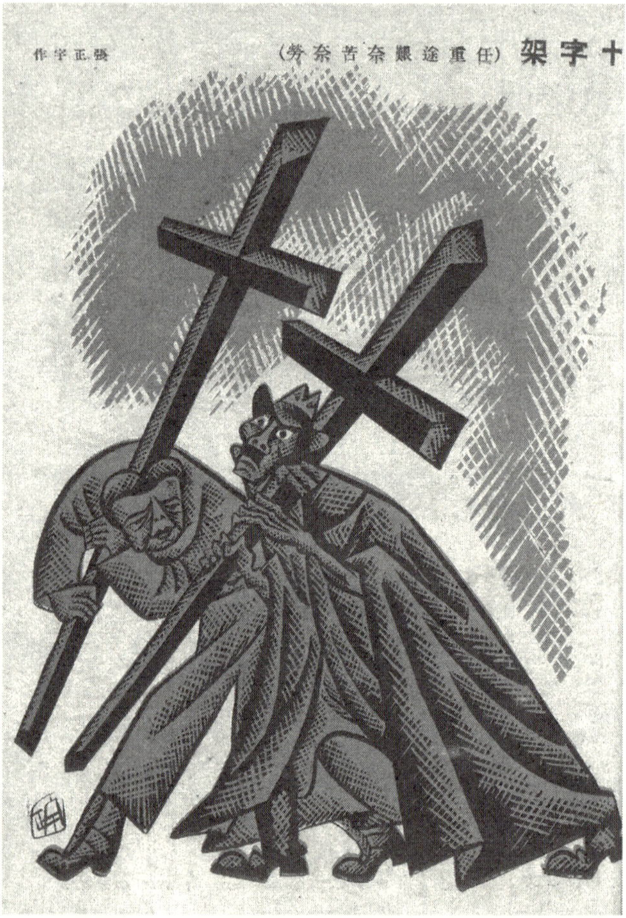

Figure 3.3. Cartoon of Wang Jingwei and Chiang Kai-shek by Zhang Zhengyu, entitled *Shizijia* (Crucifix). Featured in *Duli manhua* [Oriental puck] 2 (1935). Courtesy of the East Asia Library, Stanford University.

new agencies illustrated their accounts with prewar news photography of him.[23] In early 1939, Wang Jingwei was a name, a voice, and an opinion but not a publicly visible figure. Such invisibility would only intensify following the failed attempt on Wang's life by resistance agents in March 1939.

At the same time, Wang bore the brunt of extensive visual and rhetorical attacks from resistance-affiliated sources. Chiang Kai-shek instructed his cultural workers to launch what visual cultures theorists would today refer to as "image-weapons" against Wang, following his declaration of intent to negotiate a peaceful resolution with Japan.[24] Such calumny was not focused purely on Wang's actions. It was, just as importantly, directed at Wang himself. Muralists envisaged Wang's mutilation. Slogans calling for Wang to be "pushed into a grave" were scrawled across walls.[25] Many depictions from this period took prewar visual markers associated with Wang's apparent urbaneness and translated them into signs of feminine weakness—the gendering of "traitors" was a common theme in resistance vitriol. Wang was commonly drawn in drag, for example; in order to undermine Wang's claims to a revolutionary heritage, artists such as Zhang Guangyu depicted Wang as a ghost haunting the graves of martyrs in Guangzhou.[26] Another common trope took the very notion of the gaze and combined this with satire concerning Wang's apparent self-consciousness: Wang would often be drawn beside a mirror (only to have an animal or demon staring back at him) (figure 3.4). In such depictions Wang's raised eyebrows might be accentuated to create an impression of fear, fatigue, or naivete, and his nostrils could be enlarged to achieve a porcine appearance.[27]

This was also a period in which an entire genre of anti-Wang sculpture was initiated. The crafting of kneeling statues (*guixiang*) of Wang, upon which civilians would be encouraged to spit (in order to express their scorn for him in absentia), was started in 1939 with this purpose in mind.[28] The most celebrated kneeling statue in China prior to the Japanese invasion had been that dedicated to Qin Kuai (a Song-dynasty chancellor who had long been presented as the archetypal traitor in Chinese history due to his role in his kingdom's capitulation to the Jin empire).[29] The making of similar statues for Wang thus linked him to this figure. Resistance artists such as Xu Fubao published designs for the crafting of these anti-Wang statues in periodicals associated with the National Salvation Cartoon Propaganda Corps (Manhua xuanchuandui), for example.[30] Kneeling statues of Wang were subsequently built throughout unoccupied China from 1939 onward.

From mid-1939, however, various groups began to take part in the creation of new, sympathetic representations of Wang Jingwei. These included Mabuchi Itsuo's Propaganda Corps, Japanese news agencies such as Mainichi, and even pre-RNG client regimes.[31] Perhaps most important in the visual repackaging of Wang in this period, however, was one of the main vehicles of the Peace Movement—Lin Baisheng's Shanghai-based *Central China Daily News*. In the summer of 1939, this newspaper unveiled a new photographic portrait of Wang that would become one of the most frequently used and definitive images of him for the remainder of the war. Though the

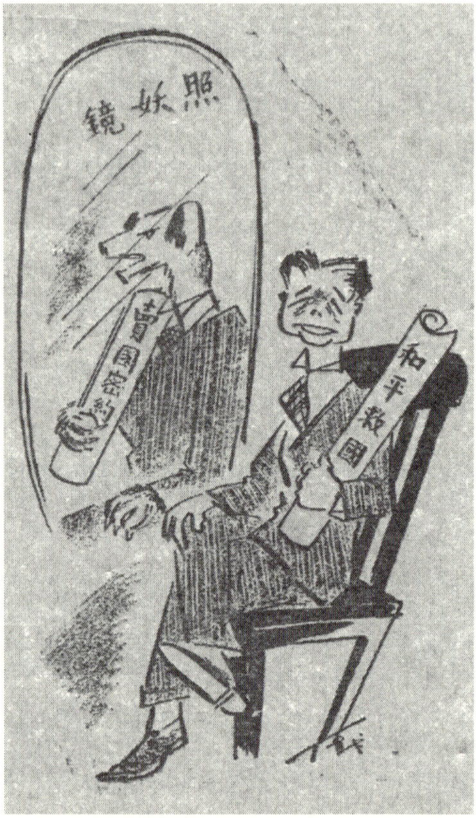

Figure 3.4. Unattributed cartoon image of Wang Jingwei sitting in front of a mirror, included in a 1939 anti-Wang leaflet produced by the Kuomintang. Courtesy of the KMT Party Archives (yi ban, 537/21).

provenance and precise date of the production of this portrait are difficult to determine through extant sources,[32] it was almost certainly taken during or shortly after Wang's stay in Shanghai in late May 1939, when Wang was engaged in formal negotiations with the Japanese.[33] As with many early portraits of Wang produced in the 1939–1940 period, it was never formally attributed to a single photographer. It first appeared in the *Tairiku shinpō* over a month prior to its first appearance in the *Zhonghua ribao.*[34]

In this image, Wang was dressed as he had been in most portraits produced in the 1930s—that is, in a dark three-piece suit, the attire of a modern Chinese

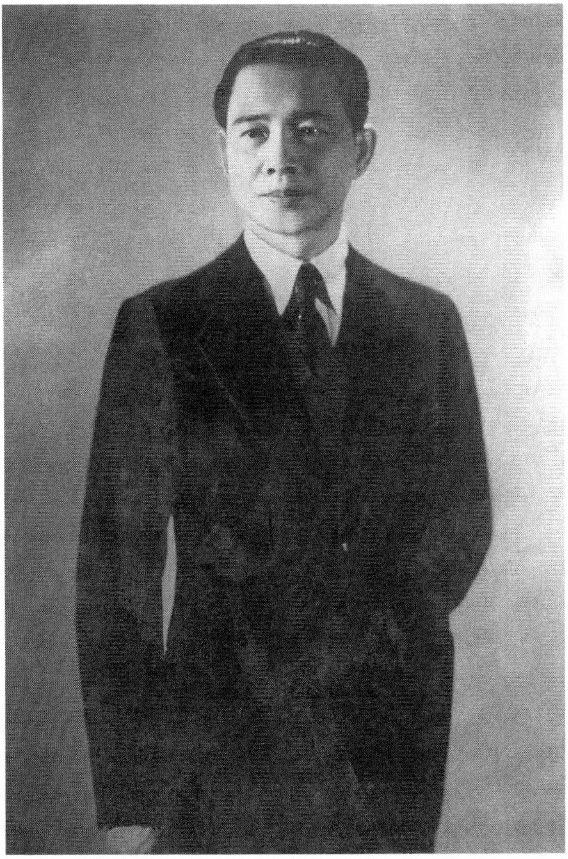

Figure 3.5. Portrait of Wang Jingwei, circa May 1939, by unknown photographer. Courtesy of The Mainichi Newspaper/AFLO.

statesman rather than a pro-Japanese activist or revolutionary. Indeed, the image looked not unlike the glamour portraits of Chinese celebrities that were common in Shanghai pictorials in the 1930s. Split lighting rendered the left side of Wang's face dark and drew attention to his brilliantined hair. The soft focus of the image and the pose assumed by Wang gave the photograph an almost pictorialist quality. Wang gazed off camera into the right middle distance with an expression that suggested idealism and purpose, but with the same raised eyebrows that had typified the 1935 Kwong Hwa studio portrait (figure 3.5).

This new portrait presented a defiant image of Wang. It offered visual proof that Wang had survived the assassination attempt by resistance agents just a few months earlier. By showing most of Wang's body in its three-quarter framing, it emphasized that Wang was in good health, despite the attempt on his life and the deluge of visual attacks on his image by cultural workers in the southwest. Descriptions of the image—such as an extended essay that accompanied it in a September 1939 issue of the *Kabun,* entitled "Tingshen fenqi heping jiuguo" (Lifting himself upright to save the nation through peace)—stressed Wang's corporeality but also his supposed vitality.[35] As Wang was rising from the (almost) dead, so too was an occupied China rising from the ashes of war.

The nondescript background of this image was matched by a lack of props or symbolic accoutrements in Wang's outfit. It is this austere and almost timeless quality that may explain the portrait's longevity. This image was the preferred choice in Chinese-language media when such outlets were reintroducing their readers to Wang in the second half of 1939, and a number of newspapers used it on their front pages to mark Wang's assumption of power on March 30, 1940.[36] Occupation newspapers were still using it some four years after its production as a generic image that could illustrate Wang-themed news, especially during periods later in the war when Wang's health was deteriorating.[37] On the recognition of the RNG by Germany and Italy in 1941, the same portrait was placed by Mainichi editors alongside photographs of Adolf Hitler and Benito Mussolini. For the RNG itself, this image continued to be used as the frontispiece for MoP publications well into 1941,[38] as well as the basis for murals and banners of Wang (figure 3.6).

This was not the only studio portrait of Wang to be produced in this early period, however. A number of new portraits, also unattributed and undated, presented a quite different image of Wang and were used for different purposes. In January 1940, for example, a new head shot of Wang, this time gazing directly at the viewer (as he had done in the 1935 portrait) began to be circulated. This new image showed a more fully lit Wang in a slightly clearer focus. The defiant and slightly romantic air of 1939 was replaced in this image by an expression of amiable solemnity, though the prominence given to his hair marked one commonality between the two images (figure 3.7).

This portrait was distributed precisely as Wang's imminent return to Nanjing was being openly discussed in the Chinese press. Its circulation was almost certainly timed to coincide with the conclusion of the Qingdao Conference (Qingdao huiyi) in January 1940, when the structure of Wang's nascent administration was being decided. The *Kabun* used a colorized version of this portrait on the cover of the issue it published to celebrate the inauguration of Wang's regime, as did the MoP, which used it as the cover image of one its very first publications, a bilingual (Chinese and English) program produced to mark the festivities of March 1940.[39]

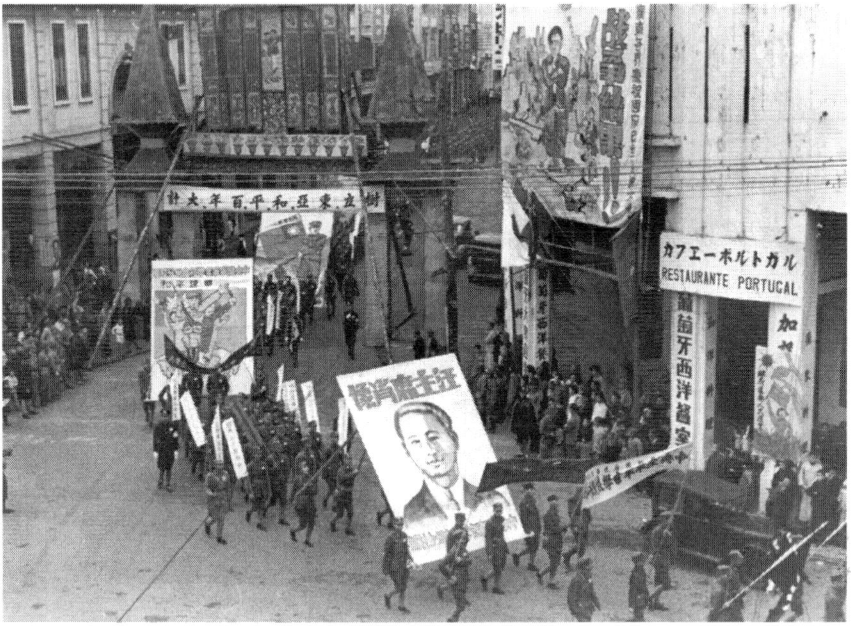

Figure 3.6 (top). Crowds in Guangzhou carrying a banner of Wang Jingwei, circa 1940. Photo by *Asahi shimbun* via Getty Images.

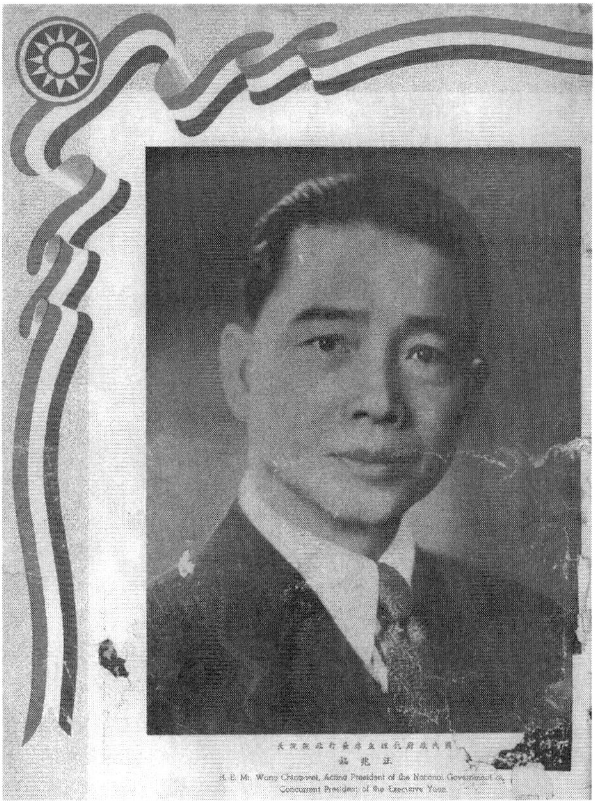

Figure 3.7 (right). Cover of Ministry of Publicity, *Special Commemoration Issue: Return of the National Government of the Republic of China to Its Capital* (Nanjing: Ministry of Publicity, 1940), featuring studio portrait of Wang Jingwei. Courtesy of Shanghai Library.

These studio portraits did not represent the full extent of Wangiana emerging in or around the *huandu,* however.[40] As the return of the RNG looked increasingly imminent in the winter of 1939–1940, organizations in and around Nanjing scrambled to produce a coherent view of what Wang looked like. This included groups that had had little to do with Wang previously, such as the Daminhui. The Daminhui's March 1940 pamphlet *Mr. Wang Jingwei and the New Central Government* (*Wang Jingwei xiansheng yu xin zhongyang zhengfu*), for example, included stylized illustrations of a bare-chested, muscular Wang bearing a torch and the Daminhui flag, looking not unlike a revolutionary worker. It also, however, included cartoon images of Wang in his lounge suit, with a full head of hair and his now trademark upturned eyebrows.[41] In Wuhan, hastily manufactured posters of Wang that drew on prewar photography but also included a distinctly Manchukuo flavor appeared in the first weeks of 1940. These posters showed Wang in oratory in front of a city wall emanating the light of dawn. Wang was also transformed into a metaphor: a lantern lighting the path to a new China, or a colossal arm distributing peace to the people.[42]

Japanese government agencies, news agencies, and even commercial advertisers also attempted to shape Wang's image in a variety of ways in this period. Just prior to the *huandu,* for example, unnamed Japanese painters were commissioned to produce life-size oil paintings of Wang (and other RNG leaders)—a process that, it appears, RNG officials themselves had little say in (figure 3.8).[43] In other cases, Japanese artists such as Asai Kan'emon were flown to Nanjing to paint portraits in oils of Wang in 1940 (figure 3.9).[44] Few of the resulting prototypes survived the RNG's first year, and many of the images produced in this period have been largely lost.[45] They nonetheless demonstrated that the Japanese government saw the benefits in making Japanese cultural workers contribute to the Wang personality cult.

Not all Japanese interventions were aligned with RNG sensibilities, however. The 1939 *Central China Daily News* portrait, for example, was recycled by the Japanese pharmaceutical firm Rohto. This company published a lithographic version of the portrait in a newspaper advertisement on the very day of the *huandu,* using it to promote "the world famous eyedrops of great men."[46]

The Militarization of Wang's Image

As I have argued elsewhere, the cult of personality built around Wang by his courtiers following the *huandu* was initially manufactured with the aim

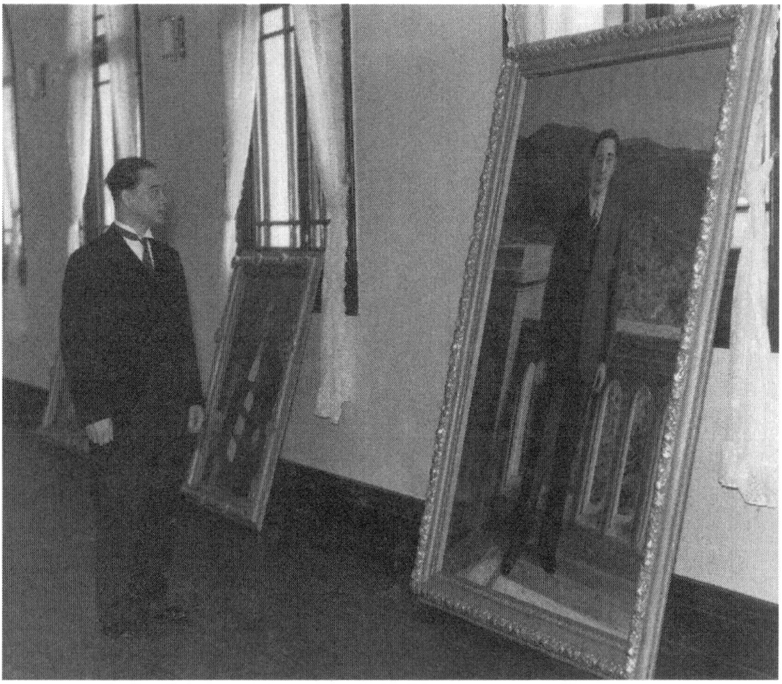

Figure 3.8. Photograph of Wang Jingwei admiring an oil painting of himself by an unidentified artist, circa 1940. Chu Minyi Collection (Lot 11700), Prints and Photographs Reading Room, Library of Congress.

of drawing a distinction between Wang and Chiang Kai-shek.[47] This attempt at what Jan Plamper has called "contradistinction"[48] has been noted in scholarship on the ideologies of the early RNG before,[49] but the visual implications of such a strategy have rarely been considered.

The Japanese invasion of 1937 had led to an explosion of rhetorical and pictorial depictions of Chiang Kai-shek as a national savior within resistance ranks. This was thanks particularly to the work of the Political Department of the Military Affairs Commission (PDMAC) (Junshi weiyuanhui zhengzhibu). This arm of the Nationalist state, restructured in January 1938, was managed by intellectuals such as Guo Moruo but included artists of diverse political proclivities.[50] In the early war years, it was tasked with producing posters, pamphlets, and murals of Chiang. As a result of such efforts, Chiang Kai-shek sat *alongside*, rather than below, Sun Yat-sen in the visual pantheon of Chinese strongmen after 1938, a fact that found expres-

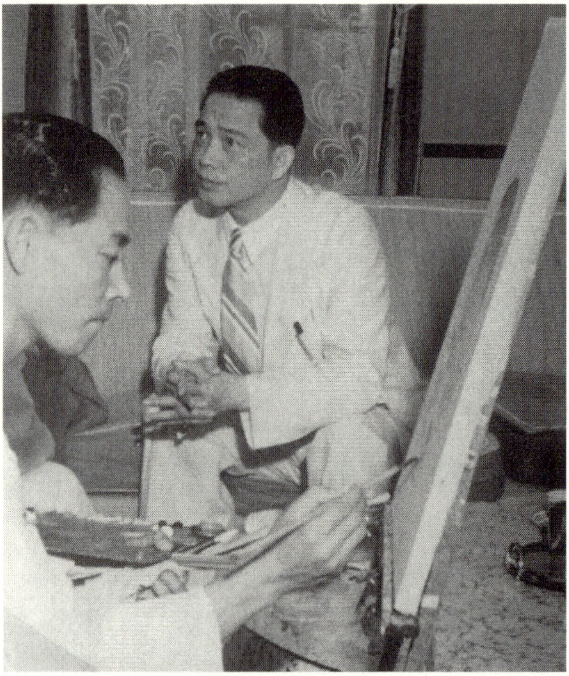

Figure 3.9. Photograph of Wang Jingwei having his portrait painted by Asai Kan'emon, August 1940. Denshō Digital Repository (ddr-njpa-1-1067), Hawai'i Times Photo Archives. Courtesy of the Hawai'i Times Photo Archives Foundation.

sion in the wartime rewriting of regulations on the production and use of Chiang's image and name in areas beyond Japanese influence.[51] The focus placed on civilianism by groups such as the *Zhonghua ribao* and the MoP was therefore clearly used to distinguish a "peaceful" and humble Wang from the aggressive and self-important Chiang that was being imagined by the PDMAC at the same time.

However, such contradistinction began to wane following the first anniversary of Wang's return in the spring of 1941. It was at this stage, according to the RNG official Luo Junqiang, that Wang was convinced by Lin Baisheng to adopt a more overtly militaristic approach to his public persona—to be seen to frequent military march-pasts, for example—in an attempt to promote the RNG as a quasi-Axis power. It was certainly the case that Lin's MoP stressed the need to celebrate the foundation of the armed forces

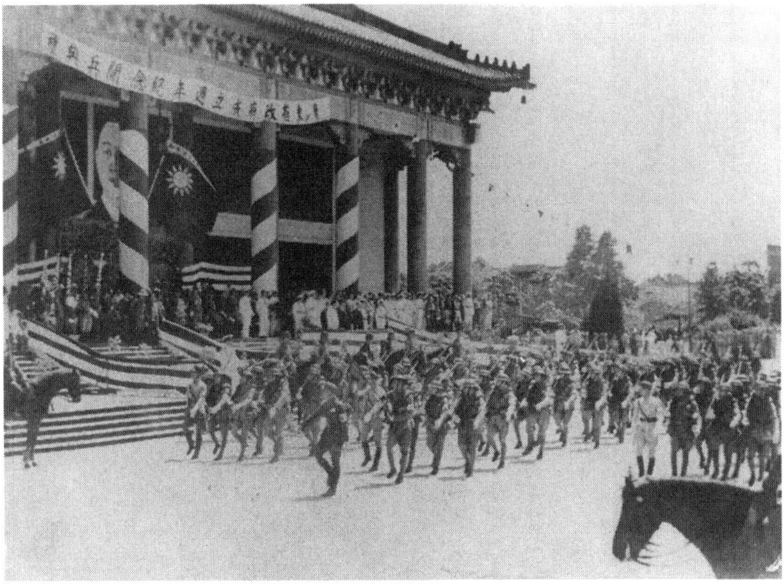

Figure 3.10. CNA photograph of military march-past in front of a large portrait of Wang Jingwei, in Guangzhou, circa 1941. Courtesy of Academia Historica.

(*jianjun*) and the modernization of the army under Wang in propaganda directives published in March 1941.[52] Many of the surviving images of Wang saluting troops date from this "Axis turn" in RNG visual cultures at around the same time (figure 3.10).[53]

Over the summer of 1941, the MoP also published new documentary images of Wang that sought to emulate early wartime depictions of Chiang Kai-shek in the PDMAC style. These were linked to the start of the Rural Pacification campaigns and specifically to Wang's multiple inspection tours (*xunshi*) of pacified areas in the Lower Yangtze delta that year. "President Wang Ching-wei in uniform" was the name given to this new entity,[54] as regime-backed pictorials showed Wang dressed in a field officer's uniform and cap, inspecting villages cleared of communist banditry (figure 3.11). Wang rode in sedan chairs, studied maps, and inspected RNG cadres. It was in this guise that some of the most frequently recycled images of Wang were produced, almost certainly by Japanese photographers. One of these, dating from October 1941, showed a uniformed Wang on location while touring a pacified area, saluting to unseen individuals to the right of the image.[55] It was also during these inspection tours of pacified areas, how-

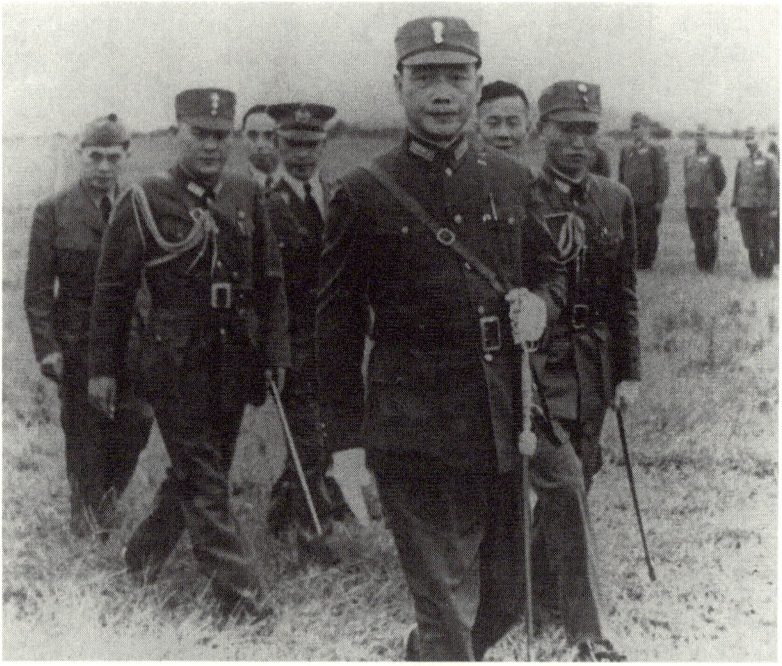

Figure 3.11. Photograph of Wang Jingwei during an inspection of Rural Pacification areas in 1941, possibly by Chen Guoqi. Courtesy of Academia Historica.

ever, that CNA photographers such as Chen Guoqi were tasked, for the first time, with pictorially documenting Wang's presence in the countryside.[56]

Rural Pacification also provided the context for the manufacture of a new and very different set of portraits of Wang. In the fall of 1941, the MoP approached a commercial purveyor of studio portraiture, Bann's Studio, to craft a new set of images of Wang Jingwei to align with Rural Pacification. It was one of Bann's Nanjing-based photographers, Liang Boping, who was responsible for this new set of 1941 "President Wang in uniform" portraits. These would be subsequently reproduced in significant number during the occupation (figure 3.12).

Aesthetically, there is little remarkable about Bann's portraits from 1941. In terms of their composition, for example, they represent nothing unusual or innovative in the grander scheme of studio portraiture in Republican China. The manufacture of these new portraits, however, did mark an important departure in the framing of a leader who had spent his entire career cultivating a civilian persona and who had been repackaged by his support-

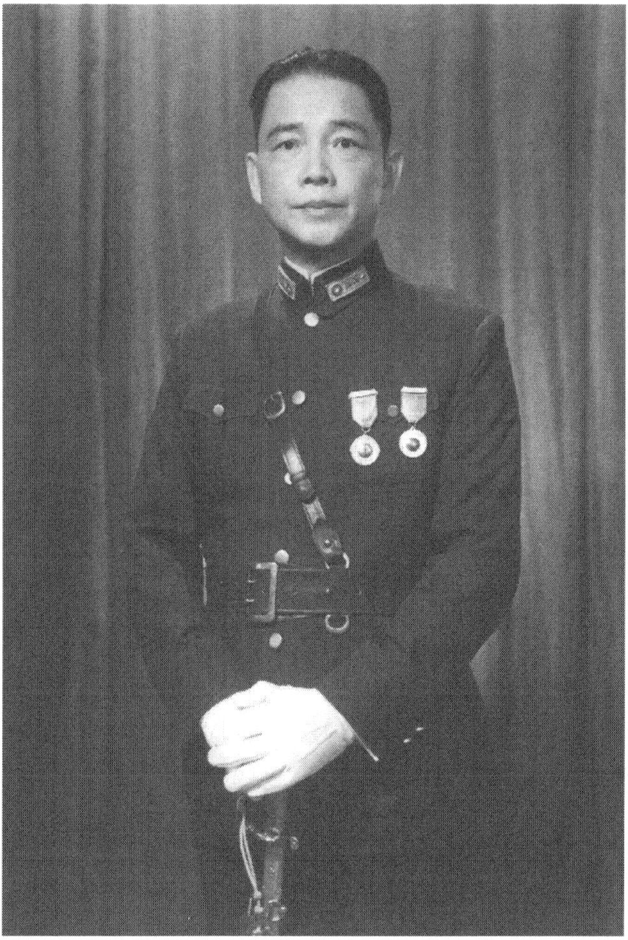

Figure 3.12. Liang Boping studio portrait of Wang Jingwei in Rural Pacification mode, 1941. Wang Jingwei and Lin Baisheng Photograph Collection. Courtesy of the East Asia Library, Stanford University.

ers in 1939 in a decidedly civilian, if romantic, fashion. Prior to 1941, Wang had never been photographed in a studio while wearing a military uniform.

In these new portraits, a be-medaled Wang was shown dressed in the uniform of a field officer. Some of the portraits were three-quarter-length images, while others showed Wang from the shoulders up. In some cases, Wang held a ceremonial sword in gloved hands. In all cases, Wang gazed directly at the viewer—his face fully lit and bearing what can only be described as a neutral and unemotional expression with none of the vaguely idealistic or romantic features of the 1939 portrait. Far less emphasis was placed on Wang's brilliantined hair in these portraits; indeed, in a number of these images, Wang wore a military cap.

In their inclusion of medals, collar insignia pins, buckles, and belts, these new portraits adopted elements of the iconic imagery of Chiang Kai-shek that had been produced early in the war, and in the name of resistance. Wang in 1941 was dressed in a similar uniform to the one that Chiang had often worn in early wartime propaganda. Yet these new portraits also presented Wang in a far less idealistic guise. Under much fuller lighting and using a far sharper focus, Liang Boping revealed the circles under Wang's eyes and the impurities in his facial skin. The hazy but timeless idealist of 1939 was thus replaced by an older but more thoughtful military leader. Wang had visibly aged during his almost two years in power, and the claims to martyrdom that RNG cadres made about him were now in full view, etched in his very face.

This militarization of Wang's image in late 1941 laid the basis for a wave of Wang hagiography under the NCM from the start of 1942. An important part of the NCM was the dissemination of leader worship throughout occupied China. References to Wang as the supreme leader (*zuigao lingxiu*) became commonplace, and members of the RNG Youth Corps were expected to publicly swear "to follow the Three Principles of the People, partake in the New Citizens Movement, and fulfill the Chinese revolution under the guidance of the supreme leader."[57] MoP staff also started experimenting with new methods of representing Wang in this period. At the second anniversary of the *huandu* in March 1942, for example, cadres created half-bodied (*banshen*) cutouts of Wang, each standing more than thirteen meters high, to be erected in central Nanjing.[58] In Shanghai, former Daminhui artists such as Wang Chuan produced photorealist woodcut portraits of Wang for NCM leaflets distributed by the municipal government.[59] This was also a period in which Wang's frequent trips to Japan—undertaken ostensibly to negotiate further autonomy for his regime—resulted in copious amounts of news photography (much of it produced by Japanese news agencies), all of which showed Wang as a competent, if compliant, statesman.[60]

In the context of such adulation, iconoclasm was viewed particularly seriously. When an RNG army cadet was arrested for having defaced an image of Wang, for example, the case was considered serious enough to

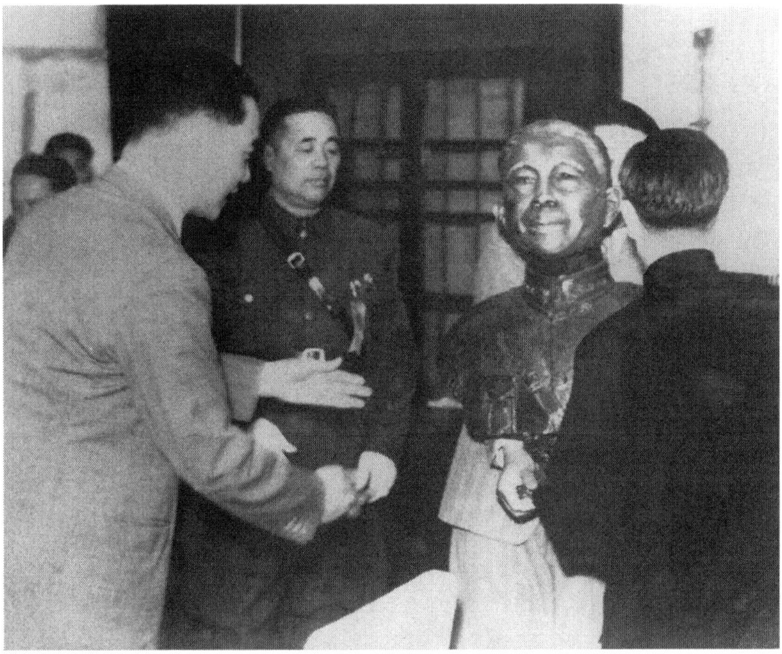

Figure 3.13. Photograph of Wang Jingwei accepting a bust of himself, circa 1943. Courtesy of Academia Historica.

prompt the Executive Yuan (Xingzhengyuan) to become involved, ordering that schools and educational bureaus throughout the RNG realm inform pupils of the gravity of such an offense.[61] In other cases, RNG agencies became increasingly nervous about the unauthorized reproduction of Wang's face by non-state actors. A local merchant in Hangzhou was found to have been selling unauthorized badges featuring Wang's image in June 1942. While the badges themselves contained nothing offensive, the fact that this was being done without state permission worried MoP personnel, and the practice was stopped.[62] In early 1943, Wang Jingwei himself also ordered an immediate halt to the unregulated production of busts of his likeness (some based on the 1941 Bann's Studio portraits) after learning that local elites in Suzhou, in a practice common in prewar political culture, were commissioning such objects as a means of currying favor with government officials (figure 3.13).[63]

This obsession with public reactions to Wang's face (both on the part of the RNG and on the part of Wang himself) was telling. In cultivating a metonymic relationship between Wang and the regime he led under the NCM, MoP cadres had equated devotion to Wang's likeness with loyalty to the RNG cause. This is why, by 1942, Wang began to take on a more overt pictorial association with the RNG navy.[64] A striking photolithographic portrait of a saluting Wang in full naval uniform was produced on the front cover of the *Kabun* in May 1942, for example. The pose adopted in this image of Wang was matched in its NCM-infused, militarized nature only by the image of an unnamed youth, adopting the exact same pose, in an advertisement for the pharmaceutical company Jintan on the inside cover of the same issue.[65] In other cases, Wang was photographed aboard naval vessels or alongside maritime props, such as ship's wheels. So prominent are photographs of Wang Jingwei flanked by RNG naval officials and dressed in the uniform of an admiral in the Wang Jingwei and Lin Baisheng Photograph Collection (housed today at Stanford University's East Asia Library)—images largely produced by the CNA photographer Chen Guoqi—that it would seem Wang himself was at the very least acquiescent in (if not fully supportive of) the promotion of this visual link (figure 3.14).[66] Indeed, given the riparian geography of this regime (discussed in chapter 1), naval-themed photography could pictorially underline the metonymic link between Wang and his government.

There was a clear connection between this NCM-era "naval Wang" and the "President Wang Ching-wei in uniform" of the Rural Pacification campaigns, produced a year earlier. In fact, under the NCM, these two Wangs were conflated. Liang Boping's portraits were added to NCM-era photomontages in 1942 and 1943, for example. The field uniform portrait of late 1941 provenance was deployed to illustrate special GEACPS-themed issues of the *Changjiang huakan* in 1942;[67] the republic's national day in 1943 was marked in Shanghai pictorials with photomontages using Rural Pacification–themed photographs of Wang from late 1941.[68]

Such developments were accompanied by practical strategies to spread Wang's image in ways that looked remarkably similar to Axis propaganda of the time. For example, the MoP revived programs it had started on a much smaller scale earlier in the war, and reproduced Wang's image on lapel badges.[69] Lin Baisheng ordered the production and compulsory wearing of badges bearing Wang's image as a means of "expressing respect and esteem for our one and only leader" in the summer of 1943, for example—a technique that was said to be borrowed from "advanced countries." "Come

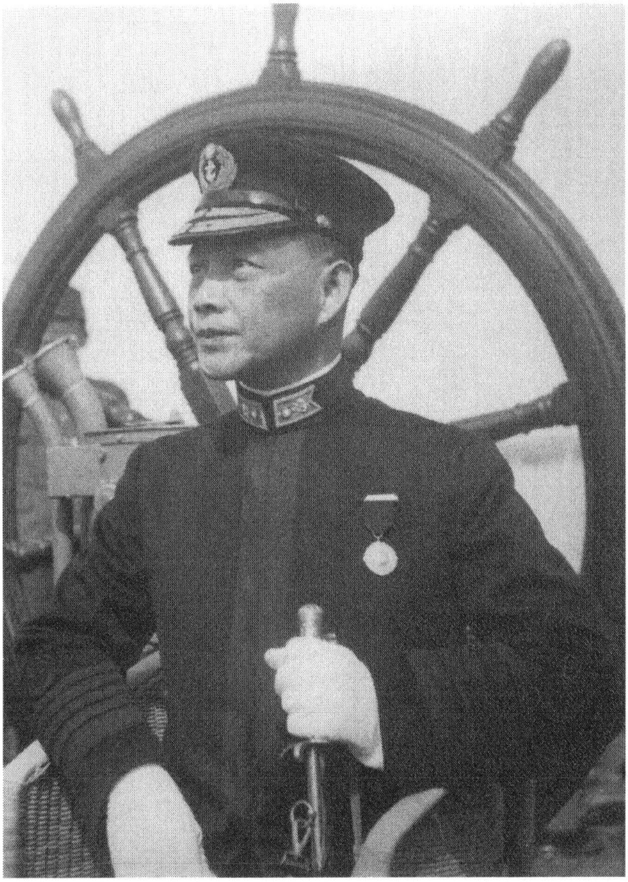

Figure 3.14. Portrait of Wang Jingwei in admiral's uniform by unknown photographer, circa 1942. Wang Jingwei and Lin Baisheng Photograph Collection. Courtesy of the East Asia Library, Stanford University.

on!" called MoP workers. "Let's make sure that the Chairman's image can be seen on every collar!"[70]

It was still in the realm of photography, however, that this late-war image of Wang was most frequently promoted. For example, the Greater East Asia Conference of November 1943, for which Wang traveled to Tokyo, became a major source of new Wang iconography. While this event was dismissed even by those in Japan who reported on it as having nothing more than propaganda value,[71] it marked a major development in RNG celebration of its leader. Dressed in his morning suit, Wang stood together with figures such as Ba Maw and José P. Laurel at this event, thus being presented as not merely a Chinese statesman but also a GEACPS leader. Wang in this GEACPS mode was a product of Japanese news photography.

Often overlooked, however, is just how important photographic depictions of Wang's interactions with other Japanese-sponsored Pan-Asian figures came to be for the RNG in late 1943. The visit to Nanjing of Subhas Chandra Bose, the leader of the Indian National Army (INA) and Azad Hind, was a much publicized event in occupied China. Despite its brevity, it resulted in the production of numerous images by RNG and Japanese photographers that conflated RNG nationalism and leader worship with new notions of Pan-Asian brotherhood and the aesthetics of "Asian-style fascism." Bose had become a common feature of RNG pictorials in late 1943, his garrison-capped head superimposed over images of INA troops or used in photomontages celebrating the end of British imperialism in Southeast Asia.[72] The visit of Bose to the Sun Mausoleum in November 1943, however, led to the creation of new images that thrust Wang and Bose into the same frame. Reprising his Rural Pacification field uniform, Wang was pictured from a low angle by RNG photographers such as Chen Guoqi alongside—though slightly higher than—a saluting Bose. Images of Bose's presence at this most revered of sites in Nanjing helped lend to the "supreme leader" Wang an entirely new significance. Alone, the uniformed Chinese leader evoked memories of the Rural Pacification campaigns of 1941; standing beside the Netaji, however, he brought the symbols of Republican nationalism firmly into the orbit of GEACPS propaganda. In such imagery, it was almost as if the RNG was aspiring to the same image of "militant patriotism centred on a strong leadership" that Bose had successfully circulated for himself around the Axis world (figure 3.15).[73]

As suddenly as Wang had appeared on the GEACPS stage in late 1943, however, he disappeared from public view. In March 1944, Wang left for Japan to seek medical treatment for multiple myeloma—believed, at the time, to have been caused by shrapnel he carried in his body from the 1935 attempt on his life. None of this was hidden from the Chinese public. Indeed, some of the last photographic images we have of Wang alive are those apparently taken while he lay on an operating table, surrounded by Japanese surgeons (figure 3.16). Photographic evidence of the pain and discomfort

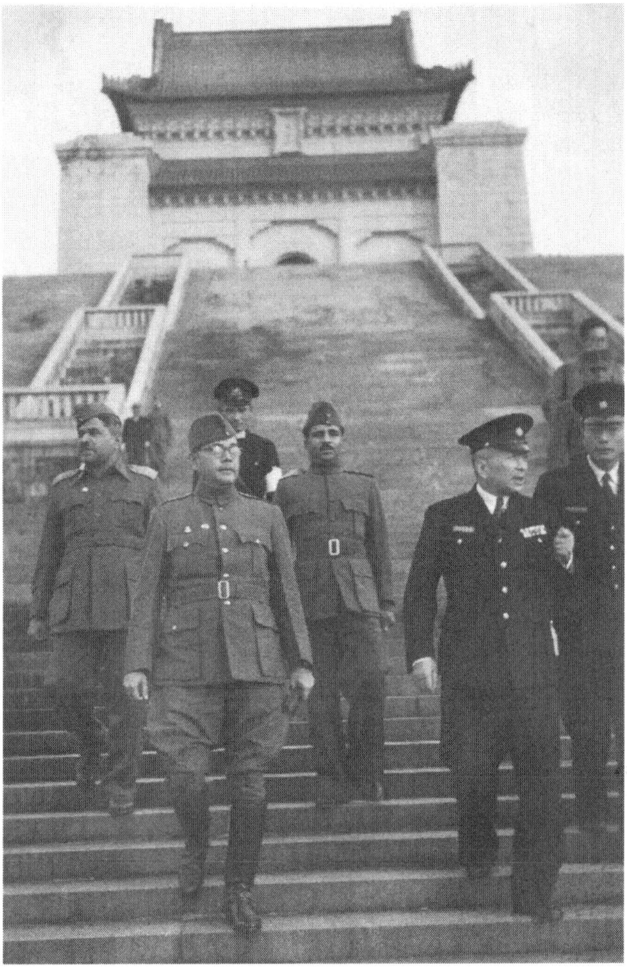

Figure 3.15. Photograph of Subhas Chandra Bose, Chu Minyi, and other INA and RNG officials on the steps of the Sun Yat-sen Mausoleum, November 1943. Chu Minyi Collection (Lot 11700), Prints and Photographs Reading Room, Library of Congress.

that Wang was willing to go through to remove bullet fragments from his back could be (and was) presented as proof of the broader selflessness that this "martyr-in-waiting" supposedly embodied.[74] It also visually recalled images from 1935 of a wounded Wang lying in a Beijing hospital bed as he recovered from the same attack.

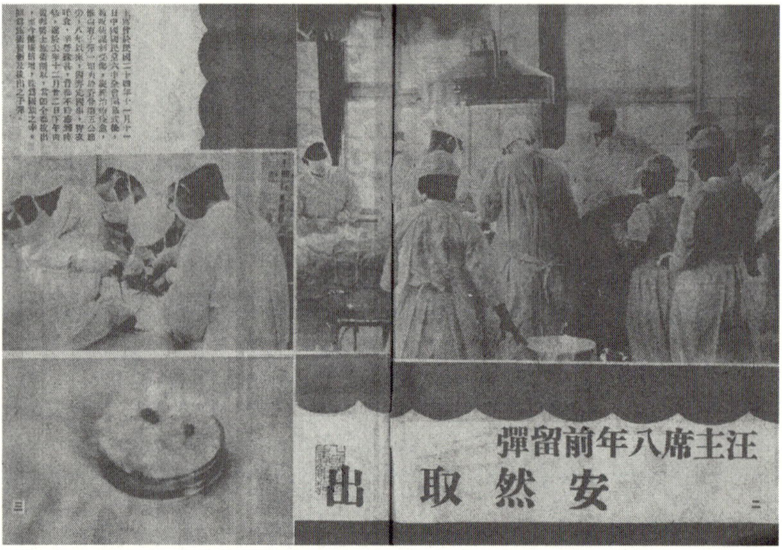

Figure 3.16. Photographic feature showing Wang Jingwei undergoing an operation to remove bullet fragments from his body. *Zhonghua huabao* [China pictorial] 2, no. 1 (February 1944): 2–3. Courtesy of Shanghai Library.

"The Spark Which Kept the Peace Movement Alight Was Gone"

Wang Jingwei died on the afternoon of November 10, 1944, in Nagoya Imperial University Hospital. While the RNG would remain in existence until August 1945, Wang's death was seen as major setback in terms of regime morale. As one employee of the regime phrased it in a retrospective account, "the spark which [had] kept the Peace Movement alight was gone."[75] To be sure, Chen Gongbo accepted the mantle of RNG leader and continued to rule as a temporary chairman (*dai zhuxi*) of the national government until August 1945.[76] But the departure of the one individual who had been so central to the supposed validity of the RNG project undermined any attempt by this regime to reinvent itself. Thus, while Wang's demise does nothing to contradict Henrietta Harrison's argument that "during the Republican period, the death of a political figure was a crucial moment for defining his subsequent image," Wang's death was far more significant than earlier deaths.[77] In light of the changing dynamics of the war in 1944 and a general belief that Japan was headed for defeat by this stage, this was a crucial moment for defining the RNG itself ahead of expected postwar retribution.

Posthumously, therefore, Wang's public image would be manipulated in 1944–1945 to fit certain ideas about his significance and the meaning of the regime he led. Such efforts started within days of Wang's death, for he had died just two days before the seventy-eighth anniversary of Sun Yat-sen's birth (November 12). This was almost certainly one factor in determining that news of Wang's death was not publicly reported in occupied China until the late afternoon of November 12 (i.e., well after commemorative events marking Sun's birthday had concluded).[78] This unplanned coincidence of Wang's death and Sun's birth (brought closer together via the delayed announcement of the former) represented an opportunity for the RNG. The calendrical overlap of the two dates could be made to suggest a cosmological connection between the two men. This implied connection would, in turn, infuse many aspects of the ways in which Wang's death was presented by RNG authorities.

Wang's body did not lie in state upon its return to China, and no new images of Wang prior to his death were circulated—although a newsreel of his body's return to Nanjing was made by the Nippon Newsreel Company (Nihon Nyūsu Eigasha).[79] This physical invisibility, however, meant that sections of the RNG administration could begin to rewrite a narrative of Wang through ritual, spectacle, and even funerary architecture—rather than portraiture. According to the archival record, Chen Bijun took the lead in many of these efforts. It was Chen, for example, who insisted that initial discussions about a state funeral for Wang—publicly discussed the day following his death—be set aside. Wang's "laying to rest" (*anzang dianli*), Chen suggested, should instead emphasize the qualities of humility and self-sacrifice that the late leader had apparently embodied when alive (the hagiography of the NCM seemingly long forgotten). "The regal practices of the feudal times of old were something that the chairman [i.e., Wang] had always loathed," wrote MoP bureaucrats. How could an ostentatious state funeral be appropriate for someone who thought only of the people?[80] Rather than bury Wang as a great GEACPS leader then, Chen was appealing for a return to earlier hagiography that had presented Wang as a martyr. Given that Japan's defeat in the war was, by late 1944, fully expected, this made sense. A return to the notion of Wang as a martyr to the cause of peace underlined the notion that the RNG and its leadership were themselves victims of, rather than complicit in, foreign occupation.

The subsequent burial of Wang on November 23, 1944, was a highly choreographed affair. The day's proceedings were designed to communicate specific meanings about Wang's life in the wider story of the Chinese Republic. Accordingly, every facet of the day's agenda was accounted for.[81] The day commenced at half past six in the morning at the central government compound. Inside, the room was decorated with a photographic portrait of Wang in his morning suit that had been produced on the occasion of his visit to Japan in 1941. It was in this hall that RNG civilian and military officials, together with Japanese and diplomatic representatives, bowed in respect before Wang's flag-draped coffin, which was adorned with a naval portrait of Wang (in contrast to the civilian portrait at government headquarters). A cortege led by RNG soldiers on horseback bearing KMT and ROC flags, but including Wang's widow and other family members dressed in dark mourning clothes, then took Wang's casket through central Nanjing, past the bronze statue of Sun Yat-sen in Xin Jiekou, and eventually to Purple Mountain.

As reference to the statue of Sun suggests, RNG authorities managed to weave into the visual and textual narrative of Wang's funeral overt parallels with the funeral of Sun Yat-sen in 1925. This was something that Japanese news agencies were only too happy to oblige. A Japanese journalist who had been present at Sun's funeral even penned an article that made explicit connections between both events, recalling Wang's presence at Sun's funeral in 1925 as he described the scenes that unfolded during Wang's funeral in 1944.[82] More importantly, however, Sun's legacy could be felt in the siting of Wang's tomb. Wang was buried in a plot of land within the wider Purple Mountain area, but in a specific location that was christened by the RNG as "Meihuashan" (literally, "Plum Blossom Mount"). This was a grand name—deliberately reminiscent, so Wang's postwar detractors later claimed, of Huanghuagang in Guangzhou[83]—for what was little more than a knoll, a short distance from the Ming tombs and the Sun mausoleum.[84] The site was planted with plums—the plum blossom had been the ROC's national flower (*guohua*) since 1929—only after the decision was made to bury Wang there.[85] However, the design of Wang's tomb was clearly planned to suggest Wang's subservience to (rather than parity with) Sun. Indeed, the tomb was conspicuous in its austere scale.[86] Wang's tomb was a circular, grass-topped mound about eight meters wide and four meters high.[87] It looked not remotely like the Sun Mausoleum. Instead, it recalled the graves of earlier Republican statesmen in

Nanjing, such as Tan Yankai, suggesting an attempt at visual continuity with distinctly Nationalist political traditions.[88]

Crucially, however, the official narrative about Wang's death did not present this site as a permanent resting place. Sun Yat-sen's funeral in Beijing in 1925 had been but a temporary solution until permanent interment in a mausoleum in the capital of a unified China could be achieved. Wang's burial on Plum Blossom Mount would thus also be presented as a provisional measure. In accounts published by the CNA, Wang's apparent desire to be ultimately laid to rest not in Nanjing but in the city of his birth, Guangzhou, was explicitly mentioned. Indeed, clear instructions about this were given in the authoritative account published shortly after the burial:

> It was Chairman Wang's wish that he be buried in Guangzhou with already deceased revolutionary comrades. He had thus chosen a burial plot below Baiyunshan in Guangzhou. In order that the Chairman's wishes, and the orders of the national government, be respected, a temporary burial shall take place on Meihuashan, in front of the Ming tombs, in Nanjing. A state funeral shall be held [in Guangzhou] after full peace is achieved.[89]

As Wang had been *almost* martyred in 1910, it was only fitting that, some three decades later, his body would be eventually destined for burial, not with so great a figure as Sun, but with other martyrs from the city that had been key to the birth of the Republican movement. Wang was so selfless, such claims suggested, that he wished, not to be commemorated individually in death, but to be laid next to (other) Cantonese martyrs in a communal grave.[90] By destroying the supposedly temporary tomb in Nanjing with dynamite in 1946 and burning Wang's body thereafter, Chiang Kai-shek's returning Nationalists ensured that this wish would never be fulfilled.[91]

Very few images of Wang's tomb survive today. I am aware of only two publicly accessible images of the site. One is held by the Central News Agency in Taipei; another (uncaptioned and unattributed) image can be found among the photographs of Chu Minyi, now held by the Library of Congress in Washington, D.C. (figure 3.17). Chiang Kai-shek's attempts at rendering this site invisible through its physical destruction in 1946,

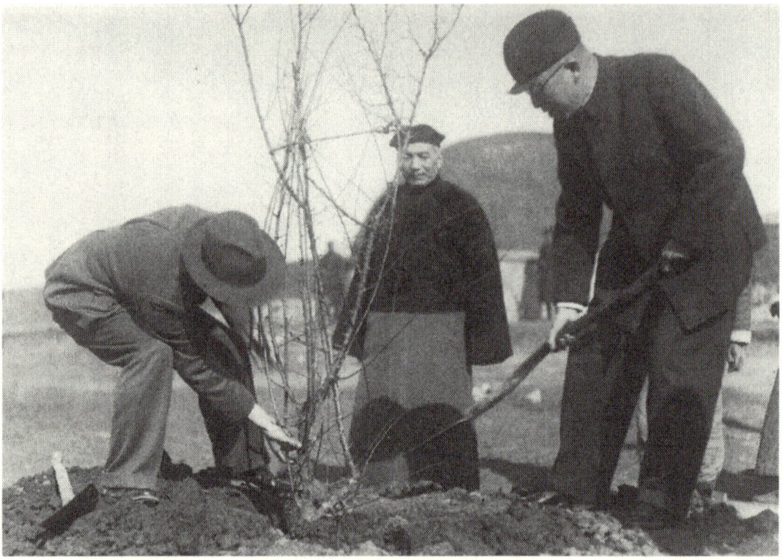

Figure 3.17. Chu Minyi overseeing the planting of plum trees, possibly in front of Wang Jingwei's tomb, circa 1944. Chu Minyi Collection (Lot 11700), Prints and Photographs Reading Room, Library of Congress.

therefore, seem to have been largely successful. Such invisibility has also had consequences for the scholarship, which has continued to feed false assumptions about the RNG's attempts to posthumously honor Wang. Contrary to a number of frequently made assertions in the secondary literature, for example, no "huge new mausoleum was built on top of the Purple and Gold Mountain just outside Nanjing [*sic*]" for Wang.[92]

In contrast, visitors to Nanjing today will still frequently encounter reproductions of the 1939 *Zhonghua ribao* portrait of Wang. The timeless quality of this image, together with its lack of a clear provenance, have ironically given it a longevity that perhaps even Lin Baisheng would not have expected, for it is now included on explanatory boards at tourist sites in the city.

The invisibility of Wang's tomb suggests that some of Wang's own apparent fears about iconoclasm were well founded. The continuing use of the 1939 portrait today, however, also suggests that the iconographies of occupation at least partially achieved what they were designed to do. Wang was reimagined by the Peace Movement as rising from near death in Hanoi and leading a resurgent, if occupied, China. That the visual ephemera of such efforts are now used to illustrate sites designed to educate Chinese tourists about Wang's treason ironically underlines the efficacy of such imaginings. The physical traces of Wang's body have long been destroyed, but the ephemeral traces of his wartime personality cult remain.

If we observe the Wang cult in 1940, we find a fairly typical set of Republican Chinese visual symbols associated with a leader claiming validity via rhetorical and spiritual proximity to Sun Yat-sen. For all the attempts to make a contradistinction between Wang and Chiang Kai-shek in wartime, the RNG inherited and deployed many of the same practices of leader worship that had been developed by Chiang Kai-shek in the Nanjing decade.[93] It is in this regard that we see just how *Chinese* the RNG aspired to look. Indeed, in light of precedents set by earlier client regimes—some of which emulated Japanese methods of leader and emperor worship (Manchukuo, for instance)—the early wartime Wang Jingwei personality cult is remarkable in its reliance on distinctly modern Chinese modes of visuality. In commissioning studio portraits by the likes of Bann's Studio, for example, the RNG was simply following a modern tradition of leader worship perfected by Chiang Kai-shek in the 1930s. The *Zhonghua ribao* and Bann's Studio portraits thus helped the RNG sustain an occupied gaze that looked remarkably different from that imposed on China by the Japanese.

However, in the changing narratives written around Wang through these images, and in the shifting visibility of Wang himself from 1944 onward, we also witness just how reliant the RNG was on its relationship with Tokyo for putting this gaze into practice. Changes to the Wang cult, and to the use of different types of visual media designed to spread the products of that cult, reflected changing policies that were not initiated in Nanjing itself and over which the RNG had little control. How could Wang's supporters establish a coherent image that could be sustained throughout the life of this regime when they were continually responding to Japanese policies, attacks from the resistance, and attempts to attain greater levels of autonomy? Over the course of only five years, therefore, we see the development of a polysemic cult—one that was visualized by a diverse community of cadres, editors, photographers, and artists and that saw Wang represented in a wide variety of often contradictory ways. Wang was a peacemaker, a brand ambassador, a field officer, a Pan-Asian statesman, and a humble martyr. Throughout all of these changing roles, however, he would remain the face of the RNG.

CHAPTER 4

Gendered and Generational Archetypes

The role of women in resisting or "collaborating" with the Japanese in wartime China is a lively realm of inquiry, and the topic has already inspired a significant literature. The important contributions of scholars such as Liu Jiurong and Yun Xia have highlighted the gendered ways in which "collaboration" was and continues to be condemned by its critics.[1] While our understanding of the gendered discourse of collaboration has improved as a result of such scholarship, however, there have been far fewer attempts to address gendered archetypes that developed, or were imposed, under occupation. Nicole Huang's analysis of the image of urban Chinese women in wartime Shanghai's print culture is one of the few examples we have of scholarship that seriously addresses such questions.[2]

Contrast this lack of research to the rich literature on gender in the historiography of occupation in modern Europe and the Middle East. On wartime France, scholars such as Francine Muel-Dreyfus have suggested that the transformation of the image of French women under occupation, achieved through the mobilization of older, prewar icons of motherhood, was one of the central pillars of the Vichy project; the "Vichy mother" was equal in importance to the creation of the personality cult around Marshal Pétain.[3] Similarly, gender historians have shown how American occupation authorities and their allies in Iraq in the early 2000s sought to grant agency to women through the creation of new female archetypes, as a means of downplaying notions of female victimhood.[4]

This chapter draws on such scholarly innovations from other contexts as it traces the recycling of older gendered archetypes and the invention of new ones—both male and female—under the RNG. The RNG encouraged new debates about gender and the role of both women and men following its return in 1940. Such debates were not limited to the written word, however. They found their way into imagery and iconography. Gendered archetypes served not simply to provide normative messages about how men and women might behave in Wang Jingwei's China; they also became outlets through which various individuals, groups, and institutions could promote sometimes conflicting agendas about what a future, post-war China—and Chinese people—might become.

New Women and Modern Girls

The redefinition of gender roles—and especially the role of women—under Japan's new order had been central to the propaganda programs of a number of client regimes in China prior to 1940. In many cases, however, this meant, not the creation of entirely new roles for women, but the reinforcement of existing ideas that had developed all over East Asia in the decade or more prior to 1937. As Prasenjit Duara notes of the region as a whole, "The advent of war brought women out of the home in increasing numbers to fulfill the goals of the wartime state [in Japan, China, and Manchukuo]. But the fundamental conceptions of women and strategies for directing their role in society appear to have not so much changed as intensified, extended, and expanded to deal with new circumstances."[5] One such figure that was "intensified, extended, and expanded" in wartime China was the "new woman" (*xin nüxing*). As Louise Edwards has shown, the new woman first emerged during the May Fourth period as a reformist challenge to traditional conceptions of Chinese womanhood and was imagined as being "politically aware, patriotic, independent, and educated." Yet the same figure could also be used by the advertising industry for entirely commercial purposes, being presented in the 1920s and 1930s as "glamorous, fashionable, desirable, and available." The tension between these two understandings of the new woman—between "substance and superficiality"—would mirror wider debates about China's modernization throughout the Republican period and would remain unresolved at the time of the Japanese invasion in 1937.[6]

Duara's suggestion that war intensified archetypes such as the new woman is supported by evidence left by regimes like the PGROC. As I have demonstrated elsewhere, for example, the Xinminhui embraced one particular interpretation of the prewar Chinese new woman that had been promoted by conservative Chinese nationalists through the New Life Movement (Xin shenghuo yundong), introduced under Chiang Kai-shek.[7] By calling on New Life ideas, the Xinminhui also set itself apart from Manchukuo, where, as Norman Smith has demonstrated, the "new woman" was generally frowned upon in official discourse in favor of other, more conservative archetypes, such as the "good wife, wise mother" (*liangqi xianmu*).[8] The Xinminhui called openly for the liberation (*jiefang*) of women, opposed polygamy, and sought to involve young educated women in propaganda activities.[9] It also manufactured an occupation archetype that I have described as the "PGROC new woman."[10]

In east China, the Daminhui articulated quite different notions of gender. This organization inherited far more conservative ideas about the role of women directly from Manchukuo. For example, the Daminhui celebrated the role of women in occupation nation-building but did so within the bounds of Manchukuo formulae.[11] This Daminhui creation looked almost identical to her Manchukuo sister, and her contributions to "new China" were measured by her willingness to resist "communist" notions of female agency.[12]

Despite the differences between the "PGROC new woman" and variations of the "good wife, wise mother" adopted by the Daminhui, these two pre-RNG occupation archetypes looked remarkably similar. Both adhered to a set of vestimentary norms that were of pre-occupation provenance. They were depicted in occupation print culture and calendar art (*yuefenpai*) in cheongsams that were austere and monochrome in design. They lacked cosmetics and jewelry, and both were groomed conservatively. While both figures were often shown to be in good physical health—their faces were always visible, though they tended not to stare directly at the viewer—they were not seductive.[13]

There was a competitor to such Xinminhui and Daminhui notions of womanhood, however. The Japanese military and Japanese news agencies maintained their own views about what Chinese women under occupation should look like. Such views often differed markedly from those expressed by Chinese collaborators, fitting more closely with an "imperial strategy to rhetorically and symbolically feminize—and thereby emasculate—the colonial subject," through what E. Taylor Atkins and others have referred to as the colonial gaze.[14] From the very start of the occupation, photographs and posters of unnamed *guniang/kūnyan* (young women) were reproduced in significant quantity,[15] with Japanese-language pictorials such as *Dōmei gurafu* featuring sexualized photographs of Chinese women in this mode, often "on location" at famous Chinese landmarks. Such photographic material found parallels in the wistful images of Chinese "modern girls" in the cartoons of the Shanghai-based *Tairiku shinpō*.[16] Others were featured in poster art and broadsides celebrating Japanese success (figure 4.1).

The *guniang/kūnyan* of the Japanese gaze overlapped with figures created in the advertising industry for a decidedly male, Chinese audience. This included a prewar archetype that had inhabited the medium of calendar art in the cities of China's coast and that Tani Barlow has identified as the

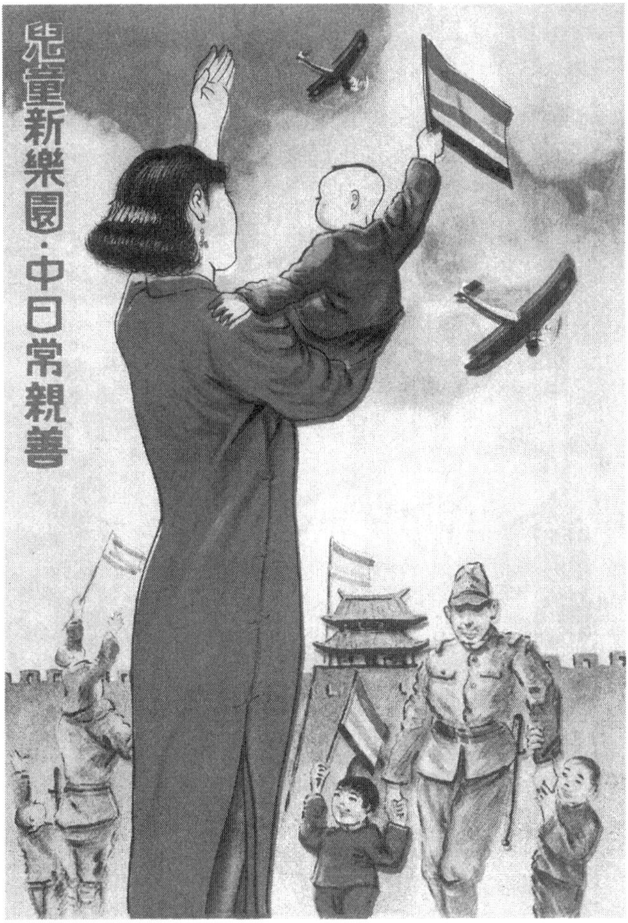

Figure 4.1. Undated (circa 1937) propaganda leaflet showing a "new woman" with a male child welcoming Japanese soldiers in north China. © The Trustees of the British Museum.

"sexy modern girl."[17] For Chinese intellectuals of both the Left and the Right, the modern girl in this guise "contained all of the vices of modernity that were believed to bring forth moral degeneration and hinder China's national salvation."[18] As Hsiao-pei Yen has explained: "She [i.e., the sexy modern girl] symbolised the commoditisation of modernity, without the political features of modernity that a truly enlightened woman would have. She was the enemy of nationalism and a threat to China's nation-building."[19]

Some scholars have suggested that this modern girl of prewar provenance enjoyed a fraught history under Japanese occupation. In Madeleine Y. Dong's view, for example, the much publicized case of Zheng Pingru—an individual associated with the modern girl image who, in working for the resistance, inspired the plot of Eileen Chang's *Lust, Caution*—sullied the very notion of the modern girl in the RNG and led to this figure being frowned upon under Wang Jingwei.[20] Given the prominence of literati culture under this regime, it might also be assumed that an archetype associated so closely with commercialism would not be welcomed in RNG China.

In examining the visual record, however, it is clear that this is not the entire story. The modern girl played a number of roles before, during, and after the *huandu*. For example, as had been the case prior to the war, the sexy modern girl could be invoked by the commercial sector simply for marketing purposes. The addition of an alluring modern girl to posters, calendars, or newspaper advertisements could help to project a business-as-usual message. This was something that both Japanese and Chinese firms were keen to underline after the *huandu*. Newspapers (and, of course, periodicals like the *Kabun*) were full of advertisements that made use of the modern girl image to sell cigarettes, cosmetics, and (most importantly) pharmaceuticals in 1940.[21]

In other cases, real-life celebrities reprised the role of the sexy modern girl in print advertising. Li Xianglan—that "enduring symbol of the Chinese culture produced within Japanese-occupied Manchuria"[22]—had played *kūnyan*-esque characters as well as PGROC new women for Japanese cinema audiences prior to the *huandu*.[23] In addition, she had been a frequent feature of pictorial propaganda built around the notion of the "harmony of the five races" (*gozoku kyōwa*) in Manchukuo.[24] She had also been made the face of marketing campaigns for Japanese brands such as Shiseido.[25] Such flexibility may explain why Li was chosen to play the role of "modern girl" in advertising that conflated occupation policies and consumption in the lead-up to the RNG's return. Posing in a tight, short-sleeved cheongsam as she applied eyedrops, Li Xianglan was pictured regularly in print advertisements for the Japanese pharmaceutical firm Rohto in 1939 and 1940 that blurred the boundaries between marketing and political communications (figure 4.2).

Li Xianglan's emergence as the quintessential modern girl in commercial advertising—promoting cosmetics, eyedrops, and occupation itself—underlines the importance of Japanese news agencies in the circulation of this archetype. Indeed, it was Mainichi, through its flagship *Kabun*, that took the opportunity presented by the signing of the Treaty concerning Basic Relations in November 1940 to craft a new, south China modern girl

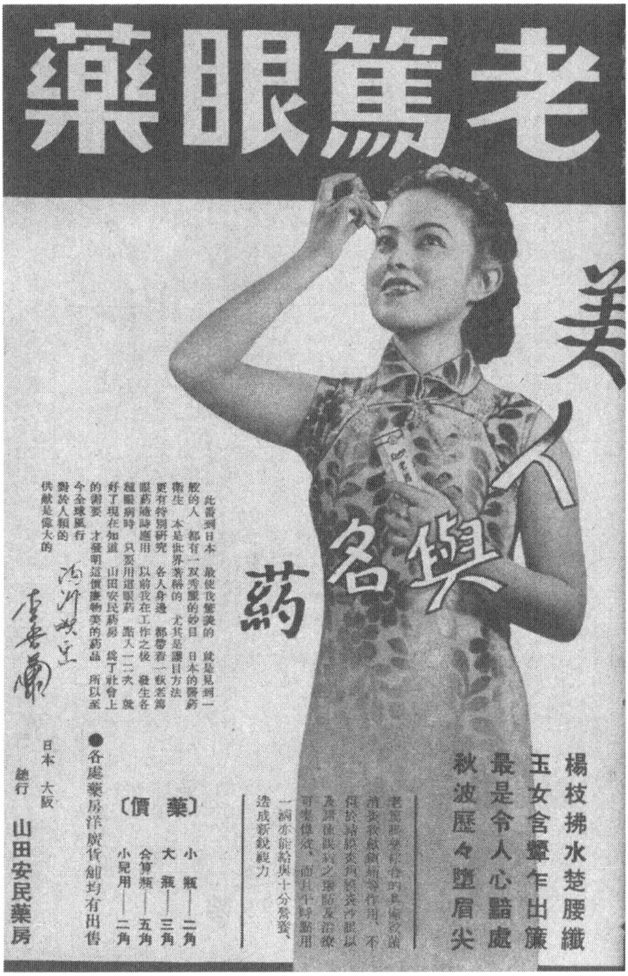

Figure 4.2. *Kabun* advertisement (1940) featuring Li Xianglan applying Rohto eye drops. Courtesy of Rohto Pharmaceutical Company.

who would sell the occupation to the Chinese reading public. The result was Li Huizhen. Li may never have been a real person, but she was presented by Mainichi as a nineteen-year old, Guangzhou-based journalist when she was first featured in a staged photo shoot designed by the *Kabun* as a "movie on paper" (*zhishang gongying*) at the start of 1941.[26] Her image would appear again in various occupation outlets over the following months (figure 4.3), often in association with the phrase "*Zhong-Ri tixi*"

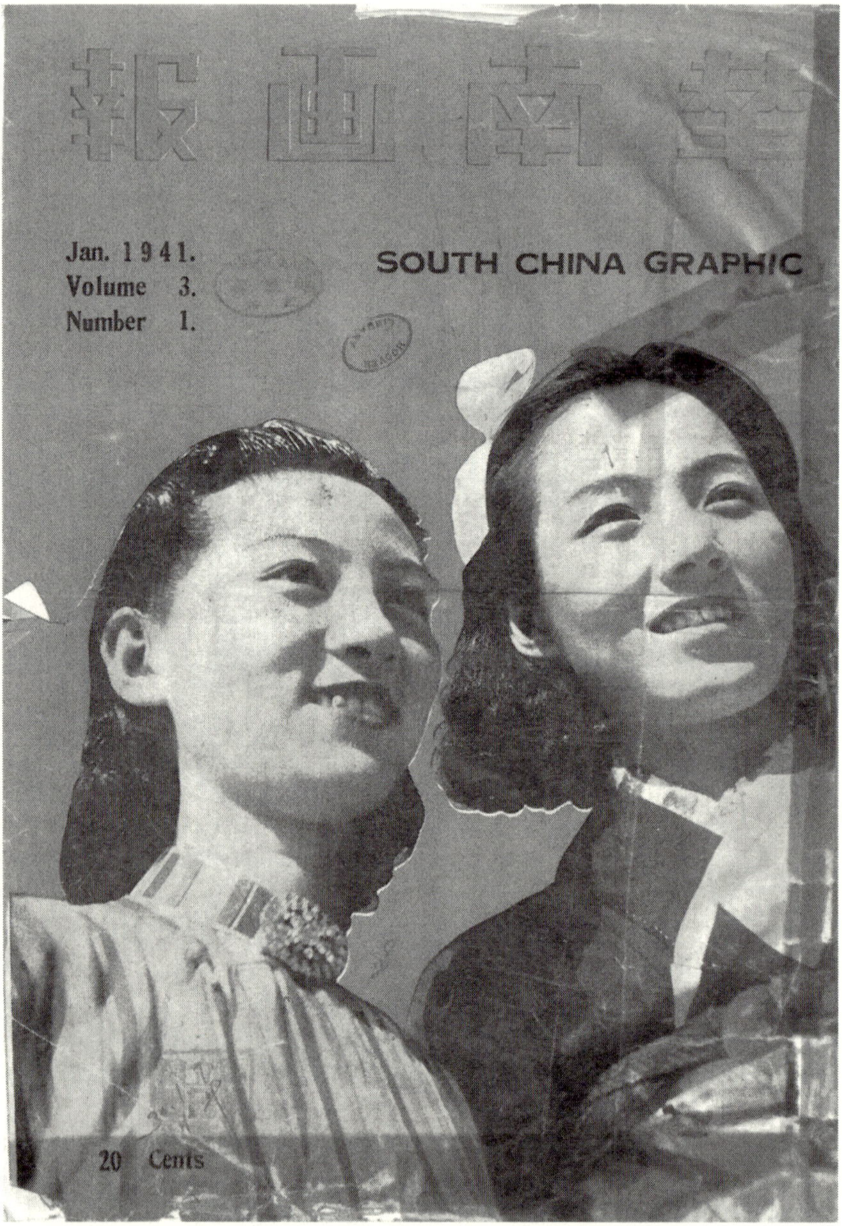

Figure 4.3. Cover image of Dōmei-published *Huanan huabao* (South China graphic), 1941, featuring Li Huizhen (*left*) and a Japanese companion. Courtesy of the East Asia Library, Stanford University.

(Sino-Japanese mutual assistance), a slogan that had been common in the Daminhui and Xinminhui lexicons.[27]

Dressed in a sleeveless cheongsam and high heels and wearing her hair in a style reminiscent of Li Xianglan, Li Huizhen was a composite of modern girls who had been featured in 1930s calendar art and *huandu*-era medicinal advertising. Pictured alongside a kimono-clad woman by the name of Nobukuni Tamiyo, however, Li was every bit the symbol of the *occupied* modern girl. The photo shoot depicted Li showing Nobukuni prominent sites in Guangzhou that spoke to RNG sensibilities, such as the Sun Yat-sen Memorial Hall (Zhongshan jiniantang) and the city's bund on the Pearl River. The two were photographed next to a wall adorned with a mural of a plump Chinese child and slogans extolling the leadership of Wang Jingwei.

At first glance, there is nothing remarkable about Li Huizhen. In invoking her only in the presence of her Japanese peer, however, the *Kabun* was attempting to graft the basic elements of the sexy modern girl of 1930s print culture onto a genre of propaganda art first developed in Manchukuo in conjunction with the aforementioned *gozoku kyōwa* (harmony of the five races) idea. Images of Chinese and Japanese women enjoying leisurely pursuits in each other's company had been experimented with in occupied Nanjing prior to the *huandu,* most noticeably under the Daminhui.[28] In reviving this trope through Li Huizhen, however, the *Kabun* was suggesting that the Chinese modern girl could have a stake in occupation and that "Sino-Japanese mutual assistance" could be made appealing and glamorous. This was a predictable trajectory for this archetype to follow under occupation. If, as Ellen Johnston Laing has shown, the modern girl could be used to "sell happiness" in 1930s Shanghai,[29] then she could just as easily be employed to sell "Sino-Japanese cooperation" in 1940s Guangzhou.

If modern girls could be invented by Japanese news agencies, however, they could just as easily be appropriated from other spheres. This is precisely what occurred with one female celebrity who would eventually become the unofficial face of the RNG in its modern girl incarnation—Nancy Chan (Chen Yunshang). In the historiography of Chinese cinema, much is made of the sudden rise of this actor by virtue of her lead role in the 1939 Bu Wancang–directed film *Mulan congjun* (Hua Mulan joins the army). This movie was commercially successful in Shanghai because of its allegorical criticism of the Japanese invasion, for it revived the historical fable of Hua Mulan, a female warrior who secretly joins an army to help repel a foreign force.[30] As Poshek Fu has pointed out, Chan achieved stardom as the embodiment of resistance via her role in this film.[31] This film also helped Chan establish an extra-diegetic public persona as a "thoroughly 'modern' girl: athletic, vital, and 'Western.' "[32]

Much less commented upon, however, is the extent to which Chan was so easily transformed into a feature of occupation visual culture and, indeed, propaganda.[33] Within a month of the RNG's return, the occupation press was remarking on this "chaste bird of peace" (*heping de zhen qin*), whose "mind used to be full of anti-Japanese thoughts" but who "has now completely changed into a star who believes in supporting peace and the new central government."[34] In this early post-*huandu* period, Chan was transformed from a "south China star" (*Nanguo xiaoxing*) into an "East Asian" celebrity.[35] And as her fame rose, so too did her attraction as a potential mascot for the RNG. Her place in the pantheon of occupation celebrities would be confirmed when she was recruited into the Japanese-backed China United Productions (CUP) in April 1942.[36] Within two years, Chan had eclipsed Li Xianglan as the most lauded modern girl in the occupation culture industry, her face gracing some of the most blatantly pro-occupation pictorials,[37] but also numerous film magazines. Chan's transformation from a symbol of patriotic resistance into a mascot of occupation underlined just how easy it was for existing archetypes to be given entirely new significance under occupation. Nothing had changed in the manner of Chan's appearance pre- and post-*huandu*. Through association with the CUP, however, Chan had become an entirely acceptable modern girl for RNG China (figure 4.4).

Nancy Chan was one of many female celebrities whose glamour portraits were featured on the covers of film magazines published in Shanghai *and* occupied Nanjing (as well as other cities in the RNG realm), for the modern girl remained a central feature of commercial filmmaking.[38] This helps explain why Chinese graphic artists associated with the RNG were able to make names for themselves by experimenting with imagery derived from Shanghai film culture. Dong Tianye, for example, specialized in caricatures of movie stars like Nancy Chan for the occupation press from 1942 onward. Incorporating photomontage techniques that had been developed by a number of prewar Chinese cartoonists, Dong's illustrations (appearing in many of the same movie-themed magazines that featured photography of Nancy Chan) were composed of a photo-realist, oversized likeness of a female star's face set atop a caricatured representation of the sexy modern girl's body.[39] Other artists experimented extensively with more-generic modern girl imagery. When he was not teaching at the Central Propaganda

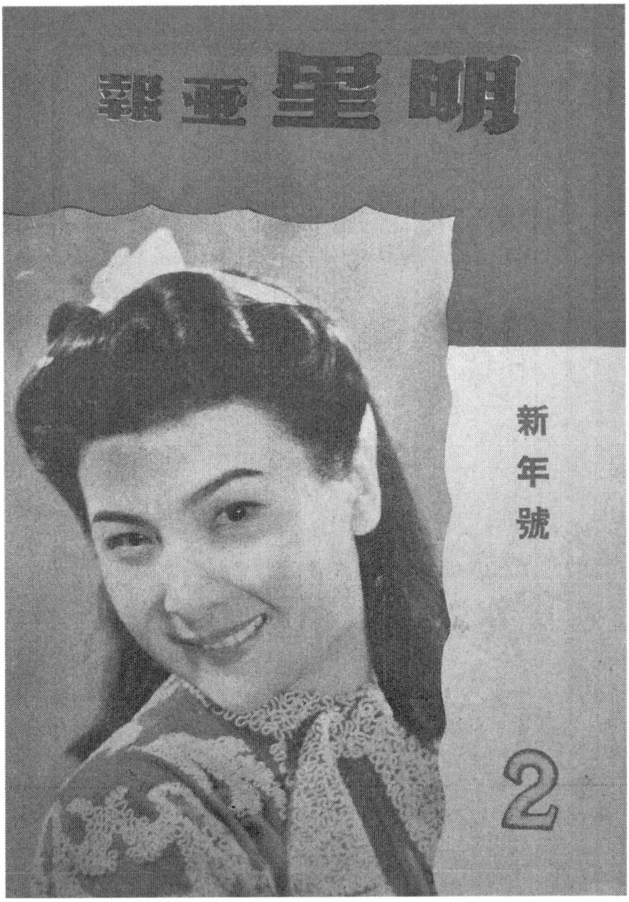

Figure 4.4. Cover image of film magazine *Mingxing huabao* 2 (January 1943), featuring a portrait of Nancy Chan. From the Paul Kendel Fonoroff Collection for Chinese Film Studies. Courtesy of the C. V. Starr East Asian Library, University of California, Berkeley.

Institute (CPI), for example, Cao Hanmei produced graceful line drawings of modern girls to accompany serialized fiction in the *Kabun*.[40] Ma Wu and his Japanese peer Miura Noa filled dozens of regime-sponsored pictorials with bawdy and voyeuristic images of modern girls. Such examples show how the occupation modern girl could not simply provide an overt propagandistic message but could also be deployed as a highly sexualized, comic, or supposedly apolitical distraction for an occupied male gaze.[41]

Over the course of 1942, however, the significance of the modern girl in occupied China's print culture began to shift. The overtly sexual (*seqing*) depictions of this figure became a topic of discord in the creative industries.[42] With the mobilization of female students through the NCM, it became difficult to justify escapist or sexualized depictions of Chinese women more generally. Photographs of Li Huizhen strolling breezily through Guangzhou had fitted perfectly well with calls for peace in late 1940. By late 1942, however, such imagery contradicted the new focus on austerity, activism, and May Fourth nationalism demanded under the NCM. How could a figure formerly revered as either a symbol of peace, treaty port glamour, or escapism be sustained in an RNG that was lamenting the persistence of compradors?[43] In directives published by the CNA, modern girls were criticized for having wasted resources on luxury clothing and cosmetics at a time when they should have been contributing to nation-building. "What does it take for a woman to be called beautiful?" asked an anonymous CNA cadre. "Does she need high heels, a perm, face powder, and curved hips to be beautiful?" For the CNA, beauty lay not in the accoutrements of the modern girl but in the role that occupied China's women could play in defending the nation and increasing levels of industrial production.[44]

This is not to suggest that the modern girl simply disappeared in the face of NCM nationalism, however. On the contrary, if this figure had proven malleable enough to be used in promotion of diverse understandings of occupation in earlier months and years, she could also be worked into the new realities of a post–Pearl Harbor China. Attempts were made by illustrators affiliated with the CCA, for example, to politicize the modern girl so that she might be reimagined as an RNG combatant. In late 1942, for example, Dong Tianye reinvented his modern girl muse—Nancy Chan—in a newly belligerent and decidedly NCM light. In a comic strip published in *Chinese cartoons*, Dong depicted Chan as apprehending and subsequently punching a bomb-throwing resistance agent on the rooftops of Shanghai.[45] Captioned "Exterminate villains" (*pumie qunchou*), a cartoon by Shi Ping in the same journal shows a modern girl (who bears a striking resemblance to Li Lihua) killing ghost-shaped "terrorists" with an insecticide sprayer (figure 4.5). The image directly references early 1930s advertising imagery in China for the iconic Flit gun.[46] In such an iteration, the modern girl could serve as a nostalgic—and perhaps ironic—referent to prewar print culture, while still being presented as a loyal subject of the Wang regime. The modern girl could even be transformed into a mascot of Rural Pacification. In a series of print advertisements produced by the Japanese

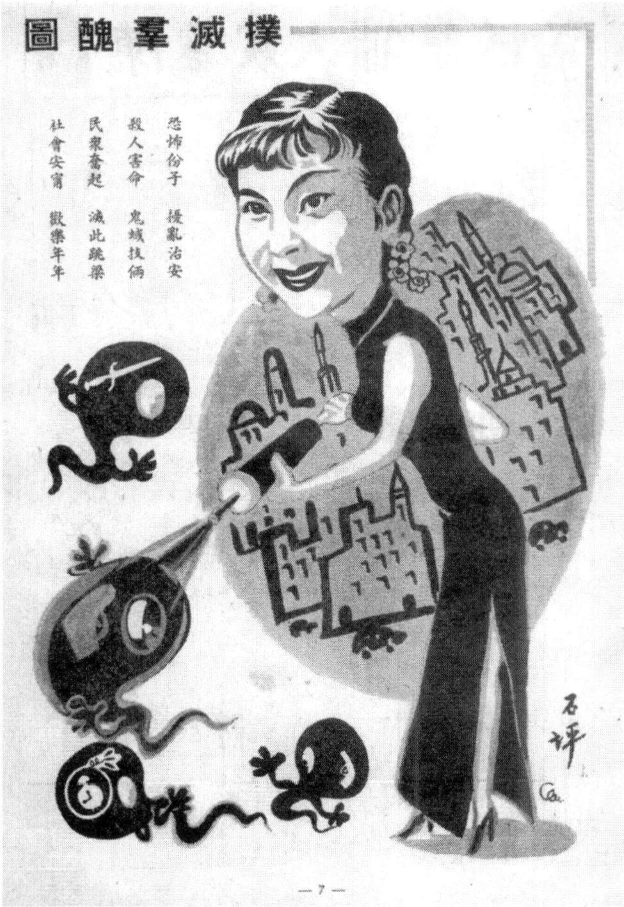

Figure 4.5. A modern girl helps rid Shanghai of (anti-RNG) "terrorists." Shi Ping, "Pumie qunchou" [Exterminate villains], *Zhongguo manhua* [Chinese cartoons] 1 (September 1942): 7. Courtesy of Shanghai Library.

pharmaceutical company Jintan in May 1944, for example, a lithographic portrait of a smiling modern girl—indistinguishable from any number of modern girls drawn from prewar calendar art—was superimposed with an exhortation to "rapidly unite for Rural Pacification" (*su tuanjie, da qingxiang*) in an advertisement for Jintan household medicines.[47]

If artists working in media such as cartoons tried to reinvent their muses in the context of the Axis turn, however, those working in other media simply expunged them. The development of woodcuts and photojournalism in occupied China, for example, largely followed the trajectory already set early in the war in areas outside Japanese control by choosing *not* to explore the frivolous modern girl after 1942. In her place were revived representations of Chinese women that fitted better with the needs of an RNG at war. In the context of Rural Pacification, for example, images of austere working women and female peasants were favored (notwithstanding the interventions of Japanese pharmaceutical companies). Such imagery drew on depictions of new women that had filled the pages of Xinminhui and Daminhui publications earlier in the occupation, yet it also betrayed a common heritage in the leftist woodcut movement of the prewar years. Just as the prewar exponents of this form had consciously sought to differentiate their craft from the garish, mass-produced commercialism of advertising art,[48] so too did RNG woodcut specialists speak to a rural (albeit "pacified") audience far removed from the stylized modern girls that had exercised their peers in Shanghai's newspapers.

This post–Pearl Harbor period also witnessed the rise of the "graceful beauty" (*shinü*) that Nicole Huang has identified as a common feature of wartime print culture in Shanghai. Paintings of "Pan-Asian" Chinese women "wearing either everyday costumes or dramatic clothing," were invoked in this period largely at the expense of the modern girl. Huang explains: "As the Japanese took control of the International Settlement in December 1941 . . . both the enigmatic 'modern girl' and the transnational presence of Hollywood images on the covers of Shanghai's pictorial publications disappeared. Instead. . . . Pan-Asian images dominated the visual culture of occupied Shanghai."[49] Where Shanghai magazine covers had once featured lithographic images of glamorous modern girls à la Li Huizhen or Nancy Chan, they now included images of "graceful aristocratic ladies" produced using the "stylistic traits of traditional figure painting." Such imagery was often produced by female Chinese artists themselves, who did this as a means of "conveying a distinct 'Chinese-ness' within the context of a 'Greater East Asia.'"[50] As modern girls became harder to justify in the context of the Pacific War then, Chinese artists explored new ways of carving out gendered archetypes of occupation that were acceptable to Pan-Asian sensitivities yet could still express a distinctly Chinese vision.

Nevertheless, the modern girl refused to disappear. On the contrary, even as she was being purged from sections of the print media, she was revived in an increasingly escapist commercial Chinese cinema. The creation of the CUP under Japanese leadership in the spring of 1942 and the formation of the China

United Motion Picture Company (CUMP) in the following year, may well have heralded a cinema that was supposedly Pan-Asian in outlook. The 1943 movie *Eternity* (*Wanshi liufang*)—a film that starred those quintessential modern girls of occupation Li Xianglan and Nancy Chan depicted in a *shinü* mode and that described Chinese resistance to British imperialism during the First Opium War—is often mentioned in studies of occupation-era cinema.[51] *Eternity* was the exception rather than the rule, however, for many of the dozens of films produced in late-war Shanghai featured Chinese celebrities reprising modern girl roles, even when these roles were entirely at odds with official RNG discourse. "If the themes of some films were antiforeign," Edward Gunn Jr. noted in *Unwelcome Muse*, "the life style portrayed in most movies was not." Escapist films featuring the likes of Nancy Chan and Li Lihua—together with pictorials that celebrated these stars by including stills from such movies—provided a space in which the modern girl could thrive.[52] In such cases, she could continue do what she had done for advertising campaigns in the early *huandu* period: serve as an apolitical and escapist figure removed from occupation politics.

Roar, China!

Occupied Nanjing is perhaps the last place one would have expected people to appreciate a Soviet stage play. This is precisely what they did, however, when a production of Sergei Tret'iakov's mid-1920s drama *Roar, China!* (*Nuhou ba Zhongguo*)—based on the Wanxian Incident of 1926, during which a British gunboat had shelled a town on the upper reaches of the Yangtze[53]—was staged by the Nanjing Theatrical Society (Nanjing juyishe) in January 1943.[54] The overtly socialist provenance of this play was all but forgotten in reports on the production's success.[55] *Roar, China!* was identified as an excellent vehicle through which to stir anti-Western sentiment (much as the abovementioned film *Eternity* would be a few months later with its cinematic reinterpretation of the First Opium War). Despite premiering in Shanghai some weeks earlier, the 1943 Nanjing production of *Roar, China!* had been modified for the RNG capital by Zhou Yuren (deputy head of Nanjing's publicity bureau) with the assistance of CPI graduates such as Lei Yimin.[56] It started with newsreel footage of Wang Jingwei's declaration of war on the Allies. The play was also interspersed with monologues delivered by an elderly narrator who claimed to have witnessed the 1926 incident upon which the play had been based.[57] So happy was the MoP with the modified version of this play that it ordered scripts to be distributed to all publicity bureaus throughout the RNG realm.[58]

One would be justified in reading the production of this piece of theater—written by a Soviet constructivist playwright and depicting Chinese boatmen defying imperialist aggression—as a brave RNG attempt at allegorical resistance.[59] Indeed, given the widespread knowledge that *Roar, China!* was not only a Soviet play but also the title of a famed 1936 woodcut by Li Hua (inspired by popular anti-imperialist sentiment),[60] one might assume that the play's production was a clever exploitation of wartime imagery in the service of a subversive Chinese nationalism.

I would argue that the January 1943 production of *Roar, China!* had a quite different significance, however. This play brought to the stage an important figure that RNG graphic and woodcut artists had been experimenting with under the NCM but that could be found in occupation-era art going right back to the *huandu* and earlier.[61] Such depictions grew far more common in 1942, as the May Fourth nationalism inherent in the NCM began to exert a greater influence on cultural production, particularly that sponsored (as *Roar, China!* was) by the MoP. Imagery of coolies, boatmen, and rickshaw pullers was a frequent feature of the work of Chinese woodcut artists included in early issues of the journal *Zhongguo muke* after it commenced publication in December 1942 (i.e., one month before the staging of *Roar, China!*).[62] Intriguingly, even the woodcuts of Li Hua would be included in regime-sponsored pictorials in 1942. In other words, RNG-sponsored publications rebranded the icons of the anti-Japanese resistance as symbols of an amorphous NCM anti-imperialism.[63]

By bringing onto the stage the RNG working man—employed, fittingly for this riparian regime, on the Yangtze—the MoP was linking existing imagery both to prewar anti-imperialist texts (most noticeably the Li Hua woodcut) and to the realities of the RNG's transformation into a belligerent force in the Pacific War. The "roaring" boatmen who defied Western traders in this 1943 stage production could be conflated with the blindfolded figure of Li Hua's woodcut who, as Xiaobing Tang suggests, had "issue[d] an urgent order that the nation must cry out."[64] These potentially controversial references to prewar salvationist patriotism could be justified if they were made to align with Pan-Asian anti-imperialism. Indeed, by invoking Yangtze boatmen as the embodiment of Chinese resistance to imperialism, this riparian regime was claiming ownership of the defiance that had theretofore been the monopoly of resistance cultural production "upstream."

Following the RNG declaration of war, the "roaring man" image would be depicted with increasing frequency in regime-sponsored publications. In fact, rather than being granted an individual personality as Li Huizhen had been, the RNG working man would often be named after the Tret'iakov

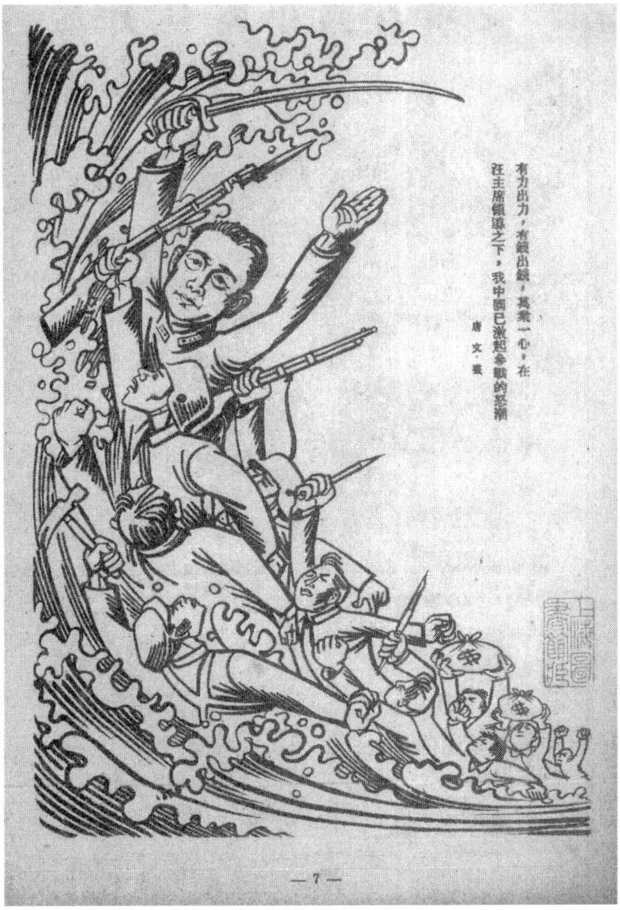

Figure 4.6. Line drawing of Wang Jingwei and RNG men rising up in anger. The text reads: "Those who have strength should contribute it; those who have money should contribute it. We are all of one heart. Under Chairman Wang's leadership, the people of China have joined the crest of the wave to join the war." *Zhongguo manhua* [Chinese cartoons] 5 (March 1943): 7. Courtesy of Shanghai Library.

play (and the Li Hua artwork) itself, as "Roar, China" (Nuhou Zhongguo). He would commonly be drawn as muscular and open-mouthed, roaring in rage at enemies unseen. In other cases, he would be linked to the figure of President Wang in uniform, as angry RNG men rose up (possibly on the waters of the Yangtze) to combat imperialism (figure 4.6).

The working man "on the docks" (*matou shang*) was a particularly favorite topic for members of the Association of Chinese Woodcut Artists who published their work in Wang Yingxiao's *Chinese Woodcuts*.[65] He also appeared in Wang Yingxiao's "first collection of propagandistic woodcuts to be produced in the Rural Pacification areas."[66] To be sure, many of the images that Wang produced in this collection were rural rather than strictly riparian in theme. Nonetheless, the first image in this collection looked remarkably like Li Hua's *Roar, China* woodcut of 1936. Wang's bare-chested prisoner was bound by chains to pillars bearing the Union Jack and the Stars and Stripes. A few pages later, Wang depicted the same figure freed from his chains, so that we see the thrashing of his dynamic body as he stabs two oversized, ursine hands that are imprinted with the characters *Mei* (America) and *Ying* (Britain). Wang wrote as the caption to this image: "Move to action! Strive to cast off the evil grasp of the British and American invaders." In other images in the same collection, raised fists—looking remarkably like the socialist realist imagery we now associate with 1960s China—were produced, as Wang called on people to "fight for the liberation of the Republic of China!"

Like the militarization of Wang Jingwei's image from 1941 onward, the invention of the roaring man represented a direct RNG response to what Yun Xia has described as "resistance-based masculinity" in wartime China. Attacks on those labeled by the resistance as traitors commonly took on a gendered nature, as "Chinese war propaganda uniformly depicted *hanjian* as individuals lacking in masculinity."[67] By creating this new and highly aggressive male archetype, the RNG was challenging the forced "feminization" of the regime by the resistance.

If the roaring man was imagined in illustrations and woodcuts, far more Japanese-inflected interpretations of the occupation man were represented in media such as photography. This was particularly the case when it came to depictions of Chinese men in the RNG armed forces. As we have seen, the navy took on a special significance for Wang's regime. In occupation pictorials, then, images of RNG sailors, seamen, and coastguardsmen were given particular prominence from the summer of 1941 onward—that is, around the same period in which Rural Pacification commenced. Much of the resulting imagery was derivative of Japanese propaganda of the time, itself highly influenced by Soviet precedents. Andrea Germer has shown, for example, that Soviet-derived techniques such as photomontage and photo collage were adopted to the constructivist and socialist realist aes-

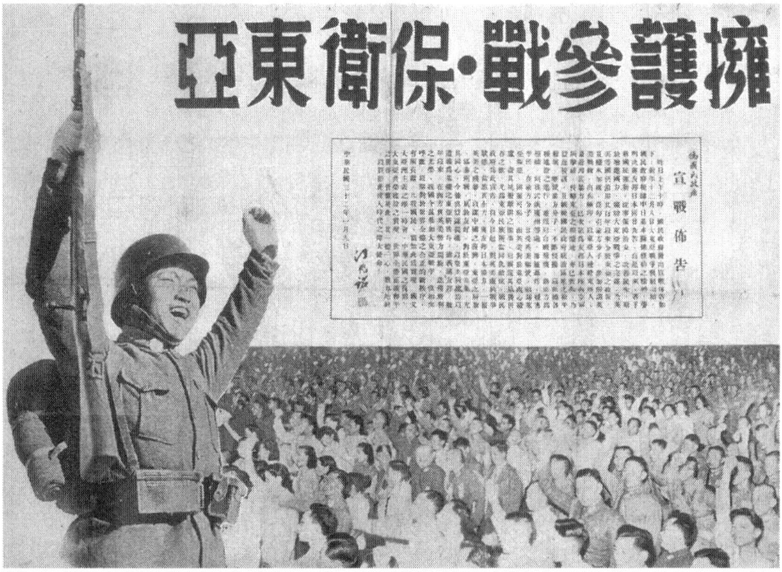

Figure 4.7. Ministry of Publicity poster celebrating the RNG's declaration of war and featuring an RNG soldier. Courtesy of the Hoover Institution Archives (Hoover Poster Collection, CC 102), Stanford University.

thetics that saturated Japanese wartime pictorials from 1942 onward. In turn, such bricolage influenced the design of occupation pictorials in China. The result was that heroic Chinese marines and soldiers were commonly presented as part of photomontages in the pages of regime-sponsored pictorials, pictured (as their Japanese peers were) from a low angle and superimposed over images of faceless crowds or battle scenes in a "co-prosperity realist" style (figures 4.7 and 4.8).[68]

Just as closely derived from Japanese precedents were images of unnamed RNG soldiers who emerged within the propaganda portfolios of the Rural Pacification campaigns. Pictorials included images of the "warriors of new China" (*xin Zhongguo de doushi*)—described as *xiongzi* (manly) or *yingzi* (dashing)—standing guard over the villages that had been purged of communist resistance.[69]

In other cases, however, these RNG soldiers were conflated with their Japanese brethren. A photograph of an unnamed Chinese soldier dressed as a Japanese warrior, for example, was first pictured on the cover of the October 1942 issue of *Dōmei gurafu* (a pictorial designed for a

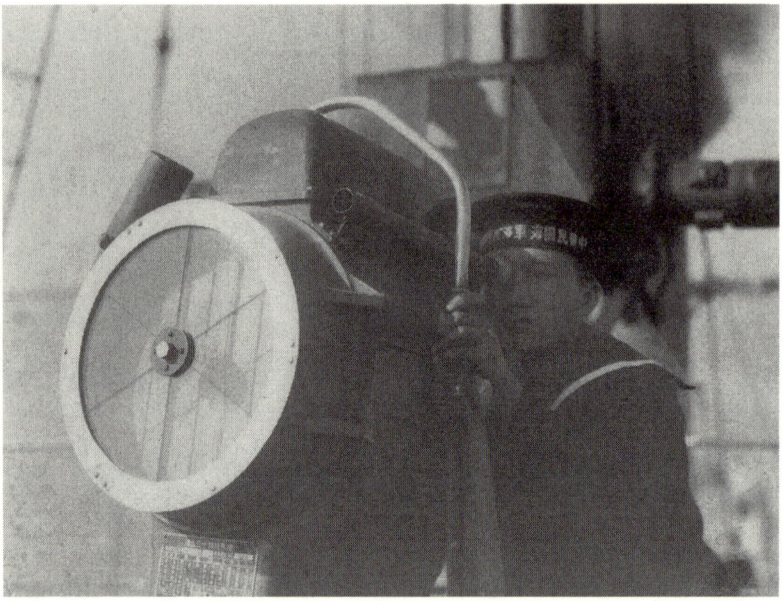

Figure 4.8. Undated photograph of RNG seaman. Courtesy of Academia Historica.

Japanese readership). There is more than a hint of socialist realism in this image's composition, with the soldier being photographed from a low angle, his body dominating the frame and the muscles of his right arm bulging as he grasps his weapon. He stares defiantly into the middle distance to the right of the lens. The only thing that distinguished this sword-wielding Chinese warrior from any number of Japanese soldiers depicted in imperial propaganda of the same period was the inclusion of a small and negligible Nationalist ensign on his cap—a feature that may well have been added after the photograph was taken. In every other sense, this RNG soldier owed much to the canon of wartime Japanese pictorials such as *Shashin shūhō* (Photographic weekly report). Fascinatingly, however, this very same image was used on the cover of the September 1943 issue of the *New China Pictorial*—possibly the only male figure to be pictured on the cover of this magazine (figure 4.9). MoP cadres were willing to appropriate Japanese imagery of Chinese men only if the images could fit into a late-war narrative about RNG masculinity.

The Pan-Asian soldier of the RNG armed forces and the roaring man of Wang Yingxiao's woodcuts made for strange bedfellows. They represented two opposing archetypes of occupation. The former followed orders. He

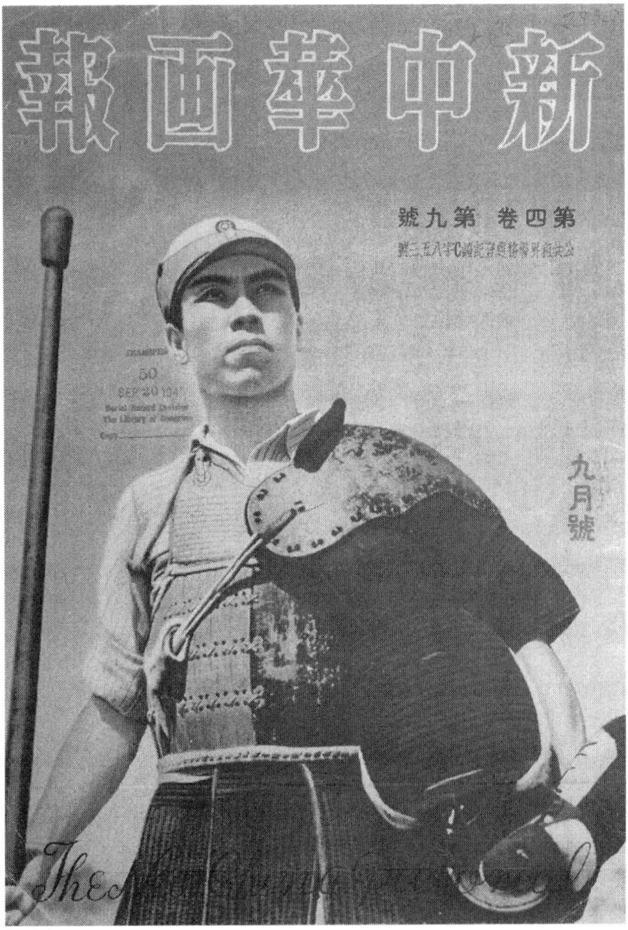

Figure 4.9. Cover image of the *New China Pictorial* in 1942, featuring an RNG soldier. *Xin Zhonghua huabao* 4, no. 9 (September 1942). Asian Reading Room, Library of Congress.

was a decidedly Japanese vision of the Chinese man, "Pan-Asianized" by Dōmei designers and inspired by the uniformity perfected in the armed forces of Japanese-occupied Asia, especially Manchukuo.[70] The latter, in contrast, spoke of spontaneous agency and righteous anger against foreign invaders (expressed, in 1943, as "the West"). Yet this tension was indicative of RNG iconography as a whole. Despite the RNG's best efforts to graft Chinese perceptions of Pan-Asianism onto Japanese imperialism, the conformity and unity inherent in the culture of the GEACPS was never entirely compatible with the revival of May Fourth Chinese nationalism experienced through the NCM. Such tensions would also be felt in depictions of Chinese youth.

The Cult of Youth

When it was inaugurated in January 1942, the NCM was presented as a renewal of the revolutionary spirit that had exercised young Chinese in 1919. It combined the anti-imperialist rhetoric of the May Fourth movement with Japanese interpretations of Pan-Asianism. To be sure, the NCM drew on an array of prewar Republican imagery and ritual. Much of this was derived from the very same Nanjing-decade programs that the RNG had, earlier in the war, decried as violent (most noticeably those aligned to the Blue Shirts, or Lanyishe).[71] It also drew on earlier, pre-RNG campaigns in occupied north China that had survived the *huandu*,[72] as well as youth groups organized in east China by the RGROC (of the sort examined by Kristin Mulready-Stone).[73] This Pan-Chinese heritage was openly acknowledged by RNG cultural workers. When, in 1943, Lei Yimin took to the radio to broadcast a speech on the ideals of the NCM for an imagined audience of young listeners in unoccupied China, he spoke sympathetically to the "youth of the resistance" who had suffered so much "in these long six or seven years [of war]." He also described the (RNG) Youth League as an occupation cognate of the San Min Chu I Youth Corps, the Eighth Route Army (Ba lu jun), and even the force that had first provoked Rural Pacification—the New Fourth Army.[74] All, it seemed, were working toward the same goal of national salvation.

Such appeals may have sounded far-fetched. In the context of the NCM, however, they made complete sense. Through the NCM, the RNG demanded of occupied China's young people many of the same overt acts of militarized patriotism that had been practiced in the name of resistance ever since the 1930s. The descriptions of youth mobilization that Stephen R. MacKinnon provides in his account of Wuhan in 1938, with their "overtones of European-style fascism," could fit just as easily with NCM activities in 1943.[75] All such groups marched in formation, shouted slogans, and swore allegiance to uniformed leaders.

In occupied China, joining the Scouts, the Youth Corps, or the Youth League was tantamount to being transformed into a living icon of the RNG itself. Such groups were visually marked by their dress and behavior. Membership of such groups, for example, entailed the public utterance of an oath of loyalty to Wang Jingwei and the Chinese Revolution in the presence of

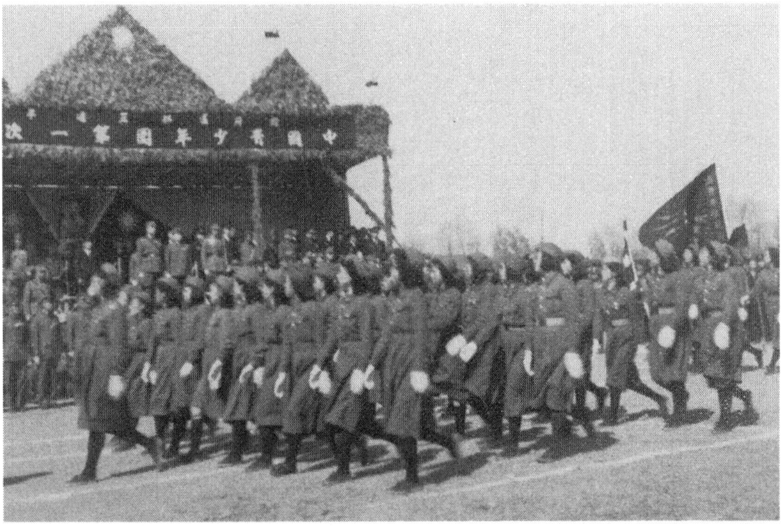

Figure 4.10. Youth groups marching in the presence of Wang Jingwei in 1943. Wang Jingwei and Lin Baisheng Photograph Collection. Courtesy of the East Asia Library, Stanford University.

others.[76] Members were required to dress and groom themselves in a strictly proscribed manner so as to achieve visual uniformity. In September 1942, the Sun Yat-sen tunic was cannily rebranded the "New Citizens uniform" (*xin guomin zhifu*) and deemed the preferred manner of dress for NCM adherents.[77] Such regulations followed an NCM-inspired *guangtou yundong* (shaved-head movement) in May 1942, through which the MoP argued that too many "gentlemen"[78] and "*xiaojiemen*" (young ladies) were wasting money and time on expensive hair care products rather than working for China's liberation.[79]

With their hair cropped and their clothing approved, occupied China's youth were mobilized by the RNG "theater state," sometimes in the thousands, at virtually all major events. By sheer weight of numbers, they became the spectacle itself. The third anniversary of the *huandu* in March 1943, for instance, was marked by the convergence of students and Youth League members on Nanjing. Many of these took part in quasi-military march-pasts in the presence of Wang Jingwei (figure 4.10). Others flooded the city's parks, where they listened to speeches by members of the RNG government itself about the need for defiance.[80] The signing of the Sino-Japanese Pact of Alliance in October 1943 was similarly marked by mass Youth League rallies—

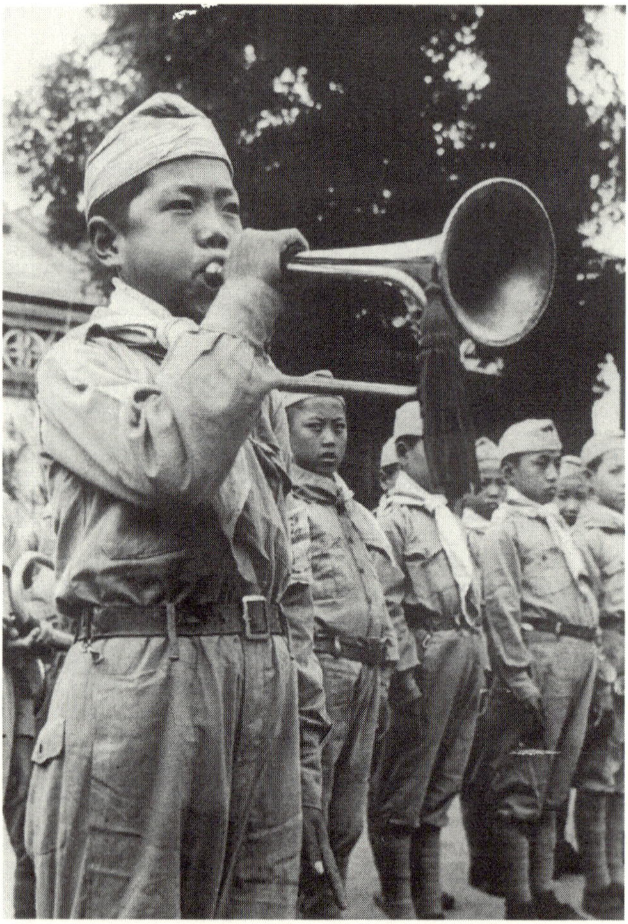

Figure 4.11. Undated and unattributed photograph of RNG Scouts. © Imperial War Museum (HU 73372).

in fact, the RNG archival record suggests that the Youth League played the central role in performing celebrations for this new agreement.[81]

As well as performing, NCM youths were also photographed. The resulting imagery is both striking and significant in the extent to which it defies identification with the RNG, however. Staged photographs of RNG Scouts from 1942, for instance, betray little evidence of having originated in a China under Japanese domination (figure 4.11). Instead, with their garrison caps, kerchiefs, and bugles, the saluting Scouts who emerge from the lenses of unnamed CNA photographers are deeply reminiscent of those pictured in quite different times and places, such as the Young Pioneers of Alexander Rodchenko's constructivist photography.[82] These subliminal references to revolutionary Russian depictions of youth were perhaps more than coincidence. Like the woodcuts of Wang Yingxiao (an artist who openly acknowledged, during the occupation, the debt he owed to Soviet artistic practices),[83] Soviet-inspired imagery of youth in occupied China could say just as much about RNG agency and Chinese revolutionary traditions as it could about Pan-Asianism.

There was more than just Soviet influence in the composition of such imagery, however. A decidedly fascist aesthetic—involving "the rendering of movement in grandiose and rigid patterns," such as those found in photographic depictions of Youth League calisthenics and marches[84]—permeated these depictions as well. This may explain why Youth League members were favored not only by the CNA but also by Japanese news agencies. Predictably, Mainichi included photo essays of Chinese youth in the *Kabun,* for such imagery fitted perfectly with the co-prosperity realist aesthetics of wartime propaganda. Dōmei publications lavished praise upon the youth of "new China" as they participated in mass rallies like their Japanese and Manchukuo peers.[85]

However, RNG youth could just as easily be turned both visually and physically against imperialism (including Japanese imperialism). Following the return of the foreign concessions, for example, photographs of an unnamed youth activist, his arm thrust into the air in anger, his gaze directed upward at some unspecified object of fury, was included in a number of regime-backed publications. In one photomontage published in the *China pictorial* to document anti-British and anti-American agitation, he was superimposed over images of student masses on the streets of Nanjing and Shanghai (figure 4.12).[86] The energy and anger that such imagery proposed may help explain the enthusiasm that members of the Youth League also displayed when physically attacking not just loathed objects of treaty port decadence (e.g., dance halls) but even institutions associated with or controlled by the Japanese, such as opium dens. As Brian Martin notes, some of the most violent protests ever tolerated under occupation were those instigated by Youth League members who, in their hundreds, ransacked opium dens in Nanjing and Shanghai in this period—and whose actions were pictorialized in the RNG press.[87] While the immediate reasons for such protests may still be debated,[88] they nonetheless demonstrated how an angry nationalism that had been framed as a form of occupation anti-imperialism, when unleashed under the NCM, could lead not simply to the mobilization of Chinese youth but also to highly visual displays of iconoclasm—even against the Japanese.

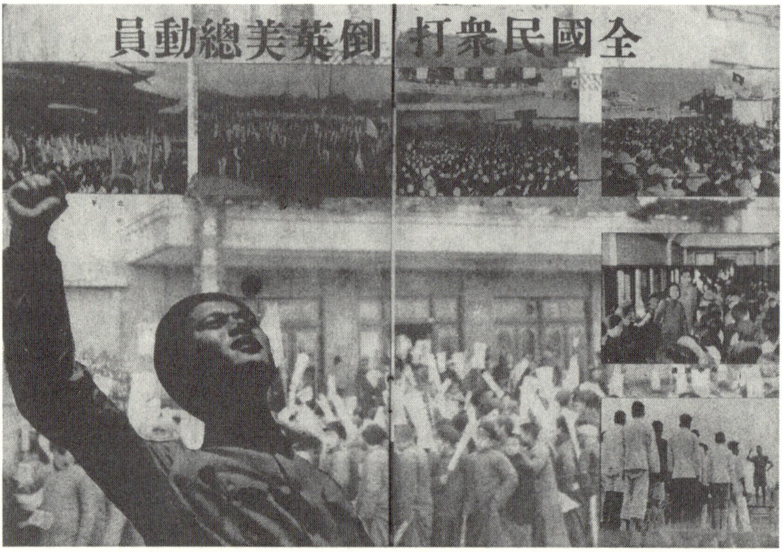

Figure 4.12. Photomontage featuring male youth activist. *Zhonghua huabao* [China pictorial] 1, no. 1 (August 1943). Courtesy of Shanghai Library.

The September 1943 edition of the *Zhonghua huabao* includes a striking juxtaposition of two photographic portraits. On the front cover is a typical NCM-era photograph of a female Youth League member. She is dressed in her New Citizens uniform and is shown, from a constructivist angle, grinning optimistically into the middle distance. She would have looked at home in a collection of Soviet photographs from the 1920s, of a rally in Wuhan in 1938, or on the cover of *Shashin shūhō*. Here, however, she is the embodiment of RNG youth militancy. On the back cover of the same issue, however, we find a sepia wedding portrait of a smiling Nancy Chan, reprinted here to mark her marriage to a Ningbo doctor (figure 4.13). This photograph of occupied China's best-loved modern girl might as well have been produced by Bann's Studio.

That both these visions of Chinese womanhood under occupation could cohabit the covers of the same MoP-sponsored pictorial speaks volumes about the conflicting ways in which different groups within the RNG themselves envisaged the Chinese. And although we have no way of determining the editorial decision that led to the publication of these two images, their juxtaposition is evidence that even diametrically opposed archetypes competed with each other within RNG visual cultures.

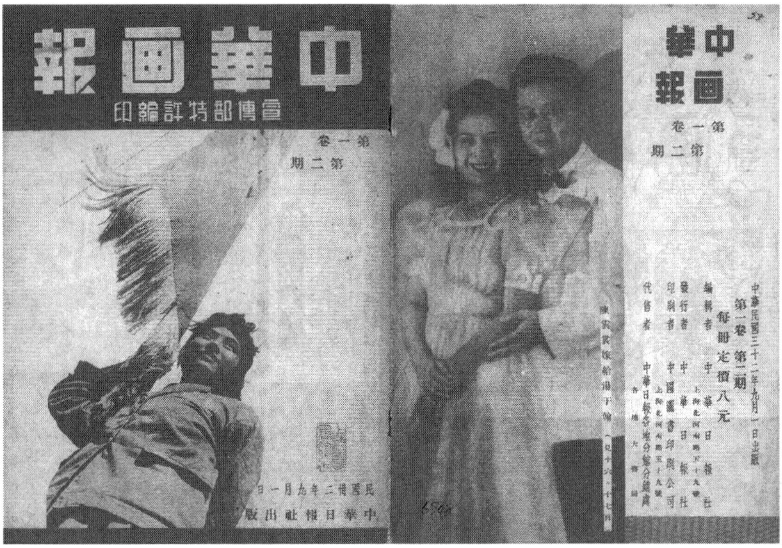

Figure 4.13. Front and back cover of the *China Pictorial* in 1943, showing image of Youth League activist and wedding portrait of Nancy Chan, respectively. *Zhonghua huabao* 1, no. 2 (September 1943). Courtesy of Shanghai Library.

The sheer familiarity of these two competing visions emphasizes how eclectic RNG iconographies had become by 1943, as well as how adept various groups within the RNG had become at adopting symbols, figures, and icons from the Shanghai International Settlement, communist Yan'an, and, of course, Japanese imperialism. Indeed, despite RNG expressions of hatred for communism, one can clearly sense in CNA photographs of Scouts and soldiers the same salvationist nationalism that animated the work of the famed communist wartime photographer Sha Fei in this very period.[89]

However, in noticing these parallels and similarities, we need not assume RNG plagiarism—even if we acknowledge the admiration for CCP propaganda techniques that are present in the RNG archival record. Instead, such parallels should prompt us to consider how similar the cultural practices, aesthetics, and modes of representation espoused by these supposedly opposing forces in this wider conflict in fact were. The organized youth of wartime Nanjing and Shanghai looked entirely at home alongside cognate youth groups mobilized throughout the "radical Right universe."[90] Equally, they could be turned into symbols of opposition to imperialism rather than supporters of it. Similarly, MoP artists shared with their communist peers an admiration for Soviet depictions of roaring men and Young Pioneers. And many of the same artists who had drawn modern girls on the pages of pictorials published in unoccupied Shanghai prior to December 1941 did precisely the same thing in an RNG Shanghai liberated from Western imperialism in the summer of 1943.

What set the RNG apart from these parallel visions of wartime China, however, was the new variable of the Japanese presence. Occupation brought with it new, external ideas about Chinese manhood and womanhood that sometimes sat uncomfortably with Republican Chinese orthodoxy. The response to such a challenge was to turn the fascist aesthetics of what Andrea Germer has referred to as "co-prosperity realism" back at the colonial gaze,[91] transforming the RNG from a docile regime of consumerist modern girls into one that was pictorially populated by revolutionary youths and dashing servicemen. If the visual record tells us anything, then, it is that gendered archetypes of occupation, like the wider iconographies of which they were a part, remained a space of contestation until the end of the war.

CHAPTER 5

Rivers and Mountains

In July 1941, following a state visit of Wang Jingwei to Tokyo, a pictorial album to commemorate the trip was published by the MoP. Edited by the filmmaker Wong Hing-sue and possibly designed by a White Russian artist, the album included a range of photo collages celebrating Wang's sojourn in Japan.[1] It also included an unattributed image on its inside cover that was aesthetically at odds with the rest of the book. A yellow and red print presented an almost clichéd picture of a timeless Chinese riverscape—complete with sailboat, sampan, and fishermen—bathed in the light of a rising sun (figure 5.1).

What is most remarkable about this print, however, is not its content or even its composition but, rather, the juxtaposition of this riparian idyll with the calligraphy in Wang Jingwei's name, which is superimposed onto it. The calligraphic script reads: "Huan women Dong Ya ren de benlai mianmu" (Return to us East Asians our original countenance). Any reader in 1941 would have been fully aware of the line's similarities with one of most commonly repeated phrases in the lexicon of the anti-Japanese resistance: "Huan wo heshan" (Return the rivers and mountains to us). This latter line of poetry, attributed to the Song-dynasty general Yue Fei, had been adopted by the Nationalist Chinese resistance to Japan since the 1930s.[2] In substituting "rivers and mountains" for something far more abstract—that is, "original countenance"—and doing so over an image of an imagined Chinese riverscape, Wang's propagandists were acknowledging the potency of the Yue Fei phrase and its invocation of landscape to the cause of wartime nationalism in China. If Wang could not publicly demand of the Japanese that China's actual "rivers and mountains" be returned to him, he could at least echo resistance propaganda that did make such demands, while at the same time imagining a historical, unspoiled China that existed only in prints and pictorials. This was a strategy that Wang's wartime administration would regularly deploy as it sought to establish its credentials as a patriotic, Chinese regime.

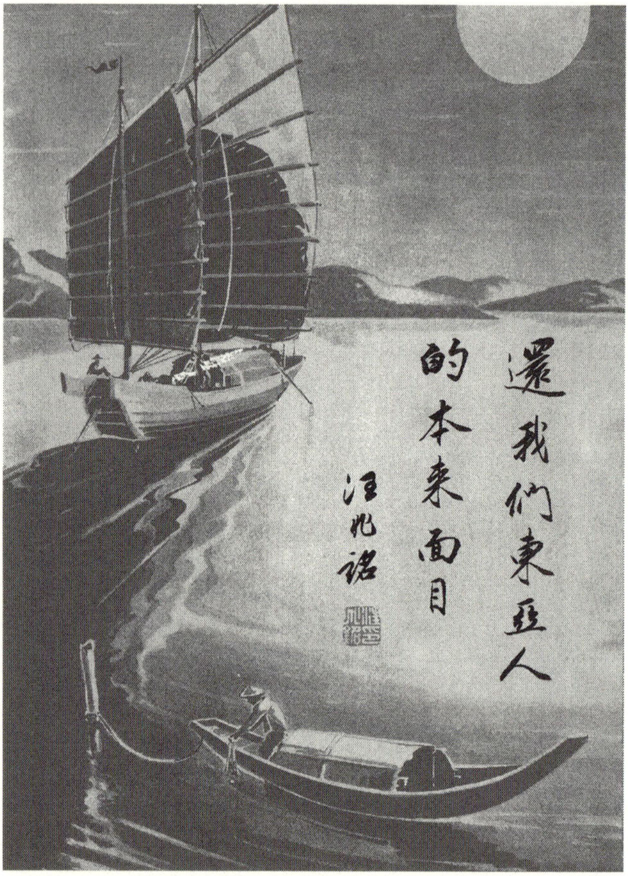

Figure 5.1. Unattributed image of sunrise over a Chinese river, featuring calligraphy by Wang Jingwei, which reads: "Huan women Dong Ya ren de benlai mianmu" (Return to us East Asians our original countenance). From Huang Qingshu [Wong Hing-sue], ed., *Wang zhuxi fang Ri jinian huakan* [Special pictorial in commemoration of Chairman Wang's visit to Japan] (Nanjing: Xuanchuanbu, 1941). Courtesy of the Hoover Institution Library, Stanford University.

The RNG was unusual among twentieth-century Chinese administrations in the limits of its irredentist claims. RNG spokespeople remained reluctant throughout the war to draw public attention to the regime's lack of territorial integrity. Nor did they publicly raise Chinese claims to Manchukuo, Taiwan, or other areas that had been carved out by the Japanese empire. This lack of revanchist aspiration can be detected perhaps most clearly in the visual realm. Indeed, it is my contention in this chapter that depictions of space under occupation—as well as a marked *avoidance* of the depiction of certain types of space—were indicative of the RNG's lack of territorial confidence more broadly. This lack of confidence would only be partially satisfied in 1943, when Shanghai's *gudao* (literally, "solitary island"—a term used to refer to those sections of the city, including the International Settlement, that were not occupied by the Japanese until the end of 1941) came under nominal RNG rule. This development was celebrated in all kinds of visual ways by the RNG. Yet, throughout the war, RNG depictions of space highlighted the fact that this regime was perpetually trapped between the demands of Japanese imperialism on the one hand and a desire to cleave to Chinese patriotism on the other.

It is in the visual realm that we see various RNG attempts to respond to this conundrum and to reimagine the "rivers and mountains" of China in ways appropriate to the occupation context. These range from a symbolic emphasis on specific mountains and rivers (namely, Purple Mountain in Nanjing and the Yangtze) to a tendency—as we saw above with the 1941 print—to re-envisage China through various forms of visual culture that avoided direct reference to national territory. The RNG also oscillated between laments about the "ruined rivers and mountains" (*heshan posui*) of China that had been prevalent in Peace Movement propaganda prior to the *huandu* (as this group sought to justify accommodation with Japan) and a pictorial celebration of China's ability to rebuild itself from the ground up. My argument in this chapter, then, is not that the rivers and mountains of China were absent from occupation iconographies; landscapes are, after all, "a cultural image, a pictorial way of representing, structuring or symbolising surroundings" and a central part of the study of political iconographies more generally.[3] Rather, the varied representations of China emerging under occupation reflected the contradictions inherent in a regime that, on the one hand, acknowledged Japanese conquest while, on the other, claimed to represent a return to Republican Chinese "orthodoxy."

Representing National Space under Occupation

As we saw in chapter 2, patronage of the fine arts continued under occupation in China. Painting in a variety of forms—particularly *guohua*—appealed to many intellectuals in occupied China for a number of reasons. For instance, the debates of the 1930s about the need to promote a national style of art in the face of foreign humiliation were entirely relevant for artists working under occupation.[4] Craig Clunas' argument that "the very act of painting the landscape, painting the *national* landscape, was in itself a political statement" makes just as much sense when we consider cultural production undertaken in areas of China under Japanese control as it does for the art of resistance produced in "Free China."[5]

At the same time, however, *guohua* could easily be celebrated for its invocation of ancient Chinese landscapes in the context of occupation.[6] As a genre that owed little to European traditions, it could even be relabeled "Pan-Asian." Michael Sullivan's account supports this argument. In his view, Chinese artists who continued to paint the rivers and mountains of an imagined China in a *guohua* mode under occupation, such as Qi Baishi, were responding to Japanese admiration for conservative forms of cultural expression.[7] Indeed, the scholarly Japanese interest in forms of cultural expression associated with the Chinese literati, such as *guohua,* "attracted the attention of many intellectuals" during this period.[8]

As Poshek Fu has shown, however, the embrace of genres within the *guohua* family, particularly *shanshuihua*—literally, "paintings of mountains and rivers"—also fitted with the self-image that many intellectuals chose to cultivate in the occupation context. In his study of the journal *Gujin,* Fu suggests that a number of prominent intellectuals of the period identified themselves as *mingshi* (unconventional scholars)—"literati whose moral idealism alienated them from society at large." In trying to emulate the *mingshi* of earlier eras, many intellectuals took up cultural practices associated with this social milieu, including a love of landscape painting. In this way, the Chinese landscapes imagined in *shanshuihua* served to express a particular response to occupation—one of withdrawal and detachment rather than conservative sentiment.[9]

None of these explanations discount, however, the very natural appeal that the *shanshuihua* form had for a regime that was constantly trying to defend itself against claims of compromised sovereignty. For example, the visualization of landscapes associated with the traditions of the literati could be utilized to project a message that Wang's regime was a protector of Chinese culture and a regime that could visualize the rivers and mountains of the country in distinctly Chinese ways. This was the narrative adopted by the Zhongguo wenyi xiehui when it reproduced the *shanshuihua* that its members—including some of the most loyal of RNG artists, such as Ma Wu and Cao Hanmei—had collected from areas beyond RNG control (all while printing congratulatory messages from the likes of Wang Jingwei himself).[10] *Shanshuihua* of the kind reproduced in *Guoyi* and similar periodicals enabled the celebration of imagined though recognizably Chinese landscapes while avoiding the discomfort implied through realist depictions of Chinese land that had been lost to the Japanese.

This also helps explain the RNG patronage of *shanshuihua* at particular moments during the war. For example, in the spring of 1943—that is, shortly after Wang's declaration of war on the Allies—and in order (officially) to reinforce Sino-Japanese artistic exchanges, the MoP arranged for some two hundred works by a Cantonese *shanshuihua* artist called Lin Meishu to be exhibited at the Nanjing office of the Sino-Japanese Cultural Association (SJCA).[11] Tellingly, this exhibition of works by an artist who had hitherto been associated with the resistance[12] was held just a few months after the organization of the Greater East Asia Exposition (Da Dong Ya bolanhui/Dai Tōa hakurankai), also in Nanjing. The exposition was a highly publicized event that the Japanese military had forced the MoP to subsidize.[13] Aesthetically, the exposition was an almost entirely Japanese affair, for it included Japanese-produced depictions of conquered Chinese landscapes, reproduced through dioramas, photography, and vast *sensōga*.[14] Such a context made a *shanshuihua* exhibition in Nanjing by a Chinese artist associated with the resistance particularly significant.

To be sure, interest in Lin Meishu's oeuvre was part of a wider fascination for *shanshuihua* under the RNG. The same SJCA had already hosted exhibitions of a number of artists working in this genre, including Guan Yide, for example.[15] This was in keeping with the tendency of the SJCA—despite its name—to support art that was distinctly Chinese in origin. Yet by juxtaposing Lin's *shanshuihua* renderings of the national landscape with Japanese *sensōga* imaginings of a conquered China, and doing so shortly after the RNG's declaration of war, the MoP was essentially using this form favored by the literati to mark itself apart from Japan's colonial gaze. This was a proudly Chinese regime that could sponsor Chinese modes of artistic production—even in the absence of territorial control over much of China itself.

If the MoP was sponsoring *shanshuihua* depictions of Chinese landscapes, however, what kinds of landscape was it simultaneously trying to hide? To reference Gil Hochberg, what was "not being seen" of China under the RNG?[16] As we saw in chapter 1, the notion of a new regime under Wang Jingwei's leadership was founded on geographic imaginings. Wang had initiated negotiations with the Japanese in 1939 on the assumption that he could establish a Nationalist government in a single region of China that lay beyond Japanese control. The end result of these negotiations, however, was a regime that was always territorially fluid and that struggled to exercise control beyond Nanjing.

It is hardly surprising, then, that few propaganda products from the MoP included maps of Chinese territory. The inclusion of maps would only have reminded viewers of the ultimate failure of Wang's negotiations in 1939 and the extent of Wang's lack of territorial control.[17] With the exception of stylized maps advertising the Yangtze-hugging routes of the Central China Railways (Huazhong tiedao/Kachū Tetsudō)[18] and the maps reproduced to demonstrate the success of specific campaigns (e.g., Rural Pacification), very few cartographic depictions were ever created by the RNG. And on the few occasions when RNG agencies did deploy maps of China in print media, they did so in such a way as to obscure China's borders.[19]

Cartographic depictions of China *were* used, however, by the Japanese military. This was especially so in the lead-up to spring 1940. Propaganda maps created by the Japanese to coincide with the *huandu* can be placed in a longer tradition, dating back to the founding of Manchukuo but peaking at the time of the Japanese invasion of China in 1937. David Nelson Rowe (an American who had been resident in Beijing that year) noted the use of stylized maps on Japanese posters, for example, while collecting numerous examples of such ephemera himself.[20] Such imagery complemented a "defeatist" message that was propagated by the Japanese military and placed an "emphasis on Japanese strength," for it was used to show how futile resistance was and how extensive Japanese control of territory could be.[21] The influence of this genre of propaganda can be seen in maps produced by the Japanese military for distribution in China in the spring of 1940. One such map divided China into two halves: occupied China (i.e., areas nominally controlled by the RNG) was bathed in light, while a dark west China of the resistance was filled with symbols of misery (figure 5.2).[22]

Similarly, representations of Chinese territory "from the air"—be they in photography or graphic art—were Japanese rather than RNG innovations in 1940. As Mark Dorrian and Frédéric Pousin have shown, the "aerial view" was a modern mode of artistic expression (especially in photography) that developed alongside aviation in the early decades of the twentieth century in Europe. The aerial view could be used to suggest a proprietorial relationship with, or control over, the spaces being represented.[23] Given the importance of aerial bombardment to Japanese war strategy—and a wartime Japanese fondness for picturing bombers in flight over China[24]—the "military utility" of such a perspective made perfect sense for Japanese propagandists. Contrarily, it made no sense for a Chinese administration that was so concerned about the limits of

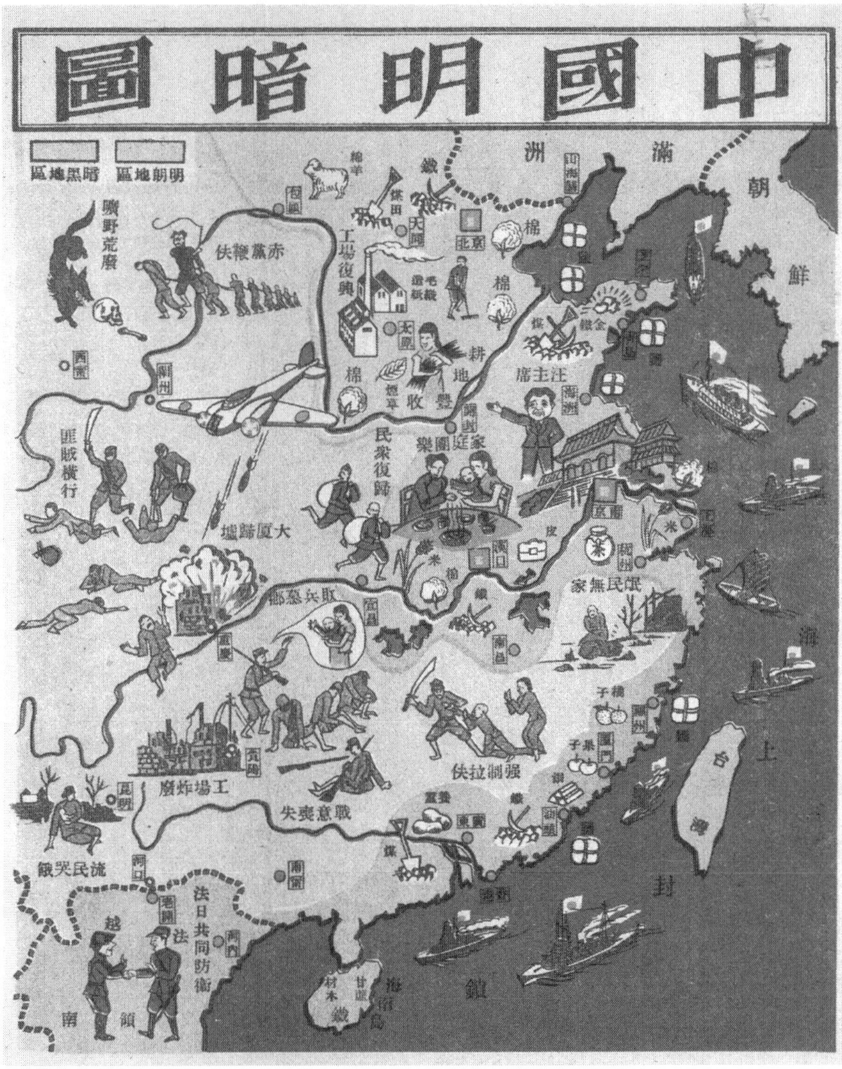

Figure 5.2. A "map of light and darkness in China" (*Zhongguo ming'an tu*) produced by the Japanese military in spring 1940, depicting those areas of China under RNG rule as being wealthy and happy. Courtesy of the Institute of National Defense Studies, Tokyo.

its territorial control and the havoc caused by Japanese aerial attacks, especially when such attacks provided content for resistance propaganda.[25]

For the same reasons, depictions of sweeping landscapes of China produced around the time of the *huandu* tended to be crafted not by members of the Peace Movement or the nascent MoP but by Japanese news agencies. In March 1940, for example, the *Kabun* marked Wang's "return" with a two-page photo spread entitled "Youjiu de Zhongguo" (Eternal China). This included unattributed photographs of some of the most iconic landmarks in China's natural and built environments: the Yellow River, the Yangtze, Mount Tai, and, dominating the page, the Great Wall of China (the latter a particular favorite of the *Kabun*'s editors, as it had also been featured on the cover of earlier issues of this magazine).[26]

From the perspective of pre-RNG Japanese pictorials, many of which had appealed to Japanese readers via notions of a vast and ancient Asian continent, this was not unusual. However, with the exception of the Yangtze—a river that was frequently invoked in RNG political iconography—the idea of an "eternal China" of mountains, rivers, and plains sat at odds with an RNG determined to avoid mention of national territory. After all, as Martin Warnke has suggested, one of the most basic functions of depictions of the landscape is the display of ownership, "like an entry in a land register."[27] If anything, then, depictions of national territory had the potential to remind occupied China's population that this land did not, ultimately, belong to China. It may also have reminded viewers of the highly militarized depictions of Chinese landscapes that had been included in so much China-themed *sensōga* earlier in the war.[28]

If Wang's administration seldom chose landscape photography, cartography, or depictions of China from an aerial view—or anything, indeed, that hinted at resistance obsessions about the country's rivers and mountains—how *did* it seek to represent the country over which it claimed stewardship? Some of the earliest CNA publications provide at least one answer to this question. Within weeks of the *huandu,* the CNA published a series of extended travelogues in which RNG journalists and photographers set out (under the watchful eye of Mabuchi Itsuo's propagandists) to travel the length and breadth of the RNG realm. One purpose of these tours, according to the MoP cadre Guo Xiufeng (who helped in their organization), was "to propagate the significance of peace, anticommunism, and nation-building." The other purpose was to inspect the "suffering of the people [*minjian zhi jiku*]."[29] In reality, the series of resulting books were field surveys of China written (rather than photographed or drawn) from the "aerial perspective." Some of the resulting accounts betray a sense of inadequacy about a lack of Chinese control. Concurrently, however, they contain expressions of awe inspired by the landscapes of the Lower Yangtze delta, as well as an undeniable sense of pride in Chinese territory.

In the first book published in the series, for example, the CNA journalist Xue Huizi wrote emotionally about the land he was flying over as he rode in an airplane from Nanjing to Wuhan on the first leg of his journey, mixing wonder for the rivers and mountains below him with ambivalent references to events that had presaged the RNG's "return":

> Every now and then, we caught a glimpse of the winding Yangtze through the clouds, hiding from us and then appearing again like some mystical dragon. As I leaned against the window to look out, I thought back to the time when Nanjing had fallen [to the Japanese], and I had boarded a ship on the Yangtze headed for Wuhan, traveling for a full seven days and eight nights.[30]

This account is justifiably nostalgic, for this was Xue's first visit to Wuhan since the city's fall in 1938. And Xue made for the perfect choice to lead and report on such expeditions. A follower of Wang's Peace Movement, Xue had originally trained as a painter before choosing journalism as his trade and had spent a period in 1938 employed as a military journalist for the *Ta kung pao*. He had been embedded with Chiang Kai-shek's forces in Wuhan that year—an experience that apparently impressed upon him the "greatness of the motherland" (*zuguo de wei da*).[31]

What is equally striking about Xue's 1940 account is the selection of pictorial representations that sat alongside his territorialized prose. Dozens of photographs by the CNA photographer Xue Diwei (possibly Xue Huizi's brother) were included in this book. A second book was published a few months later detailing a similar trip to north China.[32] Not a single one of Xue Diwei's images, however, corresponds with the aerial view present in the accompanying text. Here are pictures of children begging for food beside railway tracks; a few pages later, we see crowds waiting to purchase basic provisions. This early CNA documentary photography shows an occupied China made up of sites and landmarks—most often photographed from street level and presented in such a way as to avoid reference to wide, open spaces or the grand vistas that the *Kabun* and other Japanese outlets were publishing at this same time. Indeed, the China that emerges from the pages of such accounts is one of *places* (rather than a single, national space) all marked as part of the RNG realm by deliberate inclusion of Republican (i.e., pro-Wang) icons, such as statues, murals, and ROC flags. It is also a China that is only just beginning to rebuild after years of chaos.

These CNA field surveys were representative of an entire genre of early post-*huandu* photojournalism. Accounts compiled by Chinese journalists and their accompanying photographers traveling throughout a now partially accessible China documented the rediscovery of towns and cities after a hiatus of some years.[33] These would be illustrated with snapshots of China from the perspective of the local street. Municipalities contributed to this genre by way of books that verified the survival of sites and landmarks, as well as the resilience of people living among them.[34] Indeed, they acted as an update to the tendency of Peace Movement media in 1939 to demonstrate the futility of war by actually picturing the sites of China that had been destroyed in the conflict. The *Central China Daily News*, for instance, published a number of pictorial accounts of the "ruined rivers and mountains" in the summer of 1939.[35] Pictorial accounts produced a year after such expressions of desperation supported the narrative of the regime's return by stressing the revival of prewar morphologies—for example, through references to the famous sites and relics (*mingsheng guji*) that had survived the fighting. Nowhere was this clearer than in official depictions of the RNG capital.

New Nanjing

For the RNG—like the Nationalist government led by Chiang Kai-shek in the prewar years[36]—Nanjing was meant to serve as the ordered capital of a vibrant and modern republic. In choosing this city as its capital, the RNG was writing itself into Nationalist lore, for Nanjing was the very place that Sun Yat-sen had apparently chosen as the capital of the republic following the 1911 Revolution. Sites such as the Ming tombs were certainly important in this mythology,[37] but only insofar as they framed a capital that would encapsulate the modernity and nationalism to which the RNG aspired.

The message in 1940, then, was of a modern Nanjing being reborn under a regime that embraced peace and orthodoxy. And although the events of the winter of 1937–1938, which are now often referred to as the Rape of Nanjing, were never so much as mentioned in RNG publications, the sense that this returned regime was seeking to overcome recent trauma through rebuilding is palpable in *huandu*-era propaganda. Images of people "redecorating their houses, shops and even lamp posts" filled the pages of MoP publications in the spring of 1940.[38] Peace Movement journalists in Shanghai wrote of Nanjing being not remotely as ruined as "*gudao* propaganda" would have people believe.[39]

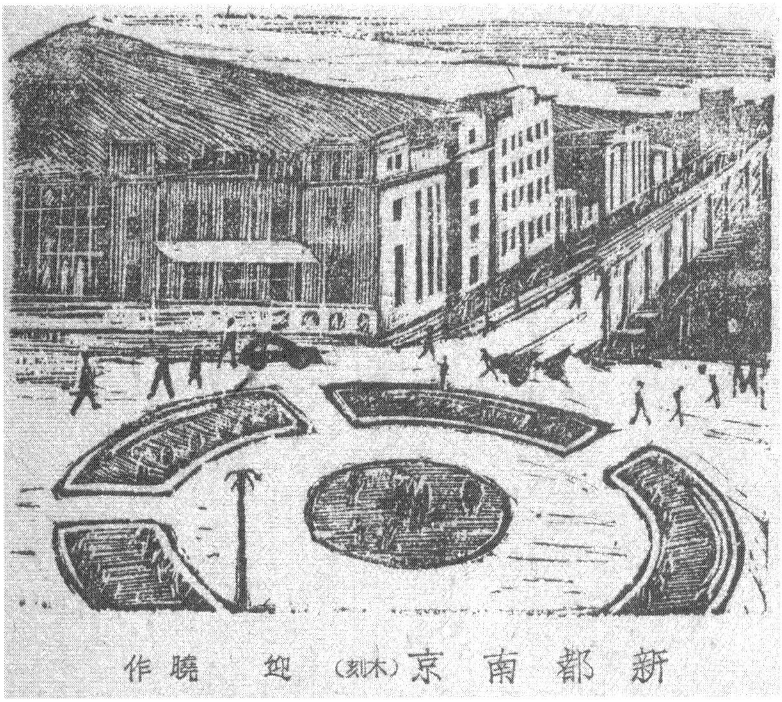

Figure 5.3. Woodcut of "new Nanjing" by Wang Yingxiao. Featured in *Huawen Daban meiri* 8, no. 7 (April 1942). Courtesy of the East Asia Library, Stanford University.

Many of these same ideas had been used by pre-RNG groups such as the Daminhui prior to the *huandu*, and Daminhui influence can be discerned in many of the textual and pictorial depictions of the "reborn" capital that were authored in the first year following's Wang's return. In the pages of Daminhui-published pictorials from 1939, unnamed artists had favored simple line drawings of modernist urban architecture when celebrating the imminent arrival of the new order. Sometimes the architecture that Daminhui artists drew would be reminiscent of actual sites in the landscape; yet just as often an unidentified office tower—one that might have been picked from the streets of any modern city in the world—was invoked as the generic symbol of the "new central government" (*xin zhongyang zhengquan*).[40]

Thanks to Daminhui artists (many of whom, like the abovementioned Ma Wu, were redeployed to RNG institutions in 1940), this old version of the "new" capital was transposed seamlessly onto the rhetoric of "peace."

RNG artists began to imagine their "new China" as one populated by imposing architectural symbols of modernity, which spoke not to Japanese contributions to China's landscape but to the urban innovations of the prewar years. The CNA even chose a modernist depiction of its own office building in the RNG capital to adorn the cover of its institutional reports.[41] This practice was not limited to Nanjing, however. In Wuhan, it was the customhouse (Jianghanguan dalou) first erected on the city's bund in 1922—one of the largest buildings to survive the destruction of 1938—that embellished early RNG publicity (figure 5.4). Lithographic depictions of this structure, which would have looked at home on the pages of any number of prewar Shanghai magazines, were reproduced on the cover of locally published RNG pictorials.[42] In Guangzhou-specific propaganda, the Oi Kwan Hotel (Aiqun da jiudian), completed just before the Japanese invasion and remaining the tallest building in the city throughout the war, was granted comparable prominence.

Other pre-RNG modes of depicting the cities of Japanese-occupied China, however, were far more problematic for the RNG. One of the most enduring motifs in the print propaganda of both the PGROC and the RGROC, for example, had been that of a radiant sun rising over a generic city wall, city gate, or pagoda. This "dreamlike scenery," as Shaoqian Zhang has described it, often showed "new China"—and its ancient architecture—under the light of a rising sun (i.e., Japan).[43] Such imagery may owe a debt to the 1930s work of Japanese war artists who experimented with the motif of the sun rising over the Great Wall of China.[44] Its more direct antecedent, however, was Manchukuo poster art, much of which deployed what Norman Smith has referred to as "sun-centered propaganda."[45] Yet as the theorist of iconography Martin Warnke has shown, this was not a purely imperial Japanese invention. "There is hardly any political situation," he argues, "that cannot be elucidated by comparisons with the sun."[46]

Produced in a linear perspective, such imagery would commonly show rays of a dawning sun shining over a horizon that split the image in two (e.g., sky and land). Often, the viewer's gaze would be drawn toward a central vanishing point of light or radiance via a path or road. In some cases, the horizon might itself be a city wall.[47] In others, a suitably "Asian" edifice would be drawn floating like fata morgana above the horizon. In the spring of 1940, this trope of a new dawn breaking over the horizons of RNG Nanjing was used to celebrate the imminent *huandu,* just as it had been in Manchukuo and north China propaganda a few years earlier. For Japanese and Daminhui artists, Nanjing's city walls—still damaged from the attacks of December 1937 but now emblazoned with large pro-regime

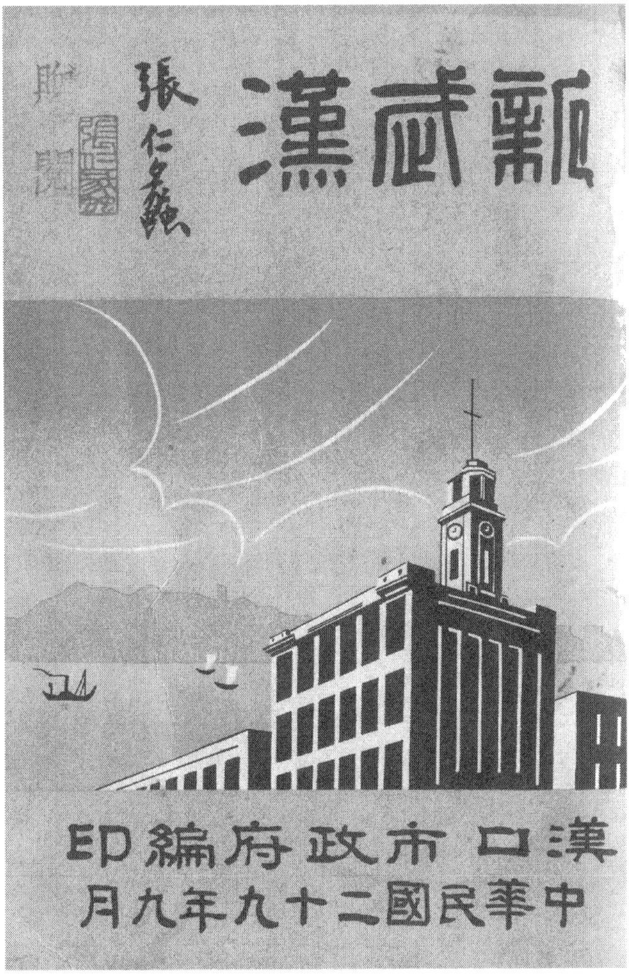

Figure 5.4. Cover of *Xin Wuhan*, including an unattributed and stylized illustration showing the Wuhan customhouse (Jianghanguan dalou) and the Yangtze riverfront. Anonymous, *Xin Wuhan* [New Wuhan] (Wuhan: Wuhan shi zhengfu, 1940). Courtesy of the East Asia Library, Stanford University.

slogans in concrete and the sun-and-moon logo of the Daminhui—could be used to frame the rays of an imagined dawn. In some instances, the characters for "peace" (*heping*) and/or "nation-building" (*jianguo*) replaced the city wall, envisaged as a three-dimensional edifice rising over the horizon like the sun itself (figure 5.5).[48]

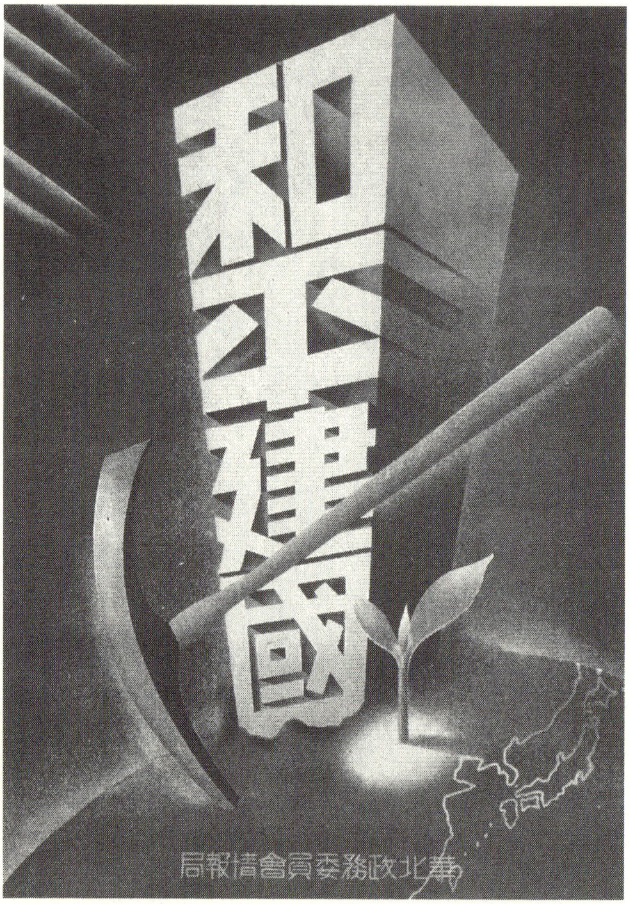

Figure 5.5. The characters for "*heping jianguo*" (peace and nation-building) emerge from the ground as an edifice emitting light in this undated poster, produced by the North China Political Affairs Commission. Courtesy of the Hoover Institution Archives (Poster Collection, CC 106), Stanford University.

The light of dawn breaking over city walls would remain a staple of propaganda art well beyond the *huandu*.[49] For Lin Baisheng and his staff, however, the sun had to be made to rise over far more modern architectural features of Nanjing's streetscapes than its ancient city walls. From the MoP perspective, the most hallowed landmark in the capital was the Sun Yat-sen Mausoleum on Purple Mountain. This building, completed in 1929, became the RNG's premier landmark. In Wang Jingwei's China, it would be this suitably modern yet Chinese edifice that would emit the light of new China's dawn.

The Sun Mausoleum's construction had been an integral part of the prewar modernization of Nanjing under Chiang Kai-shek.[50] Indeed, it had been built to serve as the "monumental, ceremonial center of the nation."[51] Just as importantly, the mausoleum had been purposefully designed as a modern Chinese monument built with Western engineering techniques. While it emulated Chinese palace architecture, it also included beaux arts elements of design and was influenced by commemorative sites beyond China, such as the Lincoln Memorial in Washington, D.C.[52] The mausoleum and Purple Mountain, upon which it had been built, could allude to RNG patriotism while avoiding reference to national space or bounded territory. This was one mountain that had, indeed, been returned.

In the RNG context, the mausoleum also served to reinforce claims to a Republican provenance for this regime and to remind the population of Wang Jingwei's personal connections to Sun Yat-sen. For an RNG obsessed with establishing political legitimacy, ownership of a mausoleum housing the physical remains of the nominal founder of the Chinese Republic mattered a great deal. Little wonder, then, that ceremonial visits to the mausoleum (a practice that had commenced as soon as the mausoleum was completed) continued apace throughout the RNG period.[53] Such visits were invariably photographed for posterity and publication by CNA photographers.[54] RNG ameliorations to the mausoleum echoed prewar practices. Much emphasis, for example, was placed on the need to beautify the site with trees—though under the RNG these would be known as commemorative peace forests (*heping jinianlin*) from 1941 onward.[55] Accordingly, entire tracts were penned to justify the need to forest Purple Mountain. Images of RNG dignitaries planting trees at the site were reproduced in many of these same publications,[56] while tree-planting activities around the site were filmed and distributed as official newsreels.[57]

As this reference to photography and newsreels suggests, the veneration of the mausoleum deserved overtly modern modes of representation. If Japanese and Daminhui artists had turned to poster and graphic art to imagine the sun rising over Nanjing's city walls, it was through photography (and photo-realist art) that the mausoleum would be celebrated. The manner in which this monument was depicted changed little throughout the RNG period. The favored mode of representation, first utilized in the lead-up to the *huandu* itself, was to picture the mausoleum from a low camera angle and to include elements of the site, such as its eight flights of steps

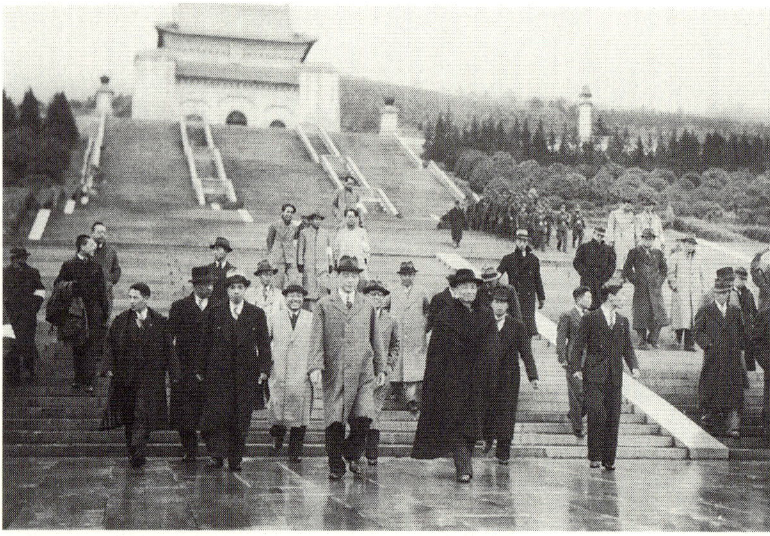

Figure 5.6. Photograph of Wang Jingwei and other Peace Movement advocates leaving the Sun Yat-sen Mausoleum in Nanjing ten days prior to the *huandu*. Photo by the *Asahi shimbun* via Getty Images.

and *via sacra* leading to its central hall. This accentuated the mausoleum's height and scale and encouraged viewers to literally look up at the mausoleum in reverence.

One of the first and most commonly circulated images of the mausoleum to be produced in this mode was a photograph of Wang and his courtiers walking down the steps from the site after paying their respects to Sun Yat-sen on March 20, 1940 (just over a week before the *huandu*).[58] This photograph recalled a similar image of Sun Yat-sen in front of the tomb of the first Ming emperor in Nanjing in February 1912.[59] In this image, almost certainly taken by an Asahi journalist, Wang and his followers are dwarfed by the sheer scale of the mausoleum site, with the steps filling most of the image and a slightly blurred central hall sitting at the top of the frame, slightly to the left of center (figure 5.6).

While this photograph was produced to document that Wang had indeed returned to Nanjing in 1940—hence the centering of Wang within it—it set the tone for many subsequent depictions, all of which presented the mausoleum as an almost sacred site for the new regime, and one that was to be looked up to in awe by the occupied Chinese. Indeed, RNG banknotes would include similarly expansive photo-realistic images of the mausoleum, with steps leading to the central hall, and the undulating silhouette of Purple Mountain in the background. The same image could also be manipulated to accentuate the mausoleum's height and Wang Jingwei's connection to it. When the editors of the *Central China Daily News* published this image in 1940, for example, they chose to crop it into a portrait orientation, thus placing Wang, and the central hall, at the center of the image.[60]

An International Settlement

Not all RNG attempts at claiming Republican-era landmarks in the existing landscape were necessarily this coherent or successful, however. Indeed, beyond Nanjing, the story of other architectural icons and their adoption by RNG agencies hints at a far more difficult relationship between Wang's regime and the Japanese. For example, when it came to the city of Shanghai, there was constant tension over how best to imagine, draw, or photograph this most cosmopolitan of centers. This tension can be illustrated with reference to one particular landmark on the Huangpu riverfront.

In Shanghai before World War II, one of the most recognizable features of the city's bund had been Henry Fehr's art nouveau Allied War Memorial, erected in 1924 and featuring at its top a statue of a winged Victory. According to Robert Bickers, this monument was so important a sight in Shanghai that it made its way into the city's culture, being included in classic films such as Yuan Muzhi's *Street Angel* (*Malu tianshi*) of 1937. This may explain why the statue came to be referred to colloquially in the city either as the angel of peace (*heping tianshi*) or the victory angel (*shengli tianshi*) during the 1930s.[61]

In 1939, however, Fehr's figure was appropriated by the Daminhui and transformed into a goddess of peace (*heping nüshen*) or even a mother of peace (*heping zhi mu*) in pre-RNG periodicals.[62] A sketch of pro–Peace Movement citizens rallying around the monument was featured in the *Zhonghua ribao* in Shanghai in July 1939.[63] And stylized sketches of Victory looking mercifully down upon the Shanghai Bund below a sky of billowing clouds were used on the covers of the Peace Movement periodical *Gengsheng* (Regeneration).[64]

In the hands of RNG-affiliated artists, however, this angel/goddess/mother was taken out of Shanghai's International Settlement and added to imagined Chinese landscapes whenever anthropomorphized references to peace were deemed necessary. In Guangzhou, children were dressed as the angel of peace when celebrating important dates in the RNG calendar. The

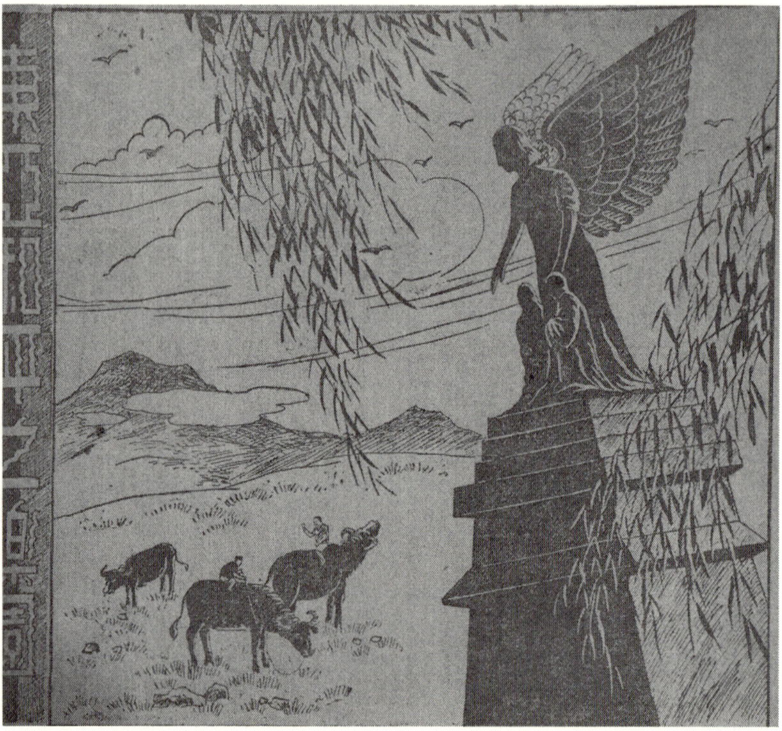

Figure 5.7. The angel of peace looks down upon oxherds riding water buffaloes in a "paradise of East Asian peace" (*Dong Ya heping leyuan*), as depicted by an unattributed artist. *Dong Ya Lianmeng huabao* [Toa pictorial] 4 (June 1941). Courtesy of the East Asia Library, Stanford University.

angel graced the front page of the Suzhou-based *Jiangsu ribao* (Jiangsu daily) when it marked China's National Day in October 1941, with the KMT sun rising behind her plinth (much as the sun had risen over Nanjing's city walls in Daminhui propaganda art).[65] In the hands of the East Asia League (EAL), Fehr's Victory could even be placed in rural Chinese landscapes as she watched over the "paradise of East Asian peace" (*Dong Ya heping leyuan*) (figure 5.7).[66]

Ironically, however, with the return of the foreign concessions to RNG rule in the summer of 1943, the angel of peace physically disappeared and was subsequently expunged from RNG visual culture. With their takeover of the International Settlement at the end of 1941, the Japanese had ordered that the residue of Western imperialism be removed from Shanghai's streets. This included, of course, Fehr's Victory.[67] Despite initially being festooned with RNG flags to celebrate the *tuihuan* in the summer 1943, this key icon that the Peace Movement and the Daminhui had visually prized from the Bund was rendered physically and figuratively invisible by the Japanese in September of the same year. Wang's regime had won Shanghai but lost its angel.

As the fate of the angel of peace suggests, the celebration of treaty port streetscapes was a field of considerable contention under occupation. On the one hand, the treaty ports (which could claim an eclectic mix of architecture, public art, and monuments) had also been the training ground for many cultural workers who were employed by RNG agencies. With the move toward "anti-imperialism" promoted from the start of 1942 onward, however, sympathetic depictions of the treaty ports—and particularly Shanghai—became problematic. How could a regime that claimed to loathe what Lin Baisheng had referred to as "compradors and slaves to foreigners" laud landmarks so closely associated with a semicolonial presence? This question only became more urgent in the summer of 1943, as the RNG faced the difficult task of balancing commemoration of what was the most important achievement of the regime to date—the return of the foreign concessions—with the increasingly nativist rhetoric generated under the NCM.

If the MoP had taken its angel of peace out of Shanghai, it had also initially chosen to ignore those areas of the city from whence she came. This was especially the case in the medium of photography. When the RNG municipal administration of Shanghai celebrated the first anniversary of the *huandu* in the spring of 1941, for example, it presented the city not as a thriving treaty port but as a miniature Nanjing. The Shanghai Bund—associated within the International Settlement, which had become part of a *gudao* beyond the reach of Japanese control—was rarely included in such accounts. At a time when "*gudao* propaganda" was feared in Nanjing, those areas of Shanghai that lay beyond RNG or Japanese control were simply not seen. Here was a city in which municipal government buildings and "new," occupied landscapes—including Shanghai's own commemorative peace forest—took precedence over the famous vistas of the International Settlement, synonymous with Shanghai itself.[68]

Such imagery sat at odds not only with the continuing prevalence of print culture emanating from the International Settlement (which, despite bans, circulated unofficially in occupied China) but also with depictions of Shanghai promoted by Japanese filmmakers. Japanese film companies that were, for all purposes, producing pro-occupation pabulum in this period, were obsessed with the streetscapes of the International Settlement. For example,

Shina no yoru (China nights), one of the most famous of the "continental films" (*tairiku eiga*) starring Li Xianglan (and released just months after the *huandu*), is spliced with newsreel footage shot on location on Shanghai's Bund (including scenes featuring Fehr's Victory), all of which presented the Bund as a dynamic and exciting space of consumption and cosmopolitanism—one possible reason behind the film's apparent popularity later in the war with Shanghai audiences.[69] Similarly, the 1941 Sino-Japanese joint production *Shanghai zhi yue/Shanhai no tsuki* (Moon of Shanghai)—a film that was supposedly "dedicated to [those] who has [*sic*] sacrificed their lives in the Sino-Japanese conflict for peace and friendship between the two countries"—used the International Settlement itself as the mise-en-scène to a story of collaboration.[70] It was precisely Shanghai's supposed "sentimentalism and eroticism," as embodied in its famed waterfront, that animated Japanese cultural production in the period around the *huandu* more generally.[71]

One can detect a clear shift of emphasis in the representation of Shanghai with the start of the Pacific War in December 1941, however. With the end of the International Settlement's special (i.e., non-occupied) status, the MoP and its local offices no longer feared direct engagement with this supposed bastion of semicolonialism. But how might this urban space be recast now that Western imperialists had been purged from it? In February 1942, the inaugural issue of the Wuhan-published *Changjiang huakan* featured on its cover a photograph of Japanese troops aboard a captured American ship moored in Pudong, with the famous buildings of the Shanghai Bund in the background.[72] This emulated similar imagery that was being promoted through the *Kabun,* in which Shanghai riverscapes were associated with naval themes. Rivers could also be worked into other visual narratives imagined by RNG propagandists, however. For example, as we saw in chapter 4, the Yangtze—apparently freed from its foreign (i.e., Western) presence—could be turned into a stage upon which the working men of occupied China could roar against imperialism.

RNG riverscapes need not always be militarized, however. In both Wuhan and Guangzhou, for example, the CNA had managed to sustain a visual narrative through the medium of pictorials and photojournalism of lively river ports replete with modern, treaty-port architecture and an urbane Chinese citizenry. Such imagery was a common feature of the *E bao,* a pictorial published by the RNG's Hubei Provincial Government from 1940 onward. Using photomontage techniques clearly inspired by wartime Japanese pictorials,[73] the very first issue of *E bao* lauded a "developing Hankou" (*fazhan zhong de Hankou*) with a photo spread of the city's bund, modern city residents framing a view of the Yangtze riverfront and customhouse.[74] Less than a year later, the Wuhan Municipal Government published a photographic collection of very similar images to mark the first year of "new Wuhan."[75] The same was the case for *Xin Guangdong* (New Guangdong), a pictorial that included photographs of a lively bund and a Pearl River bustling with water traffic. Such examples demonstrated how pictorial representations of treaty port riverscapes did not need to contradict the message of "peace, anticommunism, and nation-building" inherent in the RNG project. An occupation treaty port in which extraterritoriality was no longer exercised was entirely imaginable—in fact it had been envisaged in the Basic Treaty of 1940.[76]

If we accept the official RNG line that China attained liberty and equality through the return of the foreign concessions in 1943, then we might expect to see depictions of Shanghai replicate this bund-themed photography from Wuhan and Guangzhou. It was certainly the case that in many forms of visual media—from photojournalism to graphic art—the events of summer 1943 generated copious amounts of visual imagery. Indeed, the return of the foreign concessions to RNG rule even prompted the publication of entirely new pictorials, including the *China Pictorial*—an MoP-edited magazine that was initiated in August 1943 with the specific purpose of documenting the process of the *tuihuan*. This pictorial documented the removal of imperialist statues from the International Settlement (although Fehr's Victory was conspicuously absent) and included photographs of all the urban landmarks that a postcolonial, RNG-controlled Shanghai could now embrace.[77] One recurrent image in this and other regime publications, for example, was a photograph of the ROC flag flying above the headquarters of the Shanghai Municipal Council's office building (figure 5.8). Other landmarks, such as Broadway Mansions, also became common icons in this post-*tuihuan* period. Broadway Mansions had been a site/sight of some fascination for Japanese propagandists for some years. It had also, however, been the stage from which one of the most iconic and enduring antiwar photographs ever produced in China had been taken in September 1937—that is, Ma Yingbiao's photograph of hundreds of refugees crossing Garden Bridge (Waibaidu) to enter the International Settlement.[78] This image had been taken from the top of Broadway Mansions. Now, following the *tuihuan,* the same view could be replicated to achieve "aerial views" of a "liberated" (i.e., RNG-administered) Shanghai.[79] In other words, it was an early twentieth- century office block that enabled the RNG to see the Yangtze from the aerial perspective it had been denied prior to 1943.

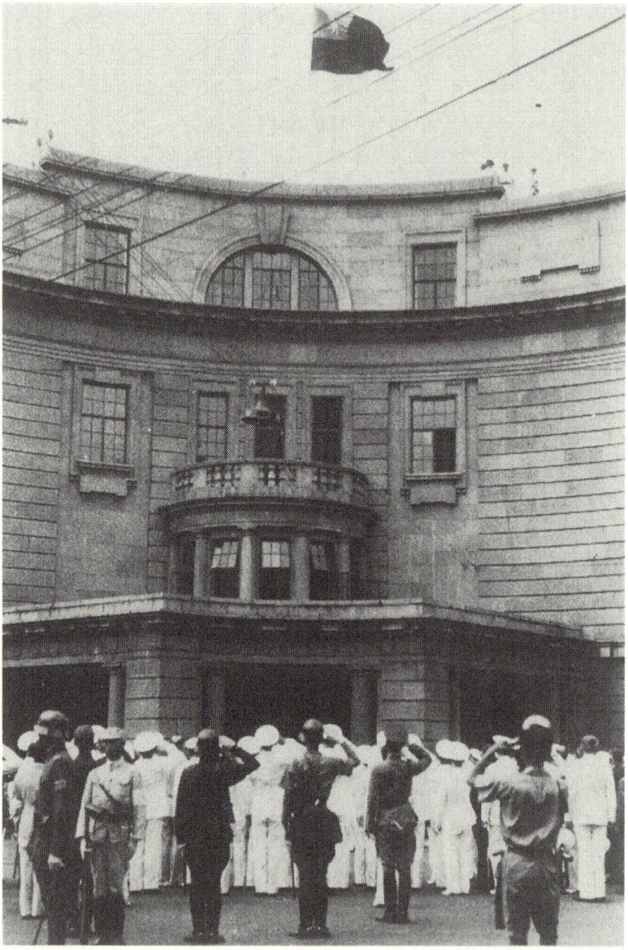

Figure 5.8. RNG troops saluting the ROC flag as it is raised above offices of the Shanghai Municipal Council in August 1943. Chu Minyi Collection (Lot 11700), Prints and Photographs Reading Room, Library of Congress.

Pacific Jiangnan

Tensions over what China should or actually did look like were not limited to depictions of urban streetscapes or riverscapes. A number of contradictory ideas about how rural China should be visually represented during wartime also developed within the RNG. This may well have been a predominantly urban regime that imagined its main support to be concentrated in the cities of China's east and south. Nonetheless, it always aspired to greater control over the countryside. In seeking to achieve this, it sought to create a visual narrative about its rural hinterland for its urban clientele. From the summer of 1941 onward, it also tried to involve rural communities themselves in the creation of a new vision of a "pacified" yet politicized countryside under occupation.

Prior to Rural Pacification, the RNG had not maintained a significant presence in rural China. Indeed, as we have seen, much of the regime's energy in the first year of its return had been spent rebuilding its capital. As a result, many of the depictions of the Chinese countryside found in early RNG art and propaganda are highly negative and are dominated by images of the ubiquitous *youjidui* (guerrilla units) of the resistance.[80] These were presented as bands of shadowy figures visiting havoc on otherwise peaceful villages and were a common feature of murals, as well as performative cultural production such as dramas.[81]

In the absence of a strong RNG presence beyond the cities, the Japanese military had maintained a monopoly over the production of visual depictions of rural China and of visual cultures in occupied rural China itself. Prior to 1941, it was Japanese artists (rather than RNG cadres) who had adorned the walls of rural towns with murals and posters touting bucolic Chinese villages. Japanese military broadsides, often aimed at local Chinese elites, showed Japanese soldiers being welcomed into villages where crops were high and skies were clear.[82]

Such imagery found its way onto the pages of pictorials such as the *Kabun*. Mainichi editors reinterpreted military visions of rural bliss through the medium of photography and graphic art. Even following the *huandu,* this Japanese tendency to visually imagine rural China as a land of contented hamlets and towns continued: publications that introduced the RNG realm to Japanese audiences included ink-wash paintings and landscape photography of temples, riverboats, and hamlets by the likes of Yonaiyama Tsuneo.[83]

A good deal of this material drew on the canon of the Manchukuo pastoral, itself highly influenced by Barbizon interpretations of rural France in the nineteenth century.[84] As Kari Shepherdson-Scott has argued, in this Manchukuo vision of Chinese villages, "the subjects [of propaganda photography] become evocative symbols of local culture . . . occupying a timeless rural landscape."[85] Like the Manchukuo villages imagined in Japanese photography of the sort Shepherdson-Scott has studied, the Chinese villages that emerged from the pages of the *Kabun* and other pictorials from 1939 onward were defined by their simplicity and innocence. They included simple shacks and fecund paddies and were peopled with happy peasants. Even the vocabulary used to describe such imagery betrayed a Manchukuo provenance. These were "central Chinese villages in which people lived in peace and enjoyed their work" (*anju leye zhi Huazhong nongcun*).[86] This "picturesque China" (*fengguang mingmei de Zhongguo*) was one of waterside vistas, pagodas, and bridges.[87] The harsh frontier feel that had typified a good deal of Manchukuo photography was replaced in east China with more languid scenes anchored firmly in the Jiangnan—China "south of the Yangtze."[88] Such imagery reflected visions of an idyllic China that had been developing in the imperial Japanese imagination for some decades prior to the war. Be it Japanese tourists to China in the early twentieth century or the main protagonists in occupation-era films such as *Shina no yoru* (China nights) (1940), "romantic idylls by the river"[89] were presented as quintessential to rural China.[90] That Japanese propagandists had become so adept at depicting the Jiangnan is hardly surprising: Mabuchi Itsuo had run propaganda work out of the Jiangnan city of Hangzhou in 1939.[91]

Other markers of rural Jiangnan presented in *huandu*-era visual cultures betrayed imperial Japanese connotations as well. In pictorials, for example, one of the most recurrent icons was that of the "peasant riding on his water buffalo—as happy as you please" (*nongcun mutong, qi niu bei shang, kuaile ziru*).[92] This obsession with peasant children herding oxen even included the publication of apparently traditional folk songs on this very theme.[93] As recent scholarship in art history reminds us, depictions of rural landscapes featuring peasants herding oxen can be dated back to at least the Song dynasty (960–1279 CE).[94] In occupied China, however, the oxherd carried with him distinctly imperial Japanese connotations. Despite its Song origins, the theme had been invoked by Japanese *nihonga* (literally, "Japanese-style paintings") artists in China such as Yokoyama Taikan prior to the war.[95] It had also been revived under Japanese colonial rule in Taiwan, with the oxherd-themed carvings and sculptures of Huang Tushui being featured in empire-wide art exhibitions and helping to popularize the water buffalo and rural child as a symbol of colonial harmony.[96] That ox herding as an artistic theme also had Buddhist connotations only helped make this image fitting for a regime that (as we have seen) found this religion to be both suitably Pan-Asian and dedicated to the same notion that had animated Wang's followers in seeking a settlement with Japan in the first place (i.e., peace).[97]

The image of the sleepy Jiangnan village with its water buffaloes, canals, and temples was not, however, the only means of imagining rural China under occupation. Indeed, this clichéd Japanese picture came under direct challenge from the RNG with the introduction of Rural Pacification in the summer of 1941. Rural Pacification prompted a fundamental shift in the ways in which RNG state actors both promoted occupation to rural China itself and promoted rural China to occupied cities. For some sections of the RNG state (especially the MoP), it involved a reordering of the imagined Chinese countryside, so that the slow and sleepy villages of the pre-1941 era could be repackaged as spaces of production and politics. Ironically, Rural Pacification also entailed increased levels of regime surveillance in the countryside and thus increased the control over what peasants themselves could actually see—even while their villages were pictorially lauded as sites of productive harvests.[98]

We can still find evidence of the visual cultures that MoP cadres sought to promote to pacified villages in the *nongcun jianshe tu* (village-building pictures) that they produced in the name of Rural Pacification—images of which survive in photographs that were reprinted in regime pictorials. A huge canvas that dwarfed even the artists who posed in front of it was hung at the entrance to the site of the MoP's First National Conference, held just as Rural Pacification was getting under way. Entitled *Revitalize the Villages and Improve the Lives of the People* (*Fuxing nongcun gaishan renmin shenghuo*), this image showed peasants leading ever-present buffaloes across fecund paddies, yet with smokestacks of industry pointing out from behind distant hills.[99] In the late summer of 1942, Chinese activists from the EAL depicted toiling peasants engaged in manual labor, foregrounding picturesque hamlets in the shadow of hills as they appealed to peasants to "return to their villages," just as the RNG had returned to Nanjing.[100]

In the CNA photography that was generated as part of the Rural Pacification campaigns, the countryside was decidedly *not* idyllic. When Lei Yimin articulated the aims of these campaigns in early 1943, for example, he described in vivid terms the countryside that he had apparently encountered as he set out to take charge of Rural Pacification propaganda work in July 1941: "The people were missing or homeless, and all the buildings had been left abandoned, their walls reduced to rubble. It was shocking to see."[101] Rural Pacification photography reflected such sentiments. While not necessarily dwelling on images of rural destitution, CNA photographers chose to present rural China as a dynamic space in which peasants were expected to perform (and be seen to perform) acts of reconstruction and political engagement (figure 5.9). Indeed, peasants themselves featured prominently in the photographs that Chen Guoqi and others produced to document Wang Jingwei's tours of the pacified zones. Rural Pacification publications

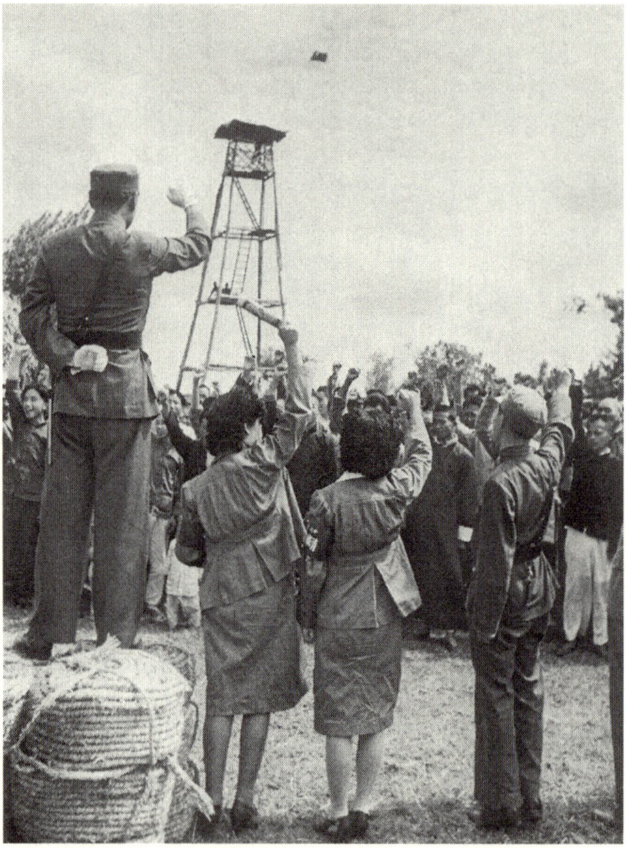

Figure 5.9. Undated photograph of unidentified Rural Pacification cadres rousing peasants. © Imperial War Museum (HU 73374).

showed peasants raising their fists in protest (at enemies unspecified) or erecting new bamboo fences that would separate their villages from communist guerrillas.[102] The symbols of the bamboo fence and the watchtower, in particular, would emerge as an integral part of the visualized countryside under the RNG: physical markers that accentuated the dichotomy between apparently happy (i.e., pacified) villages and the chaos of the ruinous, resistance-infested countryside that Lei Yimin had lamented (figure 5.10).

This image of a politically engaged countryside would even find its way into the cinema of occupied China. A small number of feature films, the plots of which revolved around *tufei* (bandits) wreaking havoc on Lower Yangtze rural communities, presented Chinese villages that cooperated

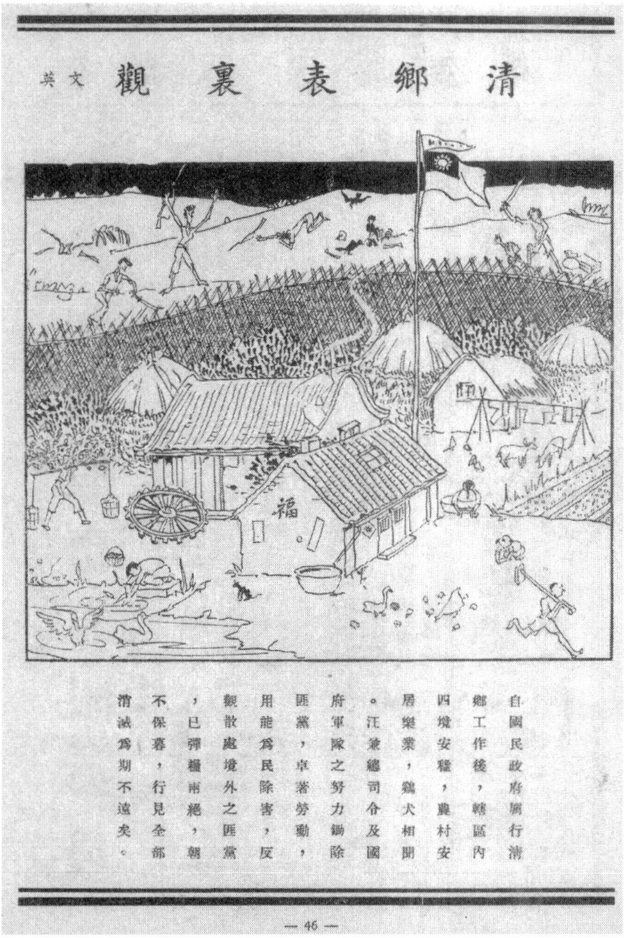

Figure 5.10. Cartoon depiction of a Rural Pacification village by Wen Ying. *Zhongguo manhua* [Chinese cartoons] 2 (October 1942): 46. Courtesy of Shanghai Library.

with the authorities and that enjoyed social harmony and high crop yields as a result. One example was the CUMP-produced film *Lai ri fangchang* (The days to come) (1943), directed by Zheng Xiaoqiu and shot in the vicinity of Changshu, near Suzhou.[103] Ironically, many of these movies—examples of what we might call "Rural Pacification cinema"—were filmed on location in the very same pacified areas that had been featured in photo shoots of Wang Jingwei's Rural Pacification tours. The actual "pacification" of

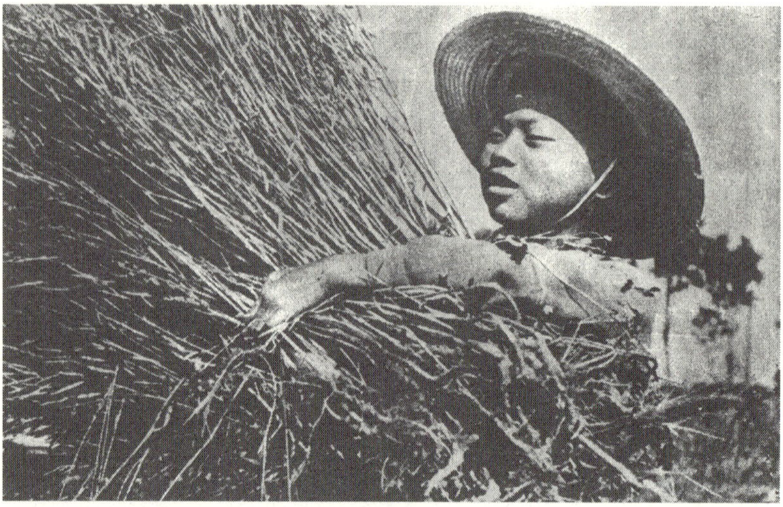

Figure 5.11. Jiangsu peasant boy collecting the harvest. *Guomin xinwen huabao* 3 (March 1942). Courtesy of Shanghai Library.

the countryside, in other words, enabled new visions of rural China to be produced for the consumption of urban RNG audiences.

By 1943, this RNG vision of the countryside was showing signs of far more direct influence from imperial Japanese propaganda praising occupation in other parts of Asia. With the start of the Pacific War, the focus in much propaganda throughout Japanese-occupied Asia emphasized agricultural production (figure 5.11).[104] In this context, Rural Pacification–themed visual propaganda, especially as it was presented in Japanese publications for Pan-Asian markets, began to conflate pacified Jiangnan with Japanese-occupied Southeast Asia.[105] Peasants pictured gathering the harvest in occupation pictorials were now as likely to be from Java as Jiangsu (figure 5.12). In photography of rural production, a clear shift toward gigantism—south China villagers growing supersized melons, just as their brethren in occupied Indonesia did—can also be detected.[106] By the end of 1944, pacified rural China had been almost entirely conflated with occupied Southeast Asia and the Pacific.

During the postwar trials of high-ranking members of the RNG staged by Chiang Kai-shek's Nationalist government in 1946, Chen Bijun berated prosecutors over the accusation that she and her husband had "sold out the nation" in 1940. How could there be a nation left to sell, asked Chen, when China had been effectively abandoned by Chiang Kai-shek over the course of

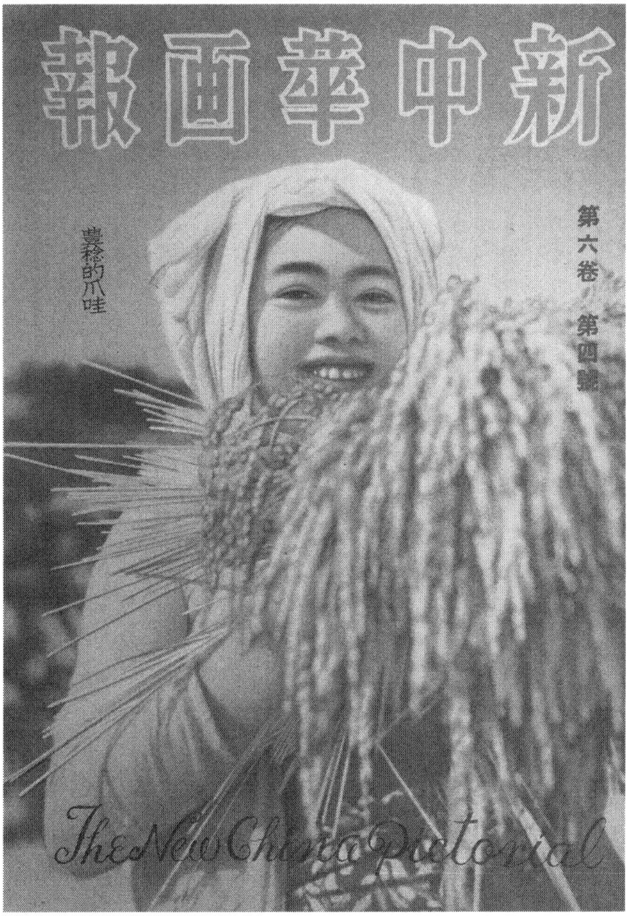

Figure 5.12. *Fengren de Zhuawa* (A bumper harvest in Java). Unattributed image featured on a *New China Pictorial* cover. *Xin Zhonghua huabao* 6, no. 4 (April 1944). Asian Reading Room, Library of Congress.

1937 and 1938? Retrospectively reinterpreted, the notion of "returning the rivers and mountains" could thus be interpreted, not as a call to arms, but rather as a justification for the creation of a Chinese regime under occupation that would ensure the restoration of partial Chinese sovereignty, as well as the resurrection of a moribund Chinese republic with its capital in Nanjing.[107]

What the visual record shows us, however, is that this is not how the situation was interpreted by many sections of the RNG state. If anything, the tendency toward avoidance of particular modes of spatial representation under occupation, particularly maps and representations of space from an aerial perspective, suggest that this regime was sensitive to the limits of its sovereignty. Just as tellingly, the RNG's sponsorship of specific modes of representing imagined rivers and mountains (e.g., in *shanshuihua*), together with its symbolic obsession with one particular mountain (Purple Mountain) and one specific river (the Yangtze), all suggest that the RNG was open to a selective appropriation of resistance iconographies when such appropriation fitted its own agenda. Just as importantly, RNG attempts to harness existing sites within the prewar built environment (e.g., Fehr's Victory) or render certain spaces invisible were sometimes undermined by Japanese policies. This demonstrates just how difficult it was for Wang's regime to maintain a consistent and coherent visual narrative that complied both with Japanese imperial designs and with Republican orthodoxy. The photographic veneration of the Sun Mausoleum thus hints, not simply at the symbolic importance of this site, but also at the fact that this was one of the few prewar monuments whose iconographic importance could be agreed upon by both the RNG and the Japanese.

In the shifting visions of rural China before and during Rural Pacification, we find further evidence of these same tensions. Wang Jingwei had established a thoroughly urban regime, turning its back on the ruralization of the resistance[108] and embracing the cities of the south and east, including those that had been so central to the prewar mythology of Republican Chinese nationalism—Guangzhou, Wuhan, and, of course, Nanjing. Under Rural Pacification, however, RNG cadres began to explore new ways of representing the hinterland, moving away from Jiangnan riverscapes so often celebrated by Japanese army artists and news agencies, in favor of the pacified village marked out by its bamboo fence.

Overall, however, we see in the visual depictions of China produced by the agencies of the RNG an administration that felt fundamentally undermined by its own lack of sovereignty. Resistance artists called on the Japanese to "return the rivers and mountains [to us]"; RNG cadres, in contrast, clung desperately to those few rivers and mountains they could find—Purple Mountain and the Yangtze—as a means of claiming some semblance of sovereignty. In doing so, however, they also ensured that much of China would remain unseen and unseeable—even to Wang Jingwei himself.

CONCLUSION

Beyond the Colonial Gaze

The seventieth anniversary of the "Victory of the Chinese People's War of Resistance against Japanese Aggression and the World Antifascist War" was marked by significant pomp in Beijing on September 3, 2015.[1] The event included a march-past by some twelve thousand Chinese troops and a speech by Xi Jinping, wearing a black Zhongshan tunic and standing above Ge Xiaoguang's famous portrait of Mao Zedong on Tiananmen.[2] This was, however, an event in which many aspects of China's wartime experience were simply ignored. In contrast to the commemorations marking the fiftieth anniversary of the war's end two decades earlier, for example, few mentions were made of Chinese traitors in official accounts.[3] Indeed, one could be forgiven for thinking in 2015 that there had been no client regime led by Wang Jingwei during the Japanese occupation.

Despite the invisibility of the RNG, one cannot help feeling that the September 2015 commemorations would have looked remarkably familiar to figures such as Lin Baisheng.[4] Military march-pasts were, of course, part of the spectacle that many wartime Chinese regimes practiced. Political portraiture was as common to the RNG as it is in the PRC today. And Wang Jingwei had worn a black Zhongshan tunic when he declared war on the Allies in January 1943 in Nanjing. Had he been there to witness the 2015 celebrations in Beijing, Lin might even have found residual references to China's "peaceful rise" (*heping jueqi*) strangely reminiscent of occupation rhetoric.

I speculate in this manner not to be flippant or to suggest that today's PRC inherited its political culture directly from Wang Jingwei's theater state. Rather, such parallels suggest that the RNG drew on a shared set of rhetoric, symbols, and icons that were common to many modern Chinese polities and that have survived into the present day. As we have seen, different "Chinas" also learned from one another during the war. The MoP envied the New Fourth Army for its propaganda prowess, even as it tried to eradicate it. May Fourth nationalism was articulated in Chongqing just as it was in occupied Nanjing. One can acknowledge the significant differences between these various wartime entities while being cognizant of the continuities in their iconographies. In his classic study of "Confucian fascism," Frederic Wakeman Jr. cited Lloyd Eastman in noting that a "larger symbolic realm of popular anti-foreignism and ethnic revivalism . . . characterized many modern movements in China." Wakeman's argument that "Red Guards and Blue Shirts . . . were not that far apart" remains entirely convincing today—but that same argument could be made even more convincing were we to consider RNG Youth League activists alongside their Republican and communist cousins.[5]

This is precisely why the RNG, despite its invisibility at the 2015 anniversary, remains highly significant. A close reading of the visual and material ephemera that this regime left to posterity can help us test many of the assumptions we make about various aspects of political culture, and cultural politics, in modern China more generally. As some of the secondary literature that has been cited throughout this book shows, political, economic, and military historians are already turning their focus toward Wang Jingwei's China so that this regime can be brought back into the wider story of modern China's development. However, in the study of wartime China's cultural history—to say nothing of the broader field of Chinese visual cultures—far fewer scholars have followed the lead that Edward Gunn, Nicole Huang, and Poshek Fu have established by taking seriously the cultural developments that occurred under Japanese occupation. Most analysis of the culture of wartime China remains heavily weighted toward the unconquered "great hinterland" (*da houfang*), the Communist base areas, or Shanghai's *gudao*. The RNG continues to be excluded from much of this scholarship.[6] As a result we have few opportunities to contrast the RNG to its cognate regimes in China's west or to other Republican entities that struggled for political legitimacy, such as Chiang Kai-shek's ROC after 1949. Nor do we have a means of properly testing how visual tropes and rhetoric crossed political and temporal boundaries both during and after the war. By not taking the RNG into account, our understanding of everything from personality cults to political theater in modern China remains incomplete.

For all its continuities with other Chinese regimes, however, the RNG is unique for what it can tell us about the resilience and adaptability of Republican Chinese iconographies. In insisting on the sanctity of the ROC flag, the figure of Sun Yat-sen, and the face of Wang Jingwei—and in seeking to present such icons through recognizably modern Chinese modes of visuality—the RNG framed itself as a distinctly Republican Chinese entity.

To be sure, this regime struggled to cast off the far more overtly Japanese representations of China that had permeated east and north China thanks to the efforts of the Daminhui and Xinminhui, respectively (e.g., poster art depicting the sun rising over city walls, or the feminization of occupied China as envisaged in the films of Li Xianglan). Nonetheless, in managing to continue to *look* Chinese—indeed, to look *defiantly* Chinese when it came to mobilizing youth activists, for example—groups such as the MoP might be said to have gone much further than other client regimes in establishing a separate visual space for their "reorganized" China.

The RNG therefore suggests that many of the icons developed in China in the prewar years were far more malleable than even the Japanese may have expected. As we saw in chapter 4, a "new woman" associated closely with both Shanghai glamour and anti-Japanese resistance (e.g., Nancy Chan) could be reinvented in the print media over the course of just a few months as an obedient symbol of occupation-era entertainment. A 1920s Soviet stage play and its ant-colonialist characters could be revived to celebrate Nanjing's declaration of war on the Allies, and could in turn provide the inspiration for a myriad of artistic representations of the occupied (and supposedly anticommunist) Chinese man. We might dismiss such instances as cynical attempts by desperate "traitors" to cling to some semblance of patriotism via prewar archetypes or visual tropes. Yet, as I have suggested throughout this book, such developments could just as easily be read as attempts by a client regime to mark itself apart from an occupying power *as well as* Chinese resisters. If a study of the iconographies of occupation tells us anything, then, it is that the Japanese invasion of China led, not to the eradication of prewar Chinese visual cultures, but to the selective and eclectic reenvisioning of China by a regime populated by veteran KMT (and, in some cases, former communist) propagandists and refugee cultural workers.

Visual History and the Limits of Collaborationist Nationalism

Citing the arguments put forward by surviving RNG leaders at trials held in 1946, a number of historians have noted the emphasis that Wang's regime placed on "the protection of people and the preservation of the nation" when explaining its decision to work with a foreign occupier as a form of patriotism.[7] In the RNG mind-set, a distinction could apparently be made between the nation and the state, with preservation of the former (even in some compromised form) being far more urgent in the circumstances of war.

To phrase it another way, "land and people were the foundation of the nation, and . . . national defense should start by remaining with them and shielding them."[8] By adopting such an ideology, the violence of war could be suspended, and a Chinese administration could ensure that people were fed and protected.

Even at the *huandu*, however, one must wonder why groups such as the MoP—if they were led by individuals who espoused a "collaborationist nationalism" that put the nation before the state—were so keen to emphasize the visual and performative trappings of the Republican state at their "return." The *huandu* may well have led to increased levels of stability for people in areas administered by the RNG. Why, however, did such an event require the mobilization of Scouts, the proliferation of Wang Jingwei portraiture (which clearly drew on prewar templates), or the revival of a largely ceremonial navy? For that matter, was the restitution of the ROC flag a prerequisite for the protection of people and land? If anything, such developments suggest a very state-centered approach on the part of the MoP in 1940. They even suggest that the RNG's leaders, rather than choosing nation over state, were proud of demonstrating just how many concessions to Republican statehood they had managed to win from the Japanese.

Another difficulty arises when we attempt to apply the logic of collaborationist nationalism to the RNG after the *huandu*. In particular, the notion that this administration embraced such an ideology is difficult to square with the realities of what I have referred to in this book as the Axis turn of 1941. If collaborationist nationalism rested on the idea that a negotiated peace would benefit the people, then the sheer amount of energy expended on political theater and symbolism seems incompatible with such a notion. Even if we accept that a good deal of these developments were forced upon Wang's administration as a result of the Japanese empire's changing fortunes during the war, we cannot deny that increasing levels of agency for the RNG only led to greater attempts to emulate the aesthetics of the Axis powers or to rebrand China as a GEACPS state. When we look at the explosion of propaganda and various other forms of cultural expression around the *tuihuan*, it would seem that concern for the safety and well-being of the people was, at the very least, matched by a desire to see—and photograph—the ROC flag flying over the Shanghai Bund.

RNG attempts to gloss over a lack of territorial control by experimenting with new and distinctly Chinese modes of representing the "rivers and mountains" also test the limits of the collaborationist nationalism paradigm. To be sure, a focus on the protection of land and people can be found in the depictions of urban and rural China that we examined in chapter 5. But so too can a deep-seated sense of inadequacy when we consider MoP avoidance of direct reference to certain types of national space. Wang Jingwei appears to have genuinely shown an interest in seeking to have the rivers and mountains of China returned to him. Until events such as the return of the foreign concessions, however, his courtiers sought specific ways of visualizing their homeland that would not remind people of the RNG's lack of territorial integrity or anger his Japanese patrons.

Such apparent contradictions that emerge from textually derived understandings of collaborationist nationalism and what I refer to as the iconographies of occupation demonstrate why a visual history of the RNG is necessary. Analyses of this regime based on the testimonies of its main proponents are certainly not invalid. They provide us with only a partial picture of the highly factionalized and changing notions of what China and "the Chinese" meant in the RNG realm, however. An emphasis on the ever-changing iconographies that were deployed by this regime complicate our understanding of the RNG, and of occupied China more generally, in a variety of ways.

First, a visual history approach helps show us how this regime lacked a single ideology—be it collaborationist nationalism, Pan-Asianism, pacifism, or anything else. To be sure, Lin Baisheng's staff at the *Zhonghua ribao* and the MoP started their work in 1939 by presenting Wang Jingwei in ways that were compatible with the notion of "peace, anticommunism, and nation-building." Yet the MoP's view of Wang developed as its own agenda changed, and its resulting visions of Wang cohabited a visual sphere that was populated by alternative representations of the leader authored by Japanese artists and Daminhui propagandists. In 1941, we find Wang the peacemaker transformed into a field commander (thanks to a private photography studio). And in 1944, Wang is buried, thanks to Chen Bijun, as a revolutionary martyr. The development of these many and sometimes contradictory Wangs over the course of the RNG's history parallel the regime more generally. This was a regime that suffered from a lack of iconographic or ideological coherence, because of its ever-changing relationship with Japan and its highly factionalized nature.

As the Wang personality cult also suggests, a visual history approach exposes just how contested the realm of the visual was in occupied China. Given that the contestation of the visual has been shown by theorists such as Gil Hochberg and Nicholas Mirzoeff to be so central to the very nature of foreign occupation in other contexts, it is surprising that this has not been noted before in the case of China. Contestation for control of the visual, and competition over what could and could not be seen in Wang Jingwei's China, meant that the RNG did not always adhere to imperial Japanese policies. We see evidence of this in Wang's obsession with the visual markers of the navy—a force that he had established against the wishes of the Japanese navy itself. We also see it in figures such as the "roaring man," who inspired RNG youth activists to attack Japanese institutions late in the war. Just as importantly, however, contestation occurred within the RNG state itself, as Nanjing struggled to rid its regional centers of residual Daminhui influence. As I demonstrated in chapter 4, even the MoP disagreed within itself on what the ideal RNG subject should look like. Was the occupied woman a glamorous starlet in a wedding gown, or was she a "co-prosperity realist" youth activist in a New Citizens uniform? There was also competition between the government and the commercial sphere for control of what could and could not be seen, with early Peace Movement reliance on the commercial print media (initiated originally to avoid censorship from "semicolonial" authorities in Shanghai and elsewhere) coming back to plague MoP attempts to drive the cultural agenda in later years. Indeed, it is perhaps more than coincidence that the notion of "seeing clearly" was so common a trope in the campaigns adopted by Japanese pharmaceutical firms, as residents of occupied China were told to see the bright future promised under Sino-Japanese cooperation if (like Wang Jingwei and Li Xianglan) they applied drops to their eyes. While such visions of occupied China did not contradict RNG policy, they trivialized MoP iconography and ultimately undermined the coherence of any messages that Wang Jingwei's government might have sought to propagate. Despite assumptions about this regime being monolithic in nature and totalitarian in aspiration—assumptions that images such as those of *Wang and Nazis* are often deployed to illustrate—the RNG was continually competing with other arms of the wider occupation state, and with itself, as it tried to visualize wartime China.

The Occupied Gaze

One of the most intriguing frames in an otherwise mundane Japanese newsreel that documents the opening of the Greater East Asia Exposition in Nanjing in late 1942 is negligible in its brevity. Thirty-six seconds into this one-and-a-half-minute film, Chen Bijun is shown entering the exposition. What is most significant about this frame is not the naval-themed *sensōga* behind Chen, however, but the fact that she is shown holding a folding camera and pointing it directly back at the unnamed Japanese camera operator who is filming her. Chen takes a photograph, then hurries sheepishly offscreen.

Chen was not alone in her fondness for photography. This was, after all, a favored leisure pursuit for many high-ranking members of the RNG, most noticeably Chu Minyi. Images of Chu and other RNG luminaries photographing events and places in occupied China are a common theme in the publications and private image collections emanating from the occupation. I have been able to write this book only because individuals such as Chu Minyi and Lin Baisheng took and/or collected photographs, and because the resulting collections are now available to researchers in public institutions. Yet the image of Chen Bijun photographing a Japanese cameraman who is in the process of filming her (as she supposedly gazes at Japanese war art depicting occupied China) speaks volumes about the complex dynamics that typified visual cultures under the RNG. Chen is not a passive subject of the colonial gaze here (though she is certainly being gazed at). She looks directly back at the occupier, even as she fulfills her role as an extra in a film of an event celebrating Japanese military conquest.[9]

Throughout this book, I have shown how RNG agencies sought to establish their own gaze over occupied China, deploying recognizably Republican Chinese modes of visuality while borrowing techniques from prewar (and resistance) Chinese, Axis, and other forms of visual propaganda. They did this even as they sought to chart a narrow course between Japanese imperial sensibilities and established notions of Chinese patriotism. What I refer to as the occupied gaze set itself apart from the visuality imposed on China by the Japanese (often via Manchukuo)—with its "sun-centered propaganda" and "harmony of the five races"—even while it sought to render non-RNG visual expressions of resistance against the Japanese invisible. The RNG was never content with being the passive subject of a colonial gaze. Like Chen Bijun with her camera, Wang Jingwei's regime gazed back.

Of course, the Chen Bijun example also demonstrates the limits of the occupied gaze. After all, though we might see Chen gazing back at a Japanese camera operator, we never see that person through Chen's lens. This is indicative of many photographic and other forms of visual representations that emerged under the RNG. While photographs of Wang Jingwei and others in the presence of Japanese officials are certainly prominent in many surviving collections, it is clear from RNG publications that depictions of Japanese officials were highly regulated, staged, and few in number. This is hardly surprising, given that Japanese military minders habitually accompanied CNA photographers and that Japanese advisers kept a close watch over the work of the MoP. Despite Chen Bijun's few seconds of photographic defiance in October 1942, the RNG gaze was therefore almost always directed at China and Chinese people rather than back at the Japanese.

The occupied gaze was also only operable as long as the Japanese military, and agents of the RNG state, were on hand to eradicate alternative ways of seeing. The oft-told story of the two-by-twenty-six-meter-long scroll entitled *Liumin tu* (Refugees), painted by the artist Jiang Zhaohe in 1943, is worth considering here. This social realist depiction of the suffering of Chinese refugees under occupation was confiscated by Japanese military officers in both Beijing and Shanghai when it was exhibited in each city and was partially destroyed in the process. An occupied gaze that exposed Chinese suffering on such a grand scale, it would seem, would not be tolerated by the Japanese military.[10] This is usually where the story of the *Liumin tu* ends. In reality, however, RNG cultural workers themselves experimented with imagery depicting the suffering of Chinese refugees and continued to circulate such images to a wide audience in occupied China, late into the war. Even the most loyal of RNG artists, such as those affiliated with the CCA and ACWA, produced cartoons and woodcuts that lamented the plight of the country's poor in 1943, even as Jiang Zhaohe's work was being censored (figure Con.1). It would appear that the content of such depictions mattered far less than who was producing it. Working under the apparent protection of RNG-sponsored and occupation-compliant institutions, some cultural workers *were* able to craft a distinct, if partial, vision of Chinese suffering—though one that has never been acknowledged since the end of the war.

The occupied gaze was not always benign, however. Indeed, despite the endless talk of China's "liberation" under Wang Jingwei, the agents of the RNG state could themselves act as belligerent occupants in lieu of the Japanese, imposing their own narrow and Nanjing-centric visions of China on communities that had no say in their own representation, and bringing such communities into partisan visions of China against their will. Rural Pacification, for example, was significant because it afforded Nanjing- and Suzhou-based cadres the opportunity to both physically and visually occupy the rural hinterland and to gaze at Chinese peasants and landscapes in ways that only Japanese military bodies had been able to do previously. Documentary photography associated with Rural Pacification and produced by the likes of Chen Guoqi was dominated by the figure of Wang Jingwei walking through the pacified landscape and by MoP cadres preaching their message to peasants. In other cases, it took its cues directly from the Japanese colonial gaze in occupied Southeast Asia. While we might see

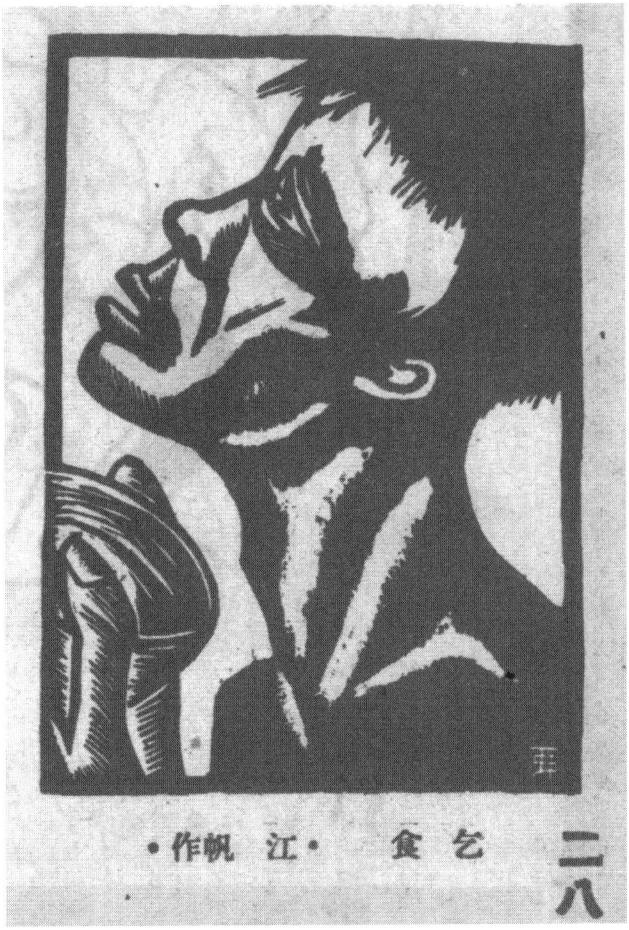

Figure Con.1. *Qi shi* (Begging for food), by Jiang Fan. In *Zhonghua huabao* [China pictorial] 1, no. 5 (December 1943): 28. Courtesy of Shanghai Library.

in this imagery a defiant response to Japanese-imagined landscapes of the early war years, we must also acknowledge that the violence and persecution that typified Rural Pacification were never allowed to be *seen* in such depictions. One shortcoming of this book, therefore, is that I have not engaged with visual cultures that were produced under, but in opposition to, RNG rule. A challenge for future scholars might be to locate and analyze the visual texts that would allow for a visual history of Rural Pacification as seen by those who lived under it.

In demonstrating how a lack of control undermined the RNG state's ability to maintain a coherent vision of China, however, the iconographies of occupation also complicate the current focus on "ways of seeing" and representation in the context of foreign occupation. To be sure, the field of critical visual studies has already moved beyond the tendency, common in earlier decades, to simply deconstruct the colonial gaze. Yet a focus on the overwhelming control of the "right to see" by occupiers—and on the spectacle of modern war and occupation—continues to shape many of the questions that scholars in this field pose.[11] What Wang Jingwei's China offers, therefore, is a case through which recent theoretical musings about the inherent difficulty in "redirecting the gaze or manipulating visions of control" in the context of occupation can be reconsidered.[12]

Although the agents of the RNG state did manage to subvert the gaze of the occupier at specific moments, the conflicting and contested iconographies espoused by this state highlight the limits of such endeavors. Occupation did not render China invisible, nor did it lead to complete control of the visual realm by a foreign power. It did, however, lead to a client regime that continually re-envisaged its leader, its people, and its territory in ways that would fit with its reliance on a belligerent occupant and its desire to *look* legitimate as an inheritor of Sun Yat-sen's republic. Only by grafting Axis aesthetics and prewar modes of visuality onto Republican Chinese icons late in the war did this eclectic regime manage to come close to achieving a unified vision.

The material and symbolic consequences of such efforts can be felt even today. Sun Yat-sen statuary still sits at the same location in downtown Nanjing at which it was first erected in 1942 under Wang Jingwei. And just as Wang Jingwei was buried temporarily in Nanjing while he awaited the peaceful unification of China, so too does the body of Wang Jingwei's longtime rival—Chiang Kai-shek—lie today in rural Taiwan, awaiting reinterment in Nanjing after the Republic of China is unified. Most importantly, however, the RNG can be felt in the reluctance to even look at the residue of Wang Jingwei's regime in a China that had, by 2015, recast the war as a life-and-death struggle between the forces of darkness and light. While so many governments have ignored the RNG or sought to erase it from the visual record since 1945, it is important that we look again at Wang Jingwei's China. In doing so, not only will we gain a more complete and balanced understanding of China's wartime experience, but we will also gain a more complex and nuanced understanding of visuality under foreign occupation more broadly.

Glossary

Aiqun da jiudian 愛群大酒店
anju leye zhi Huazhong nongcun 安居樂業之華中農村
anzang dianli 安葬典禮
Asai Kan'emon 朝井閑右衛門

Ba lu jun 八路軍
Bailaohui daxia 百老匯大廈
Bei fa 北伐
Bu Wancang 卜萬蒼

Cai Dejin 蔡德金
Cao Hanmei 曹涵美
Chan, Nancy (Chen Yunshang) 陳雲裳
Chang, Eileen (Zhang Ailing) 張愛玲
Changjiang huakan 長江畫刊
Chen Bijun 陳璧君
Chen Dabei 陳大悲
Chen Gongbo 陳公博
Chen Guoqi 陳國琦
Chen Liaoshi 陳寥士
Chen Xiaozuo 陳孝祚
Chiang Kai-shek (Jiang Jieshi) 蔣介石
chourong manmian 愁容满面
Chu Minyi 褚民誼
chuanfu 船夫

Da Dong Ya 大東亞
da houfang 大後方
Dachu bao 大楚報
Dai Tōa hakurankai 大東亜博覧会
Dai Tōa kaigi 大東亜会議
Dai Tōa Kyōeiken 大東亜共栄圏
Dai Tōa Sensō 大東亜戦争
dai zhuxi 代主席
Damin 大民
Daminhui 大民會
Diliu ci quanguo daibiao dahui 第六次全國代表大會
Dōmei gurafu 同盟グラフ
Dōmei Tsūshinsha 同盟通信社
Dong Tianye 董天野
Dong Ya heping leyuan 東亞和平樂園
Dong Ya Lianmeng 東亞聯盟
Dong Ya Lianmeng huabao 東亞聯盟畫報
Dong Ya wenyi fuxing 東亞文藝復興
Dongfang mingxing 東方明星
ducai 獨裁
Duli manhua 獨立漫畫

E bao 鄂報

Fan Tchunpi (Fang Junbi) 方君璧
fazhan zhong de Hankou 發展中的漢口
fengcai 風采
fengguang mingmei de Zhongguo 風光明媚的中國
Fengren de Zhuawa 豐稔的爪哇
Funü shijie 婦女世界
Fuxing noncun gaishan renmin shenghuo 復興農村改善人民生活
Fuzimiao 夫子廟

gaizupai 改组派
Ge Xiaoguang 葛小光
gemingpai 革命派
Gengsheng 更生
gengsheng 更生

Go So shunjū: Naka Shina gurafu 呉楚春秋: 中支那グラフ
Gonggong zujie 公共租界
gongguanpai 宮館派
gongli zhuyi 功利主義
gozoku kyōwa 五族協和
Guan Yide 管一得
Guanghua zhaoxiangguan 光華照相館
guangming zhi qiantu 光明之前途
guangtou yundong 光頭運動
Guangyi zhaoxiangguan 光藝照相館
gudao 孤島
guixiang (kneeling statue) 跪像
guixiang (return to one's native place) 歸鄉
Gujin 古今
gujun 孤軍
guniang 姑娘
Guo Xiufeng 郭秀峯
guofu 國父
guofu yizhi zhi shixian 國父遺志之實現
guohua 國畫
Guoji xuanchuanju 國際宣傳局
guomin jingshen zong dongyuan 國民精神總動員
Guomin xinwen 國民新聞
Guomin xinwen huabao 國民新聞畫報
Guoshiguan 國史館
Guoyi 國藝

hanjian 漢奸
Hankou 漢口
heping de husheng 和平的呼聲
heping de zhen qin 和平的貞禽
heping diqu 和平地區
heping, fangong, jianguo 和平, 反共, 建國
heping jinianlin 和平紀念林
Heping jiuguo jun 和平救國軍
heping jueqi 和平崛起
heping nüshen 和平女神
heping tianshi 和平天使
heping yundong 和平運動
heping zhi mu 和平之母
heshan posui 河山破碎
heyun xianlie 和運先烈
Hōdōbu 報道部
Hu Lancheng 胡蘭成
Hu Shih (Hu Shi) 胡適
Huabei zhengwu weiyuanhui 華北政務委員會
huafang 畫舫
Huan women Dong Ya ren de benlai mianmu 還我們東亞人的本來面目
huan wo heshan 還我河山
Huanan huabao 華南畫報
huandu 還都
Huang Juesi 黃覺寺
Huanghe lou 黃鶴樓
Huanghuagang 黃花崗
Huangpu junxiao 黃埔軍校
huanxiang fuye 還鄉復業
Hua-Ri jiben guanxi tiaoyue 華日基本關係條約
Huasheng yancao gongsi 華生煙草公司
Huawen Daban meiri 華文大阪每日
Huazhong tiedao 華中鐵道
huobaoju 活報劇

Ikeda Katsumi 池田克己

Jian Qing 劍青
Jiang Kanghu 江亢虎
Jiang Zhaohe 蔣兆和
Jianghanguan dalou 江漢關大樓
Jiangnan 江南
Jiangsu ribao 江蘇日報
jiaohuan 交還
jiefang 解放
jietou xuanchuan 街頭宣傳
Jiming si 雞鳴寺
Jing bao 京報
Jintan 仁丹
jiuguo 救國
jufu biaoyu 巨幅標語
Junshi weiyuanhui 軍事委員會
Junshi weiyuanhui zhengzhibu 軍事委員會政治部
Kachū Tetsudō 華中鉄道
kang-Ri 抗日
Kantōgun 關東軍
Kaoshiyuan 考試院

Katō Minosuke 可東みの助
Kawashima Riichirō 川島理一郎
kūnyan 姑娘
Kuomintang (Guomindang) 國民黨
Kyōwakai 協和会

Lai ri fangchang 來日方長
langlang tiandi 郎郎天地
Lao Du yanyao 老篤眼藥
Lei Yimin 雷逸民
Li Hua 李樺
Li Huizhen 李惠珍
Li Lihua 李麗華
Li Shiqun 李士群
Li Xianglan (Ri Ko Ran) 李香蘭
Liang Boping 梁伯平
liangqi xianmu 良妻賢母
Liangyou 良友
lianhuanhua 連環畫
liming dongyuan 黎明動員
Lin Baisheng 林柏生
Lin Meishu 林妹殊
Lishi de guaitai 历史的怪胎
Liu Haisu 劉海粟
liudong xuanchuandui 流動宣傳隊
Liumin tu 流民圖
Lü Feng 呂風
Lu Xun 魯迅
Luo Qingzhen 羅清楨

Ma Wu 馬午
Ma Yingbiao 馬應彪
Mabuchi Itsuo 馬淵逸雄
mai guo 賣國
maiban yangnu 買辦洋奴
Makita Shōya 牧田祥哉
Malu tianshi 馬路天使
Manchukuo (Manzhouguo) 滿洲國
Man'ei 滿映
Manhua xuanchuandui 漫畫宣傳隊
Mantetsu 滿鐵
Mao Zedong 毛泽东
Mao zhuxi qu Anyuan 毛主席去安源
Meihuashan 梅花山
Mengjiang 蒙疆
Miao Bin 繆斌

minglang 明朗
mingsheng guji 名勝古蹟
mingshi 名士
minjian zhi jiku 民間之疾苦
Minzhong shibao 民眾時報
Mitsui Naomaro 三井直麿
Miura Noa 三浦乃亜
modeng nüzi 摩登女子
moulüe xinwen 謀略新聞
muke 木刻
Mulan congjun 木蘭從軍

Nagai Kyūichirō 永井久一郎
Nanhua ribao 南華日報
Nanjing juyishe 南京劇藝社
Nanjing xinbao 南京新報
Nihon Nyūsu Eigasha 日本ニュース映画社
nihonga 日本画
Nobukuni Tamiyo 信國民代
nongcun jianshe tu 農村建設圖
nongcun mutong 農村牧童
Nuhou ba Zhongguo 怒吼吧中國
nuhua jiaoyu 奴化教育

Ono Isamu 尾野勇
Ōta Tenkyō 太田天橋

Peng Wangshi 彭望軾
Ping bao 平報
Pudong 浦東
Pumie qunchou 撲滅羣醜

Qi shi 乞食
Qin Kuai 秦檜
qing tian, bai ri, man di hong
青天, 白日, 滿地紅
Qingdao huiyi 青島會議
Qingnian tuan 青年團
Qingshaonian tuan 青少年團
qingxiang 清鄉
qingxiang huabao 清鄉畫報
qingxiang jutuan 清鄉劇團
Qingxiang xuanchuan zongdui
清鄉宣傳總隊
qin-Ri toudi fenzi 亲日投敌分子
qishi'er lieshi 七十二烈士

Rohto ロート

Sanmin zhuyi 三民主義
Sanmin zhuyi qingnian tuan 三民主義青年團
Se, jie 色, 戒
sensōga 戦争画
seqing 色情
Shanghai meishu zhuanke xuexiao 上海美術專科學校
Shanghai zhi yue/Shanhai no tsuki 上海の月
shanshuihua 山水畫
Shashin shūhō 写真週報
shengli tianshi 勝利天使
Sheyingshe 攝影社
Shi Ping 石坪
Shimizu Toshi 清水登之
Shina hakengun 支那派遣軍
Shina no yoru 支那の夜
shinchitsujo 新秩序
Shinsei Chūgoku no kao 新生中国の顔
shinü 仕女
shoudu fengguang 首都風光
Shōwa Kenkyūkai 昭和研究会
Song hanyi 送寒衣
Soong, May-ling (Song Meiling) 宋美齡
Soong, T. V. (Song Ziwen) 宋子文
su tuanjie, da qingxiang 速團結大清鄉
Sun Yat-sen (Sun Yixian) 孫逸仙

Tagawa Ken 田川憲
Ta kung pao (Dagong bao) 大公報
tairiku eiga 大陸映画
Tairiku shinpō 大陸新報
T'ang Leang-li (Tang Liangli) 湯良禮
Tezhong xuanchuanzu 特別宣傳組
tianyuan dushi 田園都市
"Tingshen fenqi heping jiuguo" 挺身奮起和平救國
Tōhō 東宝
tongzhong 同種
tongzijun 童子軍
Tōyō Bunko 東洋文庫
tufei 土匪
tuhua 圖畫
tuihuan 退還

Uchiyama Kanzō 內山完造
Umeya Shōkichi 梅屋庄吉

Waitan gongyuan 外灘公園
Wang Chuan 王川
Wang Jingwei zhi mu 汪精衛之墓
Wang Jingwei zhuyi 汪精衛主義
Wang Qingfang 王清芳
Wang xiansheng jiniantang 汪先生紀念堂
Wang Yingxiao 王迎曉
Wanshi liufang 萬世流芳
Wanxian canan 萬縣慘案
Wen Zongyao 溫宗堯
wenhua hanjian 文化漢奸
Wong Hing-sue (Huang Qingshu) 黃慶樞
Wu Liande 伍聯德
Wu Linzhi 伍麟趾
Wu si 五四
Wu Zhuoliu 吳濁流

Xi Jinping 习近平
xiao shimin 小市民
xiaojiemen 小姐們
Xie Xiping 谢希平
Xifang de kexue jingshen 西方的科學精神
Xin Dong Ya 新東亞
Xin funü yuekan 新婦女月刊
Xin Guangdong 新廣東
Xin guomin yundong 新國民運動
xin guomin zhifu 新國民制服
Xin Jiekou 新街口
Xin shenghuo yundong 新生活運動
Xin si jun 新四軍
Xin Zhongguo 新中國
xin Zhongguo 新中國
xin Zhongguo de doushi 新中國的鬥士
Xin Zhonghua huabao 新中華畫報
xin zhongyang zhengquan 新中央政權
xing Ya 興亞
Xingzhengyuan 行政院
Xinminhui 新民會
xiongzi 雄姿
Xu Zhimo 徐志摩
Xuanchuanbu 宣傳部
xuanchuanchu 宣傳處

Xue Diwei 薛迪蔚
Xue Huizi 薛慧子

Yamaguchi Susumu 山口進
Yan Sanyuan 顏三原
Yan Wenliang 顏文樑
Yan'an wenyi zuotanhui 延安文藝座談會
yanghua 洋畫
yanghuajia 洋畫家
ye ling 謁陵
yi zang 遺臟
yingzi 英姿
yishu xuanchuan 藝術宣傳
yishu zhaoxiang de zuigao shuizhun 藝術照相的最高水準
Yokoyama Taikan 橫山大観
Yonaiyama Tsuneo 米内山庸夫
yonghu canzhan, baowei Dong Ya 擁護參戰, 保衛東亞
yonghu Wang zhuxi 擁護汪主席
Yoshino Inosuke 吉野伊之助
youjidui 游擊隊
Youjiu de Zhongguo 悠久的中國
Yu fang 渝方
Yuan Muzhi 袁牧之
yuebing 閱兵
yuefenpai 月份牌

Zaifeng 載灃
zazhi 雜誌
Zeng Zhongming 曾仲鳴
Zhang Guangyu 張光宇
Zhang Jiangcai 張江裁
Zhang Liying 張莉英
Zhang Xianwen 张宪文
Zhang Zhengyu 張正宇
Zhang Ziping 張資平
zhanshi wenhua xuanchuan 戰時文化宣傳
Zhanshi wenhua xuanchuan zhengce jiben gangyao 戰時文化宣傳政策基本綱要
Zhao Zhengping 趙正平
Zhen Dan 震旦
Zheng Chuangu 鄭川谷
Zheng Pingru 鄭蘋如
Zheng Xiaoqiu 鄭小秋
zhengtong 正統
zhishang gongying 紙上公映
Zhong bao 中報
Zhongguo di'er lishi dang'anguan 中国第二历史档案馆
Zhongguo geming bowuguan 中国革命博物馆
Zhongguo gongchandang 中国共产党
Zhongguo manhua 中國漫畫
Zhongguo manhua xiehui 中國漫畫協會
Zhongguo muke 中國木刻
Zhongguo muke zuozhe xiehui 中國木刻作者協會
Zhongguo wenyi xiehui 中國文藝協會
Zhonghua dianying lianhe gongsi 中華電影聯合公司
Zhonghua huabao 中華畫報
Zhonghua lianhe zhipian gufen youxian gongsi 中華聯合製片股份有限公司
Zhonghua minguo linshi zhengfu 中華民國臨時政府
Zhonghua minguo weixin zhengfu 中華民國維新政府
Zhonghua ribao 中華日報
Zhonghua tongxunshe 中華通訊社
Zhong-Ri tixi 中日提攜
Zhong-Ri tongmeng tiaoyue 中日同盟條約
Zhong-Ri wenhua xiehui 中日文化協會
Zhongshan jiniantang 中山紀念堂
Zhongshan zhuang 中山裝
Zhongshan ling 中山陵
Zhongyang daxue 中央大學
Zhongyang dianxunshe 中央電訊社
Zhongyang lujun junguan xuexiao 中央陸軍軍官學校
Zhongyang xuanchuan jiangxisuo 中央宣傳講習所
Zhongyang yanjiuyuan 中央研究院
Zhou Fohai 周佛海
Zhou Yuren 周雨人
Zijinshan 紫金山
zishu 自述
zuigao lingxiu 最高領袖

Notes

Archival Abbreviations

AH	Academia Historica (Taipei)
HIA	Hoover Institution Archives (Stanford)
KMT	KMT Party Archives (Taipei)
LOC	Library of Congress (Washington, DC)
NIDS	National Institute of Defense Studies (Tokyo)
SHA	Second Historical Archives (Nanjing)
SMA	Shanghai Municipal Archives (Shanghai)

Introduction

1. These are too numerous to list in their entirety here, but for some representative examples, see John Delury, Sheila A. Smith, Maria Repnikova, and Srinath Raghavan, "Looking Back on the Seventieth Anniversary of Japan's Surrender," *Journal of Asian Studies* 74, no. 4 (November 2015): 797–820; and Yong Zhou, Vincent K. L. Chang, and Xiaohui Gong, "Recalling the War in China: The *Dahoufang* Project in Chongqing and the Restoration of a Legacy," *Frontiers of History in China* 9, no. 4 (December 2014): 611–627.

2. As evidenced, for example, in the text of Xi Jinping's speech on September 3, 2015. For the full text of this speech (in English translation), see http://www.scmp.com/news/china/policies-politics/article/1854943/full-text-xi-jinping-military-parade-speech-vows-china.

3. I borrow this phrase from David P. Barrett, introduction to *Chinese Collaboration with Japan, 1932–1945: The Limits of Accommodation,* ed. David P. Barrett and Larry N. Shyu (Stanford, CA: Stanford University Press, 2001), 1–17.

4. On this regime, see Zhang Tongle, *Huabei lunxianqu Ri-wei zhengquan yanjiu* [A study of the Japanese-bogus regime in occupied north China] (Shanghai: Sanlian shudian, 2012).

5. On this regime, see Timothy Brook, "Collaborationist Nationalism in Occupied Wartime China," in *Nation Work: Asian Elites and National Identities,* ed. Timothy Brook and Andrew Schmid (Ann Arbor: University of Michigan Press, 2000), 159–190.

6. The very name of this government remains the source of some controversy. I have chosen throughout this book to refer to it (in keeping with what is now common practice in the English-language historiography) as the Reorganized National Government (RNG). This phrase was used in English texts of the 1940s to describe it, such as

Paul Linebarger, *The China of Chiang Kai-shek: A Political Study* (Boston: World Peace Foundation, 1943), 203. In Chinese, however, the regime is not referred to in this manner. Instead, it is commonly referred to as the "bogus Wang regime" (*Wang wei zhengquan*), or the "bogus Wang national government" (*Wang wei guomin zhengfu*). The RNG referred to itself simply as the "national government" (*guomin zhengfu*).

7. On such attitudes, see Wang Ke-wen, "Irreversible Verdict? Historical Assessments of Wang Jingwei in the People's Republic and Taiwan," *Twentieth-Century China* 28, no. 1 (November 2002): 57–81.

8. This is true for popular as well as scholarly depictions. On the depiction of RNG China as a colorless place in recent cinema, see Grace Wang, "The Color of Our Emotions, or *Se, jie*," *RogerEbert.com* (blog), February 1, 2013, https://www.rogerebert.com/far-flung-correspondents/the-color-of-our-emotions-or-.

9. Hannah Arendt, *Men in Dark Times* (New York: Harcourt, Brace and World, 1968).

10. As in Julia Jackson, *France: The Dark Years, 1940–1944* (Oxford: Oxford University Press, 2001).

11. For an example of historical research that employs such a trope, see Cheah Boon Kheng, "Memory as History and Moral Judgement: Oral and Written Accounts of the Japanese Occupation of Malaya," in *War and Memory in Malaysia and Singapore,* ed. Lim Pui Huen and Diana Wong (Singapore: ISEAS, 2000), 23–41.

12. On the trope of darkness in Chinese accounts of the occupation, see R. Keith Schoppa, *In a Sea of Bitterness: Refugees during the Sino-Japanese War* (Cambridge, MA: Harvard University Press, 2012), 26.

13. As we shall see in chapter 5.

14. This is an anecdote retold in Hu Shua, "Zheng gong shouji" [Notes on political work], *Qingxiang qianxian* 2, no. 4 (June 1943): 26–28.

15. Some scholars have, admittedly, started to do this. I shall return to examples of such work throughout this book.

16. I make this statement in the knowledge that calls by other scholars for a dispassionate appraisal of "collaboration" have led to highly charged responses. On such debates, see John Whittier Treat, "Seoul and Nanking, Baghdad and Kabul: A Response to Timothy Brook and Michael Shin," *Journal of Asian Studies* 71, no. 1 (2012): 121–125.

17. See, for example, Chang-tai Hung, *War and Popular Culture: Resistance in Modern China* (Berkeley: University of California Press, 1994).

18. On this art form, see Jeremy E. Taylor, "The Sinification of Soviet Agitational Theatre: 'Living Newspapers' in Mao's China," *Journal of the British Association of Chinese Studies* 2 (2013): 27–50.

19. We will revisit this practice in chapter 3.

20. An example of such a manual is Chen Yanqiao, *Kangzhan xuanchuanhua* [Propaganda pictures for the War of Resistance] (Guangzhou: Liming shudian, 1938).

21. Linebarger, *China of Chiang Kai-shek,* 205.

22. Gerald E. Bunker, *The Peace Conspiracy: Wang Ching-wei and the China War, 1937–1941* (Cambridge, MA: Harvard University Press, 1972), 269.

23. Barak Kushner, *The Thought War: Japanese Imperial Propaganda* (Honolulu: University of Hawai'i Press, 2006), 119.

24. Parks Coble, "China's New Remembering of the Anti-Japanese War of Resistance, 1937–1945," *China Quarterly* 190 (2007): 394–410.

25. Cai Dejin, *Lishi de guaitai: Wang wei guomin zhengfu shimo* [Freak of history: The beginning and end of the bogus Wang national government] (Beijing: Tuanjie chubanshe, 2008).

26. Zhang Xianwen, *Zhonghua minguo shi (disan juan): Riben quanmian qin Hua* [A history of the Republic of China, volume 3: The complete invasion of China by Japan] (Nanjing: Nanjing daxue chubanshe, 2006).

27. One example is Li Zhongming, *Kang-Ri zhanzheng shiqi de Zhongguo wenhua* [Chinese culture during the War of Resistance] (Beijing: Tuanjie chubanshe, 2015).

28. Wang Ke-wen, "Irreversible Verdict?"

29. Liu Jie, "Wang Jingwei and the 'Nanjing Nationalist Government': Between Collaboration and Resistance," trans. Konrad Lawson, in *Toward a History beyond Borders: Contentious Issues in Sino-Japanese Relations,* ed. Daqing Yang, Jie Liu, Hiroshi Mitani, and Andrew Gordon (Cambridge, MA: Harvard University Asia Center, 2012), 205–239.

30. See, for example, Huang Meizhen, *Ri-wei dui Huazhong lunxianqu jingji de lüeduo yu tongzhi* [The economic pillage and control of the occupied areas of central China under the Japanese and the bogus regime] (Beijing: Shehui kexue wenxian, 2005); and Pan Min, *Jiangsu Ri-wei jiceng zhengquan yanjiu (1937–1945)* [A study of Japanese-bogus regime rule at the local level in Jiangsu (1937–1945)] (Shanghai: Shanghai renmin chubanshe, 2006). A thorough analysis of such work can be found in David Serfass, "Occupation japonaise et collaboration chinoise: Tendances historiographiques récentes" [The Japanese occupation and Chinese collaboration: Recent historiographical tendencies], *Revue historique* 680 (April 2016): 941–966.

31. See, for instance, Yu Zidao, Liu Qikui, and Cao Zhenwei, eds., *Wang wei zhengquan ziliao xuanbian: Wang Jingwei guomin zhengfu "qingxiang" yundong* [Selected materials from the bogus Wang regime: The Wang national government's "Rural Pacification" campaign] (Shanghai: Xinhua shuju, 1985).

32. Huang Renyuan, ed., *Wang Jingwei yu Wang wei zhengfu, shang* [Wang Jingwei and the bogus Wang government, part 1] (Taipei: Taiwan shangwu yinshuguan, 1994); and Huang Renyuan, ed., *Wang Jingwei yu Wang wei zhengfu, xia* [Wang Jingwei and the bogus Wang government, part 2] (Taipei: Taiwan shangwu yinshuguan, 1994).

33. Zhang Dianxing, *Wang Jingwei funi yanjiu* [Research on the traitor Wang Jingwei] (Beijing: Renmin chubanshe, 2008), 9–10.

34. Yingying Gao, "A Survey of Twenty-First-Century Studies of the Japanese-Occupied Areas in China," trans. Tian Xiansheng, *Journal of Modern Chinese History* 9, no. 1 (2015): 130–151.

35. John Hunter Boyle, *China and Japan at War, 1937–1945: The Politics of Collaboration* (Stanford, CA: Stanford University Press, 1972), 50.

36. Timothy Brook, *Collaboration: Japanese Agents and Local Chinese Elites in Wartime China* (Cambridge, MA: Harvard University Press, 2005).

37. Timothy Brook, "The Creation of the Reformed Government in Central China, 1938," in *Chinese Collaboration with Japan, 1932–1945: The Limits of Accommodation,* ed. David P. Barrett and Larry N. Shyu (Stanford, CA: Stanford University Press, 2001), 100.

38. Brook, "Collaborationist Nationalism," 163.

39. Dongyoun Hwang, "Wartime Collaboration in Question: An Examination of the Postwar Trials of the Chinese Collaborators," *Inter-Asia Cultural Studies* 6, no. 1 (2005): 75–97, esp. 92.

40. Margherita Zanasi, "Globalizing *Hanjian:* The Suzhou Trials and the Post–World War II Discourse on Collaboration," *American Historical Review* 113, no. 3 (2008): 738; see also Margherita Zanasi, *Saving the Nation: Economic Modernity in Republican China* (Chicago: Chicago University Press, 2006), 222.

41. Though there are notable exceptions. I will draw on many of these in later sections of this book.

42. Rana Mitter, *China's War with Japan, 1937–45: The Struggle for Survival* (London: Allen Lane, 2013), 370.

43. Poshek Fu, *Passivity, Resistance, and Collaboration: Intellectual Choices in Occupied Shanghai, 1937–1945* (Stanford, CA: Stanford University Press, 1993).

44. Zhiyi Yang, "The Road to Lyric Martyrdom: Reading the Poetry of Wang Zhaoming (1883–1944)," *Chinese Literature* 37 (2015): 135–164.

45. Nicole Huang, "Fashioning Public Intellectuals: Women's Print Culture in Occupied Shanghai (1941–1945)," in *In the Shadow of the Rising Sun: Shanghai under Japanese Occupation,* ed. Christian Henriot and Wen-hsin Yeh (Cambridge: Cambridge University Press, 2004), 327.

46. Edward M. Gunn Jr., *Unwelcome Muse: Chinese Literature in Shanghai and Peking, 1937–1945* (New York: Columbia University Press, 1980), 7.

47. Such as Carolyn FitzGerald, *Fragmenting Modernisms: Chinese Wartime Literature, Art, and Film, 1937–49* (Boston and Leiden: Brill, 2013).

48. One example is Jeffrey N. Wasserstrom, ed., *Oxford Illustrated History of Modern China* (Oxford: Oxford University Press, 2016).

49. Nicole Huang, *Women, War, Domesticity: Shanghai Literature and Popular Culture of the 1940s* (Boston and Leiden: Brill, 2005); Andrew Cheung, "Slogans, Symbols, and Legitimacy: The Case of Wang Jingwei's Nanjing Regime," Indiana East Asia Working Paper Series, 6 (July 1995); Shaoqian Zhang, "Combat and Collaboration: The Clash of Propaganda Prints between the Chinese Guomindang and the Japanese Empire in the 1930s–1940s," *Transcultural Studies* 1 (January 2014): 95–133.

50. FitzGerald, *Fragmenting Modernisms,* 5.

51. On graffiti in occupied Nanjing, see J. Thomas Rimer, "Paris in Nanjing: Kishida Kunio Follows the Troops," in *War, Occupation, and Creativity: Japan and East Asia, 1920–1960,* ed. Marlene J. Mayo, J. Thomas Rimer, and E. Eleanor Kerkham (Honolulu: University of Hawai'i Press, 2001), 181.

52. Such as Pingchao Zhu, *Wartime Culture in Guilin, 1938–1944: A City at War* (Lanham, MD: Lexington Books, 2015).

53. Gerhard Paul, "Visual History" (English version), *Docupedia-Zeitgeschichte,* July 11, 2011, http://docupedia.de/zg/paul_visual_history_v1_en_2011.

54. Horst Bredekamp, *Image Acts: A Systematic Approach to Visual Agency,* trans. Elizabeth Clegg (Berlin: De Gruyter, 2017), esp. 160.

55. Hung, *War and Popular Culture;* Henrietta Harrison, *The Making of the Republican Citizen: Political Ceremonies and Symbols in China, 1911–1929* (Oxford: Oxford University Press, 2000).

56. James A. Cook, Joshua Goldstein, Matthew D. Johnson, and Sigrid Schmalzer, introduction to *Visualizing Modern China: Image, History and Memory, 1750–Present,* ed. James A. Cook, Joshua Goldstein, Matthew D. Johnson, and Sigrid Schmalzer (Lanham, MD: Lexington Books, 2014), 3. Italics in the original.

57. Sumathi Ramaswamy, *The Goddess and the Nation: Mapping Mother India* (Durham, NC: Duke University Press, 2010), 2.

58. Christian Henriot and Wen-hsin Yeh, "Introduction. China Visualised: What Stories Do Pictures Tell?" in *Visualising China, 1845–1965: Life/Still Images in Historical Narratives,* ed. Christian Henriot and Wen-hsin Yeh (Leiden: Brill, 2013), xv.

59. I take this description from Suzanne Pepper, "The Political Odyssey of an Intellectual Construct: Peasant Nationalism and the Study of China's Revolutionary History—a Review Essay," *Journal of Asian Studies* 63, no. 1 (2004): 120.

60. Chang-tai Hung, *Mao's New World: Popular Culture in the Early People's Republic* (Ithaca, NY: Cornell University Press, 2010); and Barbara Mittler, *A Continuous Revolution: Making Sense of Cultural Revolution Culture* (Cambridge, MA: Harvard University Press, 2013).

61. Such as Jeffrey W. Cody and Frances Terpak, eds., *Brush and Shutter: Early Photography in China* (Hong Kong: Hong Kong University Press, in association with the Getty Research Institute, 2011).

62. See, for instance, FitzGerald, *Fragmenting Modernisms,* 169, in which cinema produced under occupation is denied analysis on the basis that "filmmakers in the occupied regions were unable to produce films that explored in depth the experiences of ordinary people in wartime."

63. Such as Marlene J. Mayo, J. Thomas Rimer, and E. Eleanor Kerkham, eds., *War, Occupation, and Creativity: Japan and East Asia, 1920–1960* (Honolulu: University of Hawai'i Press, 2001).

64. For an example, see Ruth Weiss, *China's War Art Front* (Chungking: China Information Committee, 1940). Cultural production under occupation (let alone in the name of occupation) is not so much as mentioned in accounts such as this.

65. John Berger, *Ways of Seeing* (London: Penguin, 1973).

66. *Watching Babylon: The War in Iraq and Global Visual Culture* (London: Routledge, 2004) was Mirzoeff's original articulation of this argument.

67. See, for example, the special issue of *Journal of Visual Culture* 5, no. 1 (April 2006), ed. Suhail Malik, which included a number of articles on the photographs and their significance.

68. Nicholas Mirzoeff, "Invisible Empire: Visual Culture, Embodied Spectacle, and Abu Ghraib," *Radical History Review* 95 (Spring 2006): 21–44.

69. See, for instance, Susan L. Carruthers, "Why Can't We See Insurgents? Enmity, Invisibility and Counterinsurgency in Iraq and Afghanistan," *Photography and Culture* 8, no. 2 (2015): 191–211.

70. Gil Z. Hochberg, *Visual Occupations: Violence and Visibility in a Conflict Zone* (Durham, NC: Duke University Press, 2015).

71. Nicholas Mirzoeff, "Introduction: For Critical Visuality Studies," in *The Visual Culture Reader,* ed. Nicholas Mirzoeff (London: Routledge, 2013), xxix–xxxviii.

72. On these topics, see Marc Olivier Baruch, "Charisma and Hybrid Legitimacy in Pétain's *État français* (1940–44)," *Totalitarian Movements and Political Religions* 7, no. 2 (2006): 215–224; Margaret Collins Weitz, "Art in the Service of Propaganda: The Poster War in France during World War II," *Religion and the Arts* 4, no. 1 (2000): 43–75; and Chris Pearson, *Scarred Landscapes: War and Nature in Vichy France* (London: Palgrave, 2008).

73. Laurence Bertrand Dorléac, *Art of the Defeat: France 1940–1944,* trans. Jane Marie Todd (Los Angeles: Getty Research Institute, 2008), 234.

74. Ibid., 287.

75. Eric Jennings, "Reinventing Jeanne: The Iconology of Joan of Arc in Vichy Schoolbooks, 1940–1944," *Journal of Contemporary History* 29 (1994): 711–734.

76. Francine Muel-Dreyfus, *Vichy and the Eternal Feminine: A Contribution to a Political Sociology of Gender,* trans. Kathleen A. Johnson (Durham, NC: Duke University Press, 2001).

77. On the subtle difference between these two terms, see Marion G. Müller, "Iconography," in *The International Encyclopedia of Communication,* ed. Wolfgang Donsbach (Malden, MA: Blackwell, 2008), 1–3.

78. Ibid.

79. Pablo Schneider, "Political Iconography and the Picture Act: The Execution of Charles I in 1649," in *Pictorial Cultures and Political Iconographies: Approaches, Perspectives, Case Studies from Europe and America,* ed. Udo J. Hebel and Christoph Wagner (Berlin: De Gruyter, 2011), 64.

80. Victoria E. Bonnell, *Iconography of Power: Soviet Political Posters under Lenin and Stalin* (Berkeley: University of California Press, 1997).

81. Horst Bredekamp, "A Neglected Tradition? Art History as *Bildwissenschaft,*" *Critical Inquiry* 29, no. 3 (Spring 2003): 418–428.

82. Matthias Bruhn, "The Warburg Electronic Library in Hamburg: A Digital Index of Political Iconography," *Visual Resources* 15, no. 4 (2000): 410.

83. Martin Warnke, *Political Landscape: The Art History of Nature* (London: Reaktion Books, 1994).

84. I borrow the notion of the "cultural biography of a portrait" from Irene Stengs, "The Commodification of King Chulalongkorn: His Portraits, Their Cultural Biographies, and the Enduring Aura of a Great King of Siam," in *Commodification: Things, Agency, and Identities,* ed. Wim M. J. van Binsbergen and Peter L. Geschiere (Münster: Lit Verlag, 2005), 301–318.

85. Schneider, "Political Iconography," 65.

86. To borrow a phrase from Sarah Kovner, *Occupying Power: Sex Workers and Servicemen in Postwar Japan* (Stanford, CA: Stanford University Press, 2012), 5–6.

87. As opposed to what Andrew Buchanan refers to as the "occupying gaze" (i.e., that adopted by occupiers themselves). On this, see Andrew Buchanan, "'I Felt like a Tourist instead of a Soldier': The Occupying Gaze—War and Tourism in Italy, 1943–1945," *American Quarterly* 68, no. 3 (September 2016): 593–615.

88. An account of this practice can be found in Liu Longguang, "Heping yu zuguo" [Peace and the motherland], *Huawen Daban meiri* 5, no. 5 (March 1941): 19–23.

89. The partial reopening of the Second Historical Archives in Nanjing has benefited this book enormously. However, many files held by that institution (including those relating to censorship under the RNG) were still not accessible to researchers at the time of this writing.

Chapter 1: Contextualizing the Wang Jingwei Regime

1. For an excellent example of the former, see Joseph Yick, "Communist-Puppet Collaboration in Japanese-Occupied China: Pan Hannian and Li Shiqun, 1939–43," *Intelligence and National Security* 16, no. 4 (2001): 61–88. The political economy of the RNG has been addressed in part 4 of Zanasi, *Saving the Nation.*

2. For an analysis of this group's origins, see Wang Ke-wen, "Wang Jingwei and the Policy Origins of the 'Peace Movement,' 1932–1937," in *Chinese Collaboration with Japan: The Limits of Accommodation,* ed. David P. Barrett and Larry N. Shyu (Stanford, CA: Stanford University Press, 2001), 21–37.

3. There is some confusion in the literature about the transliteration of Lin's name. Some texts (including some written by this author) give his full name as "Lin Bosheng." Texts from the time of the occupation, however, show that the first character in Lin's personal name was pronounced "*bai*" (rather than "*bo*"). For example, a portrait of Lin by one of the RNG's most prolific woodcut (*muke*) artists, Wang Yingxiao, is captioned (in English) "H. E. Mr. Lin Pai-sheng." This portrait appears in *Huawen Daban meiri* 9, no. 3 (August 1942): 44.

4. On RNG factionalism, see David P. Barrett, "The Wang Jingwei Regime, 1940–1945: Continuities and Disjunctures with Nationalist China," in *Chinese Collaboration with Japan, 1932–1945: The Limits of Accommodation,* ed. David P. Barrett and Larry N. Shyu (Stanford, CA: Stanford University Press, 2001), 102–115.

5. Jiang Hao, "The KMT Reorganization Faction and Its Activities in Shanghai," *Chinese Studies in History* 27, no. 1–2 (1993): 123–130.

6. On these similarities, see Barrett, "Wang Jingwei Regime."

7. Yue Du, "Sun Yat-sen as *Guofu:* Competition over Nationalist Party Orthodoxy in the Second Sino-Japanese War," *Modern China* 45, no. 2 (2019): 201–235.

8. Zhu Yayun, "Nanking: Chronology," *China Heritage Annual 2017,* 2017: http://chinaheritage.net/annual/2017/chronology/?lang=zh. While the Sun statue that is now found at this site in Nanjing is not the same statue that was placed there during the occupation, it was the RNG that initiated the use of Xin Jiekou as a site associated with Sun through statuary.

9. Cheung, "Slogans, Symbols, and Legitimacy."

10. Serfass, "Occupation japonaise et collaboration chinoise"; see also David Serfass, "Résister ou négocier face au Japon: La genèse du gouvernement de collaboration de Nankin (janvier 1938—avril 1939)" [Resistance against or negotiation with Japan: The origins of the Nanjing collaborationist government (January 1938–April 1939)], *Vingtième siècle: Revue d'histoire* 125 (January–March 2015): 121–132.

11. Serfass, "Occupation Japonaise et collaboration chinoise," 955 n45.

12. "China-Japan: Treaty concerning Basic Relations and Protocol Annexed Thereto," *American Journal of International Law* 35, no. 3 (1941): 125–128.

13. Robert Culp, "Rethinking Governmentality: Training, Cultivation, and Cultural Citizenship in Nationalist China," *Journal of Asian Studies* 65, no. 3 (2006): 529–554. In this book, I follow Culp's use of a gender-neutral term to refer to the *tongzijun* (a category that included both Boy Scouts and Girl Guides).

14. "Wang wei jiaoyubu chengqing huifu Zhongguo tongzijun zonghui an" [Files relating to the revival of the Scouts under Wang's bogus Ministry of Education], March–June 1941, SHA, 2003-1-4118.

15. Stephen R. MacKinnon, "Conclusion: Wartime China," in *China at War: Regions of China, 1937–1945,* ed. Stephen R. MacKinnon, Diana Lary, and Ezra F. Vogel (Stanford, CA: Stanford University Press, 2007), 338.

16. Frederic Wakeman Jr., "The Struggle between Western and Chinese Medicine," in *China at War: Regions of China, 1937–1945,* ed. Stephen R. MacKinnon, Diana Lary, and Ezra F. Vogel (Stanford, CA: Stanford University Press, 2007), 276.

17. Philip Jowett, *Rays of the Rising Sun,* vol. 1, *Japan's Asian Allies 1931–45, China and Manchukuo* (Trowbridge, UK: Helion and Co., 2004), 72.

18. On the importance of this city and its wider provincial hinterland in early, pre-1940 discussions, see Joseph K. S. Yick, "'Pre-Collaboration': The Political Activity and Influence of Chen Bijun in Wartime China, January 1938–May 1940," *Southeast Review of Asian Studies* 36 (2014): 58–74.

19. Controlled by the Japanese navy. See R. T. Phillips, "The Japanese Occupation of Hainan," *Modern Asian Studies* 14, no. 1 (1980): 93–109.

20. For a detailed analysis of the limited territorial spoils granted to the RNG at its "return," see Boyle, *China and Japan at War,* 256–276.

21. T'ien-wei Wu, "Contending Political Forces during the War of Resistance," in *China's Bitter Victory: The War with Japan, 1937–1945,* ed. James C. Hsiung and Steven I. Levine (Armonk, NY: East Gate, 1992), 71.

22. For a comprehensive account of RNG control in east China, see David Serfass, "Le gouvernement collaborateur de Wang Jingwei: Aspects de l'État d'occupation durant la guerre sino-japonaise, 1940–1945 [Wang Jingwei's collaborationist government: Aspects of the occupation state during the Sino-Japanese War, 1940–1945] (PhD diss., École des hautes études en sciences sociales, Paris, 2017), esp. 525–534.

23. It was left to Zhou Fohai to convince the Japanese not to transform strategically important areas such as east Zhejiang into militarized zones directly administered by the Japanese in 1941, for example. See Cai Dejin, ed., *Zhou Fohai riji quanbian, shangbian* [The complete, edited diaries of Zhou Fohai, part 1] (Beijing: Zhongguo wenlian chubanshe, 1998), 456–457.

24. Brian G. Martin, "Patriotic Collaboration? Zhou Fohai and the Wang Jingwei Government during the Second Sino-Japanese War," in *Japan as the Occupier and the Occupied,* ed. Christine de Matos and Mark E. Caprio (London: Palgrave Macmillan, 2015), 155.

25. Brian G. Martin, "Shield of Collaboration: The Wang Jingwei Regime's Security Service, 1939–1945," *Intelligence and National Security* 16, no. 4 (2001): 130.

26. Gregor Benton, *New Fourth Army: Communist Resistance along the Yangtze and the Huai, 1938–1941* (Berkeley: University of California Press, 1999), 249–250.

27. "Minguo sanshiyi niandu xiaban niandu qingxiang gongzuo yaoling" [Rural Pacification work orders for the second half of 1942], 1942, SHA, 2003-1-4000.

28. On this, see David Serfass, "L'occupation japonaise comme objet pour l'histoire de l'État chinois: L'exemple de la campagne de pacification rurale du gouvernement de Wang Jingwei, 1941–45" [The Japanese occupation as an object for the history of the Chinese state: The example of the Rural Pacification campaigns of the Wang Jingwei government, 1941–45], *Études chinoises* 35, no. 2 (2016): 123–137.

29. On this, see Guomindang qingxiangqu dangwu banshichu, *Qingxiangqu dangwu baogaoshu* [Report on party services in the Rural Pacification areas] (Suzhou: Guomindang qingxiangqu dangwu banshichu, 1942), 10–13.

30. Zhongyang dang'anguan and Zhongguo di'er lishi dang'anguan, *Ri-Wang de qingxiang* [Japan and the Wang government's Rural Pacification campaign] (Beijing: Xinhua shudian, 1995), 512–513.

31. Martin, "Patriotic Collaboration?" 158.

32. Variations of this phrase were permitted, however. See "Xuangua guoqi ying zhuyi gedian" [Take note of the following points when flying the national flag], *Zhong bao,* March 31, 1940.

33. This is taken from a bilingual (Chinese-English) publication distributed in March 1940 to mark the *huandu.* See Ministry of Publicity, *Special Commemoration Issue: Return of the National Government of the Republic of China to Its Capital* (Nanjing: Ministry of Publicity, 1940).

34. This description is taken from a contemporary newspaper account of the "lone battalion's last stand." See North China Daily News, *Five Months of War* (Shanghai: North China Daily News and Herald, 1938), 113.

35. Fu, *Passivity, Resistance, and Collaboration,* 17–18.

36. One of many intriguing revelations in Zhu Zijia [Jin Xiongbai], *Wang zhengquan de kaichang yu shouchang shang* [The beginning and end of the Wang regime, part 1] (Taipei: Fengyun shidai, 2012), 132, is that the *huandu* was marked not just by Wang-themed festivities but also by Japanese soldiers ripping down and destroying ROC flags that had been raised in Nanjing.

37. "Guofu mingling: Zi wu ri qi, chuqu guoqi huangse biaozhi" [The national government decrees that from [February] 5, the yellow pennant shall be removed from the national flag], *Jing bao,* February 3, 1943.

38. Ward, "Zhou Fohai," 38.

39. On this topic, see Du, "Sun Yat-sen as *Guofu.*"

40. Including, interestingly, a bronze mirror once used by Sun. "Wang Zhaoming dian Zhou Fohai ju Chu Minyi yun zongli you tongjing yi mian you Chi Pengji songlai zai Dongjing shi shifou jianguo" [Telegram from Wang Jingwei to Zhou Fohai asking if he saw a bronze mirror that, according to Chu Minyi, had been sent to Sun Yat-sen by Ike Kyokichi when he was in Tokyo], October 21, 1942, AH, Wang Zhaoming shiliao, 118-010100-0029-039.

41. Rudolf G. Wagner, "Ritual, Architecture, Politics, and Publicity during the Republic: Enshrining Sun Yat-sen," in *Chinese Architecture and the Beaux-Arts,* ed. Jeffrey Cody, Nancy S. Steinhardt, and Tony Atkin (Honolulu: University of Hawai'i Press, 2011), 264–265.

42. On "collaborationist nationalism" and ownership of Sun's physical remains, see Zanasi, "Globalizing *Hanjian.*"

43. Delin Lai, "Searching for a Modern Chinese Monument: The Design of the Sun Yat-sen Mausoleum in Nanjing," *Journal of the Society of Architectural Historians* 64, no. 1 (March 2005): 22–23.

44. Zhang Sheng, "Lun Wang wei dui Guomindang zhengzhi fuhao de zhengduo" [On the RNG's struggle over Kuomintang political symbols], *Kang-Ri zhanzheng yanjiu* 2 (2005): 1–33.

45. Shuk-wah Poon, *Negotiating Religion in Modern China: State and Common People in Guangzhou* (Hong Kong: Chinese University Press, 2011), 7.

46. Images of foreign dignitaries (e.g., from the Indian National Army) paying their respects at the site are included in Anonymous, "Guangdong sheng Da Dong Ya qingnian dahui" [The Greater East Asia Youth Convention in Guangdong], *Dong Ya Lianmeng huabao* 3, no. 11 (December 1943).

47. Zhongyang dianxunshe, ed., *Zhongguo canzhan yi lai dashi xiezhen zhuanji* [An album of photographs of major events in China since the declaration of war on the Allies] (Nanjing: Zhongyang dianxunshe, 1944), 82.

48. Jiaoyubu, ed., *Guomin li* [Citizens' calendar] (Nanjing: Xingzhengyuan jiaoyubu, 1941), 98–100.

49. Yang, "Road to Lyric Martyrdom," 136.

50. We shall return to this topic in chapter 5. On bunds more generally, see Jeremy E. Taylor, "The Bund: Littoral Space of Empire in the Treaty Ports of East Asia," *Social History* 27, no. 2 (2002): 125–142.

51. On the establishment and development of the RNG navy, see Zhang Shaofu, "Wo suo zhidao de Wang wei haijun" [The bogus Wang navy that I knew], in *Wei ting youying lu: Dui Wang wei zhengquan de huiyi* [A secret record of the puppet government: Memoirs of the bogus Wang regime], ed. Huang Meizhen (Beijing: Dongfang chubanshe, 1986), 186–230. See also Xu Xuehai, "Wang wei haijun jianli jingwei yu xiachang" [The complex process of the establishment of Wang's bogus navy and its aftermath], *Zhuanji wenxue* 112, no. 6 (June 2018): 30–37.

52. Clifford Geertz, Negara: *The Theatre State in Nineteenth-Century Bali* (Princeton, NJ: Princeton University Press, 1980).

53. Heonik Kwon and Byung-Ho Chung's use of this idea in *North Korea: Beyond Charismatic Politics* (Lanham, MD: Rowman and Littlefield, 2012), 63–65.

54. Ibid., 59.

55. Geertz, Negara, 13.

56. Mark S. Eykholt, "Living the Limits of Occupation in Nanjing, China, 1937–1945" (PhD diss., University of California–San Diego, 1998), 117–118.

57. Wu Zhuoliu, *Nanjing zagan* [Nanjing sketches] (Taipei: Yuanxing, 1977), 94–95. It is relevant that Wu's account details festivities in the area around the Fuzimiao, as this was also focused upon in regime photography, which showed the supposedly *renao* (lively) activities that went on in this part of the city. An example is Zhongyang dianxunshe, *Guofu huandu hou de zhengzhi qingshi* [Political trends since the return of the national government] (Nanjing: Zhongyang dianxunshe, 1941), 6.

58. Wai Chor So, "Race, Culture, and the Anglo-American Powers: The Views of Chinese Collaborators," *Modern China* 37, no. 1 (2001): 74.

59. Don Bate, *Wang Ching Wei: Puppet or Patriot* (Chicago: Ralph Fletcher Seymour, 1941), 157.

60. Bunker, *Peace Conspiracy*, 274.

61. Wen-hsin Yeh, "Prologue: Shanghai Besieged, 1937–45," in *Wartime Shanghai*, ed. Wen-hsin Yeh (London: Routledge, 2004), 6–7.

62. Rebecca Nedostup, *Superstitious Regimes: Religion and the Politics of Chinese Modernity* (Cambridge, MA: Harvard University Asia Center, 2009).

63. Li Narangoa, "Japanese Imperialism and Mongolian Buddhism, 1932–1945," *Critical Asian Studies* 35, no. 4 (2003): 492–510.

64. Yeh, "Prologue," 6.

65. Zhang Jiangcai, *Wang Jingwei xiansheng xingshilu* [A true record of Mr. Wang Jingwei's activities] (Dongguan: Baiyuantang, 1943), 8.

66. On this, see Benjamin Brose, "Resurrecting Xuan Zang: The Modern Travels of a Medieval Monk," in *Recovering Buddhism in Modern China*, ed. Jan Kiely and J. Brooks Jessup (New York: Columbia University Press, 2016), 143–176.

67. Lin Baisheng had, in fact, started speaking of the RNG as being part of an "East Asian Axis" (*Dong Ya chouxin*) in June 1941. Lin Baisheng, "Zhengzhi baogao" [Political report], in *Xuanchuanbu diyi jie quanguo xuanchuan huiyi shilu* [Record of the first national publicity conference of the Ministry of Publicity], ed. Xuanchuanbu (Nanjing: Xuanchuanbu, 1941), 15.

68. David Serfass, "Le dilemme de Nankin: Tergiversations autour de la reconnaissance du gouvernement de collaboration chinois (1940–1945)" [The Nanjing dilemma: Procrastinations over the recognition of the Chinese collaborationist government (1940–1945)], *Vingtième siècle* 133 (January–March 2017): 99–111.

69. Rana Mitter, "Contention and Redemption: Ideologies of National Salvation in Republican China," *Totalitarian Movements and Political Religions* 3, no. 3 (2002): 68.

70. Such sentiments were articulated in a guide published in association with the movement on—significantly—May 4, 1942: Anonymous, *Qingshao xunlian yu xiuyang* [The training and fostering of youth] (Nanjing: Zhongyang dianxunshe, 1942).

71. This list is paraphrased from Wang Zihe, "Ruhe tuijin xin guomin yundong" [How to promote the New Citizens Movement], in *Ruhe tuijin xin guomin yundong* [How to promote the New Citizens Movement], ed. Minguo ribao she (Nanjing: Minguo ribao she, 1942), 1–7.

72. Anonymous, *Xin guomin yundong yanlunji, shangce* [Collection of NCM speeches, volume 1] (Nanjing: Nanjing tebie shi xuanchuanchu, 1942).

73. Luo Junqiang, "Weiting youying lu: Dui Wang wei zhengfu de huiyi jishi" [Secret records of the puppet government: My memoirs of the bogus Wang government], in *Wei ting youying lu: Dui Wang wei zhengquan de huiyi* [A secret record of the puppet government: Memoirs of the bogus Wang regime], ed. Huang Meizhen (Beijing: Dongfang chubanshe, 1986), 49.

74. I am drawing here on the interviews with former students that are found in Eykholt, "Living the Limits of Occupation," 278–286.

75. "Wang wei xin guomin yundong diyi jie qingshaonian tuan shuqi jixun ying xunlian gangyao deng" [Points on the first NCM summer training camp for members of the Youth League under the bogus Wang government], 1943, SHA, 2003-1-2092.

76. Zanasi, *Saving the Nation,* 218–219.

77. William C. Johnstone, "Japan's 'New' China Policy," *Far Eastern Survey* 12, no. 19 (September 1943): 190.

78. "Guomin jingshen zong dongyuan biaoyu" [Slogans for the general mobilization of the national spirit], January 1943, SMA, R18-1-387.

79. Brian G. Martin, " 'In My Heart I Opposed Opium': Opium and the Politics of the Wang Jingwei Government, 1940–45," *European Journal of East Asian Studies* 2, no. 2 (2003): 365–410.

80. "Wang wei Xuanchuanbu guanyu Zhong-Ri tongmeng Dong Ya lianhe gongshi zhuan'an" [The bogus Wang regime's Ministry of Publicity files on the Sino-Japanese alliance and joint offensives in East Asia], 1943, SHA, 2003-1-2168.

81. On the racial nationalism in *China's Destiny,* see W. J. F. Jenner, "Race and History in China," *New Left Review* 11 (September–October 2001): 55–77.

82. In the words of Peter Duus, "Imperialism without Colonies: The Vision of a Greater East Asia Co-Prosperity Sphere," *Diplomacy and Statecraft* 7, no. 1 (1996): 70.

83. Luo ("Weiting youying lu," 49), who had served within the RNG, suggests that this was Lin Baisheng's doing and that, in light of the new realities of the war following

Pearl Harbor, Lin sought to transform the RNG into an Axis power, with Wang akin to a fascist leader.

84. Zhu Zijia, *Wang zhengquan de kaichang yu shouchang shang,* 211.

85. Madeleine Herren, "Fascist Internationalism," in *Internationalisms: A Twentieth-Century History,* ed. Glenda Sluga and Patricia Clavin (Cambridge: Cambridge University Press, 2016), 191–212.

86. So, "Race, Culture."

87. Louise Young, "When Fascism Met Empire in Japanese-Occupied Manchuria," *Journal of Global History* 12 (2017): 274–296, esp. 282.

88. Ibid., 295.

89. Zuigao guofang huiyi [Supreme Council for National Defense], "Zhanshi wenhua xuanchuan zhengce jiben gangyao" [Basic outline on policy for wartime culture and propaganda], in *Wang wei zhengquan ziliao xuanbian: Wang Jingwei guomin zhengfu "qingxiang" yundong* [Selected materials from the bogus Wang regime: The Wang national government's "Rural Pacification" campaign], ed. Yu Zidao, Liu Qikui, and Cao Zhenwei (Shanghai: Xinhua shuju, 1985), 392–398.

90. Maggie Clinton, *Revolutionary Nativism: Fascism and Culture in China, 1925–1937* (Durham, NC: Duke University Press, 2017).

91. Brook, "Collaborationist Nationalism," 187.

92. Bate, *Wang Ching Wei,* 153.

93. Torsten Weber, *Embracing "Asia" in China and Japan: Asianism Discourse and the Contest for Hegemony* (Basingstoke, UK: Palgrave Macmillan, 2018), 279–282.

94. Ibid., 286.

95. The result was T'ang Leang-li, ed., *China and Japan: Natural Friends—Unnatural Enemies; A Guide for China's Foreign Policy by Dr. Sun Yat-sen* (Shanghai: China United Press, 1941).

96. Eri Hotta, *Pan-Asianism and Japan's War, 1931–1945* (Basingstoke, UK: Palgrave Macmillan, 2007).

97. So, "Race, Culture," 79.

Chapter 2: Visual Cultures under Occupation

1. See, for instance, http://www.christies.com/lotfinder/Lot/wang-jingwei-1883-1944-calligraphy-5573876-details.aspx.

2. Frank Dunand, ed., *The Pavilion of Marital Harmony: Chinese Painting and Calligraphy between Tradition and Modernity* (Geneva: Collections Baur, 2002).

3. See https://commons.wikimedia.org/wiki/File:Wang_and_Nazis.jpg.

4. This date is confirmed in one of the many magazines that reproduced the image under occupation: *Guomin xinwen huabao* 3 (March 1942): 3.

5. Kushner, *Thought War;* Kari Shepherdson-Scott, "Race behind the Walls: Contact and Containment in Japanese Images of Urban Manchuria," in *The Affect of Difference: Representations of Race in East Asian Empires,* ed. Christopher Hanscom and Dennis Washburn (Honolulu: University of Hawai'i Press, 2016), 180–206.

6. Jeremy E. Taylor, "Cartoons and Collaboration in Wartime China: The Mobilization of Chinese Cartoonists under Japanese Occupation," *Modern China* 41, no. 4 (2015): 408.

7. For example, the RNG's Central New Agency (CNA), examined later in this chapter, included on its board high-ranking Dōmei news agency staff.

8. Kushner, *Thought War,* 77.

9. Some seventy-five artists (ranging from exponents of *sensōga*—or Japanese "war painting"—to cartoonists) who worked for the Propaganda Corps in occupied China are listed in Mabuchi Itsuo, *Hōdō sensen* [Reporting on the front] (Tokyo: Kaizōsha, 1941), 432–433.

10. On Kawashima, see Joshua A. Fogel, *The Literature of Travel in the Japanese Rediscovery of China: 1862–1945* (Stanford, CA: Stanford University Press, 1996), 294; on Ōta, see Xu Jinsheng, "Qin Hua Rijun de xuanchuan zhan: Yi Rijun di shiyi jun zhizhi xuanchuanpin wei zhongxin" [The Japanese propaganda war during the invasion of China: A study of Japan's Eleventh Army's printed propaganda materials], *Minguo dang'an* (March 2017): 112–119.

11. On the recycling of Propaganda Corps cartoons in the Wuhan-based *Dachu bao,* see Naikaku Jōhōbu, *Senden jihō (Shina kankei)* [Propaganda times (China relations)], March 10, 1940.

12. Michael Baskett, *The Attractive Empire: Transnational Film Culture in Imperial Japan* (Honolulu: University of Hawai'i Press, 2008), 32.

13. Jie Li, "Phantasmagoric Manchukuo: Documentaries Produced by the South Manchuria Railway Company, 1932–1940," *positions* 22, no. 2 (2014): 334.

14. Norman Smith, *Intoxicating Manchuria: Alcohol, Opium and Culture in China's Northeast* (Vancouver: UBC Press, 2012), 2.

15. Louise Young, *Japan's Total Empire: Manchuria and the Culture of Wartime Imperialism* (Berkeley: University of California Press, 1998), 287–288.

16. Jeremy E. Taylor, "Gendered Archetypes of Wartime Occupation: 'New Women' in Occupied North China, 1937–40," *Gender and History* 28, no. 3 (2016): 665.

17. On this organization, see Beijingshi dang'anguan, ed., *Ri-wei Beijing Xinminhui* [The Japanese-bogus regimes' Xinminhui in occupied Beijing] (Beijing: Guangming ribao chubanshe, 1989).

18. T'ien-wei Wu, "Contending Political Forces," 66–67.

19. Wen Zongyao, "Daminhui Wen huizhang gao minzhong shu" [Letter from Director Wen of the Daminhui to the people], *Xin Zhongguo* 2, no. 11–12 (December 1939): 2–3.

20. Timothy Brook, "Occupation State Building," in *China at War: Regions of China, 1937–1945,* ed. Stephen R. MacKinnon, Diana Lary, and Ezra F. Vogel (Stanford, CA: Stanford University Press, 2007), 35.

21. Zhu Zijia, *Wang zhengquan de kaichang yu shouchang shang,* 243–244.

22. Liu Jie, "Kangzhan chuqi Huadong lunxianqu qin-Ri qunti yanjiu: Yi Daminhui Zhenjiang lianhe zhibu wei zhongxin de tantao" [A study of pro-Japanese groups in occupied areas of east China in the early stages of the War of Resistance: A discussion of the Daminhui's branch office in Zhenjiang], *Zhongyang yanjiuyuan jindaishi yanjiusuo jikan* 98 (2017): 89–114.

23. And as detailed in Stephen R. MacKinnon, *War, Refugees, and the Making of Modern China: Wuhan, 1938* (Berkeley: University of California Press, 2008).

24. Such as the Daminhui's house theater company, the Yuandong jutuan (Far East Drama Troupe). On the origins of this troupe, see Mabuchi, *Hōdō sensen,* 370–375.

25. Gao Danyu and Xu Shaohong, "Nanjing wei weixin zhengfu ji qi Daminhui" (The bogus Nanjing RGROC and its Daminhui), *Minguo dang'an* 2 (2000): 89–94. A

photograph from 1938 appearing to show the Daminhui logo on the walls of Nanjing is now held by Getty Images ("The city wall of Nanking (China) after the Japanese invasion," Corbis Historical, 526781174).

26. Andrea Germer, "Visual Propaganda in Wartime East Asia: The Case of Natori Yōnosuke," *Japan Focus* 20, no. 3 (2011): 1–35.

27. Song Yuwu, "Meiguo guohui tushuguan cang Zhong-Ri zhanzheng (1937–1945) Zhongwen qikan wenxian" [Chinese-language periodicals and documents from the era of the Sino-Japanese War (1937–1945) held in the Library of Congress], *Guoshiguan yanjiu tongxun* 13 (December 2017): 129.

28. So, "Race, Culture," 70.

29. One example being Luo, "Weiting youying lu," 47–48.

30. Zhong-Ri wenhua xiehui, *Zhong-Ri wenhua xiehui Wuhan fenhui erzhounian jinian tekan* [Special commemorative edition celebrating the second anniversary of the founding of the Wuhan chapter of the Sino-Japanese Cultural Association] (Wuhan: Zhong-Ri wenhua xiehui, 1943), 27.

31. "Zhongguo Guomindang zhongyang zhixing weiyuanhui xuanchuanbu gongzuo baogao" [Work report of the Propaganda Department of the Kuomintang Central Executive Committee], December 1940, 47–48, KMT, yi ban, 715.1/415.

32. Anonymous, "Diyi ci huiyi jingguo" [Record of the first meeting], in *Xuanchuanbu diyi jie quanguo xuanchuan huiyi shilu* [Record of the first national publicity conference of the Ministry of Publicity], ed. Xuanchuanbu (Nanjing: Xuanchuanbu, 1941), 57–60.

33. Anonymous, "Guanyu xuanchuan de zuotanhui" [On a roundtable about propaganda], *Huawen Daban meiri* 6, no. 2 (January 1941): 6–9.

34. Norman Smith, *Resisting Manchukuo: Chinese Women Writers and the Japanese Occupation* (Vancouver: UBC Press, 2007), 53. Smith's analysis is one of the only ones we have in English for this important publication.

35. On the folding of the Daminhui in 1940, see Luo, "Weiting youying lu," 52.

36. Zhu Zijia, *Wang zhengquan de kaichang yu shouchang, shang,* 283–284.

37. Anonymous, "Ben kan zhu Hua banshichu zai Nanjing chengli" [The establishment of this magazine's China office in Nanjing], *Huawen Daban meiri* 7, no. 7 (October 1941): 29.

38. Wu Xuebin, "Xuerou zuocheng de changcheng: Yijiu sansan nian de xin tuxiang yu xin guannian" [A Great Wall of flesh and blood: The new imagery and new opinions of 1933], *Wenyi yanjiu* 1 (2015): 134–143.

39. Ironically, one of his cartoons on the front page of the November 1, 1939, edition of *Nanjing xinbao* (a RGROC publication) lampooned Wang Jingwei and his defection from Chongqing.

40. J. E. Taylor, "Cartoons and Collaboration."

41. Zhu Shuirong, "Gu wei jin yong: *Jin ping mei* quantu lianhuanhua quanban" [Using the past for present purposes: The complete publication of the comic version of the *Golden Lotus*], *Meishu zhi you* 1 (2003): 27.

42. George E. Taylor, *The Struggle for North China* (New York: Institute of Pacific Relations, 1940), 65–68.

43. I am translating the name of the Xuanchuanbu here as "Ministry of Publicity" (rather than as "Ministry of Propaganda"). This is how this organization referred to

itself in English-language publications in 1940. See, for example, Ministry of Publicity, *Special Commemoration Issue.*

44. "Zhongguo Guomindang zhongyang zhixing weiyuanhui xuanchuanbu gongzuo baogao" [Work report of the Propaganda Department of the Kuomintang Central Executive Committee], December 1940, 46, KMT, yi ban, 715.1/415.

45. Zhu Zijia, *Wang zhengquan de kaichang yu shouchang shang,* 132.

46. Lawrence M. W. Chiu, "The *South China Daily News* and Wang Jingwei's Peace Movement, 1939–1941," *Journal of the Royal Asiatic Society of Hong Kong* 50 (2010): 343–370.

47. On Hu Lancheng, see David Der-wei Wang, *The Lyrical in Epic Time: Modern Chinese Intellectuals and Artists through the 1949 Crisis* (New York: Columbia University Press, 2015), 158–161.

48. Zhu Zijia, *Wang zhengquan de kaichang yu shouchang shang,* 126–127.

49. "Qudi sheying huihua zhanxing banfa caoan" [Interim draft regulations on the banning of photographs and paintings], April 4, 1941, SHA, 2003-1-7320.

50. "Zhongyang xuanchuan jiangxisuo gaikuang" [The current state of affairs at the Central Propaganda Institute], *Jing bao,* December 12, 1940, 4; see also "Sheli Zhongyang xuanchuan jiangxisuo jihua" [Plan for establishment of the Central Propaganda Institute], July 22, 1940, SHA, 2003-1-2191.

51. "Gongzuo baogao" [Work report], June 1942, SHA, 2003-1-2035. In this case, the MoP notes that members of the fourth cohort of graduates were instructed to design and illustrate a range of cover images for government publications. Some of the unattributed images that we will examine in later chapters of this book from the late 1942 period may well be those produced in response to such calls.

52. Including graduates of Japanese and American universities.

53. "Wang wei Guangdong sheng xuanchuanchu renyuan renmian an" [Hiring of personnel by the Guangdong Provincial Publicity Bureau under the bogus Wang regime], 1941–1943, SHA, 2003-4-600.

54. Shuge Wei, "News as a Weapon: Hollington Tong and the Formation of the Guomindang Centralized Foreign Propaganda System, 1937–1938," *Twentieth-Century China* 39, no. 2 (2014): 118–143.

55. On Dōmei's role in Asia more generally, see Tomoko Akami, "Japan's New Empire and the Dōmei News Agency in Occupied Southeast Asia, 1942–45," *Japan Focus* 13, issue 1, no. 3 (2015): 1–28.

56. Zhongyang dianxunshe, *Zhongyang dianxunshe disan nian* [The third year of the Central News Agency] (Nanjing: Zhongyang dianxunshe, 1943), 21.

57. Andrea Germer, "Artists and Wartime Politics: Natori Yōnosuke—a Japanese Riefenstahl?" *Contemporary Japan* 24 (2012): 21–50.

58. Although, as we shall see in later chapters, CNA photographers were active even in 1940.

59. Wei Jianxin, "Qingxiangqu de huigu yu qianzhan" [A retrospective view of and the prospects for Rural Pacification areas], *Huawen Daban meiri* 9, no. 3 (August 1942): 15–17.

60. "Gongzuo baogao" [Work report], May 1942, SHA, 2003-1-2035. In this file, mention is made of the need to strengthen photography in response to the perceived combined propaganda threat posed by the United States, the United Kingdom, and Chongqing.

61. The photography of the former was featured regularly in travelogues published by the CNA, including those examined in chapter 3; examples of the work of the latter can be found in the Wang Jingwei and Lin Baisheng Photograph Collection, East Asia Library, Stanford University (https://exhibits.stanford.edu/wangjingwei).

62. Xue Huizi had started his career as a journalist in Suzhou. Zhu Jiayu, "Dai wu zi de Suzhou lao baozhi" [The old newspapers of Suzhou that carried the character "wu" in their titles], *Zhongguo difangzhi* 8 (2007): 43–45.

63. So argued the CNA in Zhongyang dianxunshe, *Zhongguo canzhan yi lai dashi xiezhen zhuanji,* 2.

64. Including fine arts academies in Shanghai and Suzhou. See Tao Kangde and Qiu Shimu, *Shenbao nianjian* [The *Shenbao* almanac] (Shanghai: Shenbaoshe, 1944), 1021.

65. Pedith Chan, "The Discourse of *Guohua* in Occupied Shanghai," paper presented at the Cultural and Intellectual Histories of Japanese-Occupied China Workshop, Asia House (London), September 16, 2019.

66. On this policy, officially introduced in June 1943, see Zuigao guofang huiyi, "Zhanshi wenhua xuanchuan zhengce jiben gangyao," 392–398.

67. Liu Zi, "Cong Shanghai manhua xiehui tan dao Huazhong manhuajie" [From the Shanghai Cartoonists Association to the cartooning field in central China], *Huawen Daban meiri* 9, no. 5 (September 1942): 43–45.

68. J. E. Taylor, "Cartoons and Collaboration."

69. The topic is explored in Hung, *War and Popular Culture;* see also Zhou Aimin, *Yan'an muke yishu yanjiu* [A study of Yan'an woodcut art] (Shijiazhuang: Hebei jiaoyu chubanshe, 2009).

70. Wang penned some twenty-eight essays expounding the form for the *Kabun*. For the final one of these, see Wang Qingfang, "Muke jiangzuo" [Lectures on woodcuts], *Huawen Daban meiri* 8, no. 5 (March 1942): 44–45.

71. Uchiyama Kanzō [Nei shan Wan zao], "Muke zhi fuxing" [The renaissance of woodcuts], *Zhongguo muke* 2 (January 1943): 1.

72. Tao and Qiu, *Shenbao nianjian,* 1021.

73. We shall return to the *Guoyi* group in chapter 5.

74. Eight "Western-style painters" (*yanghuajia*) exhibited their work in the period between 1940 and 1944. Tao and Qiu, *Shenbao nianjian,* 1020–1021; see also Anonymous, "Renwu jieshao: Yan Wenliang" [Introducing Yan Wenliang], *Zhonghua huabao* 1, no. 4 (November 1943): 14.

75. Michael Sullivan, *Art and Artists in Twentieth-Century China* (Berkeley: California University Press, 1996), 110–111.

76. Her work was promoted through pro-Wang publications even in the early 1930s. A collection of her paintings was advertised, for example, in *Nanhua pinglun* (South China weekly review), a pro-Wang publication, in 1932. See Anonymous, "Fang Junbi nüshi ji hua chuban" [A collection of paintings by Ms. Fan Tchunpi has been published], *Nanhua pinglun* 3, no. 17 (December 1932): 8.

77. Craig Clunas, "Chinese Art and Chinese Artists in France (1924–1925)," *Arts asiatiques* 44 (1989): 100.

78. Fang Junbi, *Fang Junbi huaji yice* [A collection of paintings by Fan Tchunpi] (Changsha: Shangwu yinshuguan, 1938).

79. Anonymous, "Fang Junbi youhua zhan jinri juxing yuzhan" [Preview of Fan Tchunpi's exhibition of oil paintings starts today], *Zhonghua ribao,* May 4, 1945, 2.

80. Sophie Wirth Brentini, "Fan Tchunpi (1898–1986): Between East and West," in *The Pavilion of Marital Harmony: Chinese Painting and Calligraphy between Tradition and Modernity,* ed. Frank Dunand (Geneva: Collections Baur, 2002), 70.

81. "Zhongguo Guomindang zhongyang zhixing weiyuanhui xuanchuanbu gongzuo baogao" [Work report of the Propaganda Department of the Kuomintang Central Executive Committee], December 1940, 60, KMT, yi ban, 715.1/415.

82. Poshek Fu, "The Ambiguity of Entertainment: Chinese Cinema in Japanese-Occupied Shanghai, 1941 to 1945," *Cinema Journal* 37, no. 1 (Autumn 1997): 80.

83. Jeremy E. Taylor, "Chinese Film Exhibition in Occupied Manila (1942–1945)," *Modern Asian Studies* 47, no. 5 (2013): 1588–1621.

84. The most thorough study of the industry is Lin Chang, *Yanmo de beihuan: Zhong lian, Hua ying dianying chutan* [The decline of tragedy and happiness: A preliminary study of the CUP and the CUMP] (Hong Kong: Zhonghua shuju, 2014).

85. Huang Qingshu [Wong Hing-sue], ed., *Wang zhuxi fang Ri jinian huakan* [Special pictorial in commemoration of Chairman Wang's visit to Japan] (Nanjing: Xuanchuanbu, 1941).

86. Including one quite extraordinary account of Chinese film stars' pilgrimage to Nanjing in 1942: Xiao Mi [Li Lihua], "Yingxing zai Nanjing" [Movie stars in Nanjing], *Huawen Daban meiri* 8, no. 2 (June 1942): 34–35.

87. "Wei benshi gechu ren you xuangua di Mei dianying zhaopian . . ." [On the hanging of photographs from enemy American films in various places throughout the city], November 29, 1944, SMA, R1-18-1769.

88. On Bann's prewar fame, see Chen Xuesheng, *Xunhui shiluo de minguo sheying* [Searching for the lost photography of the Republican era] (Taipei: Fukai yishu, 2015), 117–119.

89. So said one of Bann's advertisements in the *Jing bao,* November 16, 1944.

90. Sherman Cochran, *Chinese Medicine Men: Consumer Culture in China and Southeast Asia* (Cambridge, MA: Harvard University Press, 2006), 45–46.

91. Zhang Ziping, "Xin hong A zi" [New red A train], *Huawen Daban meiri* 7, no. 5 (September 1941): 21. The ellipses are all featured in the original text.

92. On the conflation of resistance messages and advertising art, see Rana Mitter, "The Visual Imaginary of the War of Resistance, 1937–1947," *European Journal of East Asian Studies* 7, no. 2 (2008): 167–192.

93. Specific examples of such advertising are presented at various points throughout this book.

94. Anonymous, "Guanyu xuanchuan de zuotanhui."

95. "Dui Yu Gong gongshi xuanchuan gongzuo baogao" [Work reports on propaganda on the offensive against Sichuan and the communists], n.d., SHA, 718-499.

96. A fascinating account of RNG Rural Pacification cadres admiring captured CCP propaganda material can be found in Hu, "Zheng gong shouji," 28.

97. Jiangsu sheng xuanchuanchu, "Xuanchuan" [Propaganda], in *Wang wei zhengquan ziliao xuanbian: Wang Jingwei guomin zhengfu "qingxiang" yundong* [Selected materials from the bogus Wang regime: The Wang national government's "Rural Pacification" campaign], ed. Yu Zidao, Liu Qikui, and Cao Zhenwei (Shanghai: Xinhua shuju, 1985), 399–403. The original document is from July 1943.

98. Wang Zhenghua, "Wanshan wanli qing: Jiashu zhong de zhanshi shenghuo" [Far apart but close at heart: Wartime life through private letters], *Guoshiguan xueshu jikan* 17 (September 2008): 86–128.

99. Toby Lincoln, "The Rural and Urban at War: Invasion and Reconstruction in China during the Anti-Japanese War or Resistance," *Journal of Urban History* 20, no. 10 (2012): 1–19.

100. Second only to the discrediting of communism in Lin's view. Lin Baisheng, "Xian jieduan xuanchuan de fendou" [The struggle in the current stage of propaganda], in *Xuanchuanbu diyi jie quanguo xuanchuan huiyi shilu* [Record of the first national publicity conference of the Ministry of Publicity), ed. Xuanchuanbu (Nanjing: Xuanchuanbu, 1941), 22–30.

101. "Xuanchuan yaodian wushisan hao: Guanyu Ri dui Ying Mei kaizhan" [Propaganda points number 53: On the commencement of war between Japan and the US and UK], December 1941, SHA, 2003-1-7155.

102. Anonymous, "Fa kan ci" [Remarks on the publication of the journal], *Zhonghua huabao* 1, no. 1 (August 1943).

103. On this, see P. Zhu, *Wartime Culture in Guilin*.

104. I am referring here, of course, to Mao Zedong's Yan'an Forum on Literature and Art (Yan'an wenyi zuotanhui) in May 1942, where the Chinese communists adopted socialist realism as their single, preferred style of cultural expression.

Chapter 3: Visualizing the Occupied Leader

Some sections of chapter 3 first appeared in Jeremy E. Taylor, "The 'Occupied Lens' in Wartime China: Portrait Photography in the Service of Chinese 'Collaboration,' 1939–1945," *History of Photography* 43, no. 3 (2019): 284–307; in Jeremy E. Taylor, "From Traitor to Martyr: Drawing Lessons from the Death and Burial of Wang Jingwei, 1944," *Journal of Chinese History* 3, no. 1 (2019): 137–158; and in Jeremy E. Taylor, "Republican Personality Cults in Wartime China: Contradistinction and Collaboration," *Comparative Studies in Society and History* 57, no. 3 (2015): 665–693. All are used here with the permission of Taylor and Francis and Cambridge University Press.

1. Indeed, his name is still attached to the RNG in the Chinese-speaking world, where this regime is often referred to as the *Wang wei zhengquan* (the bogus Wang regime).

2. On the visual veneration of Puyi in Manchukuo propaganda, see Jie Li, "Phantasmagoric Manchukuo"; on the cult of Pétain in wartime France, see Christopher Lloyd, *Collaboration and Resistance in Occupied France: Representing Treason and Sacrifice* (London: Palgrave Macmillan, 2003).

3. For example, see T'ang Leang-li, *Wang Ching-wei: A Political Biography* (Tianjin: China United Press, 1931).

4. This is recounted in Wen Shaohua, *Cong lieshi dao hanjian: Wang Jingwei zhuan* [From martyr to traitor: A biography of Wang Jingwei] (Hong Kong: Zhonghua shuju, 2013).

5. Harrison, *Making of the Republican Citizen,* esp. 133–145.

6. A number of such images can be found in the Historical Photographs of China Database at Bristol University, https://www.hpcbristol.net/.

7. Howard L. Boorman, "Wang Ching-wei: China's Romantic Radical," *Political Science Quarterly* 79, no. 4 (1964): 505.

8. Bunker, *Peace Conspiracy*, 9.

9. One example of such collections is Shao Hou, ed., *Wang Jingwei wenxuan* [Collected writings of Wang Jingwei] (Shanghai: Fanggu shuju, 1937).

10. "Huanying Wang Jingwei tongzhi xuanchuan dawang" [Propaganda guidelines on welcoming Comrade Wang Jingwei], Hubei sheng dangbu [Party headquarters, Hubei Province], 1927, KMT, bu, 10222.

11. Boorman, "Wang Ching-wei," 504–525.

12. I am thinking here, of course, of *Chairman Mao Goes to Anyuan* (*Mao zhuxi qu Anyuan*), the 1968 painting by Liu Chunhua, which is purported to be one of the most widely circulated images in history. On this, see Elizabeth J. Perry, "Reclaiming the Chinese Revolution," *Journal of Asian Studies* 67, no. 4 (November 2008): 1147–1164. The image of Wang I am describing here was printed on the cover of *Time* 25, no. 11 (March 1935).

13. Claire Roberts, *Photography in China* (Hong Kong: Hong Kong University Press, 2013), 73–75.

14. Ibid., 75.

15. As was the case with Seyuan Shu, ed., *Poems of Wang Ching-wei* (London: George Allen and Unwin, 1938).

16. He Peng, "Yi wei sheyingshi yanli de Wang Jingwei" [Wang Jingwei in the eyes of a photographer], *Shijixing* (May 1995): 34–36.

17. Zhou Anqing, "Wang Jingwei shi zenyang guizang Nanjing Meihuashan de" [How Wang Jingwei was buried on Plum Blossom Mount], *Dongfang shoucang* 1 (2012): 116–118.

18. "Wang Zhaoming qiantian zai zhongyang yiyuan bingta shang sheying (guojishe)" [Wang Zhaoming lying on a sickbed in the central hospital two days ago (TASS)], *Li bao*, November 17, 1935.

19. On this event, see Jiang Yingjing, "Hu Shi and Wang Jingwei: Discussions on Sino-Japanese Issues before and after the War of Resistance against Japan," *Chinese Studies in History* 42, no. 1 (2008): 34.

20. John A. Lent and Xu Ying, *Comics Art in China* (Jackson: University Press of Mississippi, 2017).

21. Wen Shaohua, *Cong lieshi dao hanjian*, 59.

22. On the political significance of such clothing, see Antonia Finnane, *Changing Clothes in China: Fashion, History, Nation* (New York: Columbia University Press 2008), 180.

23. For a text-heavy collection of Peace Movement propaganda from this period, see Nanhua ribaoshe, ed., *Nanhua ribao gaikuang* [The current state of affairs for the *South China Daily*] (Hong Kong: Nanhua ribaoshe, 1941).

24. Such imagery was, in fact, referred to as a weapon by observers at the time. On anti-Wang caricatures as weapons, see A. L. Bader, "China's New Weapon—Caricature," *American Scholar* 10, no. 2 (Spring 1941): 228–240.

25. For examples of this sort of material, see "Fensui Wang ni wei zuzhi zhi xuanchuan chuandan" [Propaganda pamphlets for ruining the bogus organizations of the turncoat Wang], 1939, KMT, yi ban, 537/21.

26. Such images were featured in collections such as Xu Daren, ed., *Wang Jingwei ma Wang Zhaoming* [Wang Jingwei curses Wang Zhaoming] (Cunjinqiao: Lingnan chubanshe, 1939).

27. This approach appears to have been particularly common in art produced by cartoonists associated with the CCP. See Zhongguo geming bowuguan, *Kang-Ri zhanzheng shiqi xuanchuanhua* [Propaganda images from the period of the War of Resistance] (Beijing: Wenwu chubanshe, 1990), 169.

28. "Tao Wang su jian yundong xuanchuan dawang" [Propaganda outlines for opposing Wang and traitors], April 1940, KMT, yi ban, 155/141. This document advised that such *guixiang* would depict both Wang and his wife, Chen Bijun, and that they would be erected in front of tombs for the "unnamed hero" (*wuming yingxiong*) in unoccupied China.

29. On the Qin Kuai statue in Hangzhou, see Huang Donglan, "Shrines of Yue Fei: Spaces for Creation of Public Memory," *Chinese Sociology and Anthropology* 37, no. 23 (2005): 74–112.

30. A full page of such designs and instructions on their use can be found in *Qingqi manhua* 44 (n.d.), held in a collection entitled "Zhong-Ri zhanzheng qijian shishi manhua" [Topical cartoons from the period of the Sino-Japanese War], Special Collections, East Asia Library, Stanford University.

31. One of the earliest depictions in graphic art that I have come across from 1939 is a pamphlet produced by the Xinminhui in north China, entitled *Se yanjing* [Colored spectacles] (Beijing: Xinminhui, 1939), HIA, David Nelson Rowe Papers, 78064, Box 10. Published in January 1939, this graphic text tells the story of an optometrist's store owned jointly by Chiang Kai-shek and Mao Zedong, who are selling *kang-Ri yanjing* (anti-Japanese glasses). Wearing these spectacles, the people of China are oblivious to the corruption of the Nationalists and communists but are willing to run blindly into battle as cannon fodder. Only a cartoon Wang Jingwei sees through the ploy, smashing his tinted spectacles on the ground with the words: "I don't want these!"

32. The only specific date I have been able to locate for this image is one attached to it in the Hawai'i Times Photo Archives, where a scan of the portrait lists the image (object no. ddr-njpa-1-1063) as having arrived at the offices of the *Hawai'i Times* (a Japanese-language newspaper based in Honolulu) on July 12, 1939. Available at http://ddr.densho.org/ddr-njpa-1-1063-master-4853ea7569/.

33. Bate, *Wang Ching Wei,* 146–149.

34. Intriguingly, the *Central China Daily News* (*Zhonghua ribao*) only published the image for the first time on August 31, 1939 (i.e., well after other sources had published it). The first instance of its use in that newspaper was with an article entitled "Zhongguo Guomindang zai Hu juxing diliu ci quanguo daibiao dahui" [The sixth national congress of the Kuomintang is convened in Shanghai], *Zhonghua ribao,* August 31, 1939, 1. However, the *Tairiku shinpō* credited the image to the *Central China Daily News* when it first published the image on the front page of its evening edition on July 11, 1939.

35. Tai Shi Gong, "Tingshen fenqi heping jiuguo" [Lifting himself upright to save the nation through peace], *Huawen Daban meiri* 3, no. 5 (September 1939): 4.

36. For example, see "Qingzhu guomin zhengfu huandu tekan" [Special edition to commemorate the return of the national government], *Zhong bao,* March 30, 1940, 1.

37. See, for example, Anonymous, "Wang zhuxi fang Ri zuo fan jing" [Chairman Wang returned to Nanjing yesterday after a visit to Japan], *Zhong bao,* September 24, 1943, 1.

38. Such as Xuanchuanbu, *Wang zhuxi heping jianguo yanlunji* [Collection of Chairman Wang's speeches on peace and nation building] (Nanjing: Xuanchuanbu, 1941).

39. Ministry of Publicity, *Special Commemoration Issue.*

40. "Wangiana" is a term I have adapted from Bonnell, *Iconography of Power* (in which the term "Leniniana" is used to refer to cultural products created to celebrate Lenin in the Soviet Union).

41. Daminhui xuanchuanbu, *Wang Jingwei xiansheng yu xin zhongyang zhengfu* [Mr. Wang Jingwei and the new central government] (Nanjing: Daminhui, 1940).

42. These examples are drawn from multiple issues of the RGROC-affiliated magazine *Xin Dong Ya* (New East Asia).

43. Cai Dejin, *Zhou Fohai riji quanbian, shangbian,* 262. The extant photographic record suggests that such paintings were rarely hung in public spaces. I have yet to see a photograph of an RNG office in which anything other than a photographic portrait of Wang was hung.

44. As evidenced in a photograph of Wang posing for a painting with Asai himself: *Wang Jingwei Having His Portrait Painted,* August 16, 1940, object no. ddr-njpa-1–1067 (G388.040), Denshō Digital Repository, http://ddr.densho.org/ddr-njpa-1-1067/.

45. A color woodblock print, possibly based on the 1940 Asai oil painting but produced by Yamaguchi Susumu in 1943, is held at the British Museum (item no. 2015,3025.1).

46. "Weiren yu ming shi yanyao" [The world-famous eyedrops of great men], *Zhonghua ribao,* March 30, 1940, 11.

47. Jeremy E. Taylor, "Republican Personality Cults in Wartime China: Contradistinction and Collaboration," *Comparative Studies in Society and History* 57, no. 3 (2015): 665–693.

48. Jan Plamper, *The Stalin Cult: A Study in the Alchemy of Power* (New Haven, CT: Yale University Press, 2012), 14–15.

49. This point is raised, for example, in Mitter, "Contention and Redemption."

50. MacKinnon, *War, Refugees,* 78–79. For an account of the work of the PDMAC penned by one of its employees, see Yi Junzuo, *Shengli yu huandu* [Victory and return to the capital] (Taipei: Sanmin shuju, 1970).

51. "Guofu yixiang ji zhuxi xiaoxiang zhizuo shenqing shencha banfa" [Regulations on the applications for the making of portraits of the father of the nation and the chairman], December 11, 1943, KMT, huiyi, 5.3/221.9.

52. "Xuanchuan yaodian diershiba tiao: Guanyu huandu yi zhounian jinian" [Propaganda directive number 28: On the commemoration of the first anniversary of the *huandu*], March 17, 1941, SMA, R18-1-54.

53. *Guangdong sheng zhengfu chengli zhounian jinian yuebing dianli* [Military parade celebrating the first anniversary of the founding of the Guangdong Provincial Government], photograph, April 1941, AH, Wang Zhaoming shiliao, 118-030400-0001-014.

54. Anonymous, "President Wang Ching-wei in Uniform," *Xin Zhonghua huabao* 3, no. 10 (October 1941).

55. The original image is now held by Getty Images (editorial no. 514876566) but was used in countless RNG publications in one form or another until the end of the war.

56. Anonymous, "Wang weiyuanzhang san ci xunshi qingxiangqu ji" [An account of Chairman Wang's third tour of the Rural Pacification areas], *Zhongyang daobao zhoukan* 2, no. 39 (April 1942): 19.

57. Thus stated the oath that Shanghai-based followers of the NCM were expected to read. "Xin guomin yundong wan zhong qian zhe ce" [New Citizens Movement oath to be signed by the masses], February 1942, SMA, R48-1-1445.

58. "Gongzuo baogao" [Work report], April 1942, SHA, 2003-1-2035.

59. Examples of Wang Chuan's work from this period can be found in SMA, R18-1-387.

60. Tan Qixu, *Wang zhuxi fang Ri tekan* [Special supplement on Chairman Wang's visit to Japan] (Tokyo: Yuandong yuebaoshe, 1941).

61. "Wang wei xuanchuanbu wei cheng qing chajin bu liang fenzi wumo zhuxi xuanchuan xiang" [Investigation by the bogus Wang regime's Ministry of Publicity on the smearing of the chairman's portrait by an undesirable element], July–August 1941, SHA, 2003-1-2201.

62. "Hangxian Linpingzhen gongmin Zhong Chenzong feng cheng qing chajin qiang shou yuanshou xiaoxiang jinian zhang de youguan wenshu" [Documents relating to the illegal sale of badges bearing portraits of the head of state by Zhong Chenzong and other residents in Linping Township], March–June 1943, SHA, 2003-1-2070.

63. Telegram from Wang Jingwei to Li Shiqun, March 1, 1943, AH, Wang Zhaoming shiliao, 18-010100-0047-070.

64. Barrett, "Wang Jingwei Regime," 105.

65. Suggesting a clear link between the NCM, Wang, the navy, youth, and health—exploited, in this case, by the ubiquitous Jintan. See *Huawen Daban meiri* 8, no. 9 (May 1942): front cover.

66. https://exhibits.stanford.edu/wangjingwei.

67. Wang Jingwei, "Wang zhuxi dui quanguo guangbo" [Chairman Wang broadcasts to the people of the nation], *Changjiang huakan* 1 (February 1942).

68. As was the case in *Zhonghua huabao* 1, no. 3 (October 1943).

69. On earlier (and largely unsuccessful) attempts at the manufacture of Wang badges, see Jing Shenghong, *Nanjing lunxian banian shi (xia)* [The eight-year history of Nanjing's occupation, part 2] (Beijing: Shehui kexue wenxian chubanshe, 2013).

70. "In many of the advanced countries around the world," read instructions from the Ministry of Publicity, "almost every single person wears an image of their leader out of respect. Why is it that even in this minor issue we are unable to keep up?" See "Wei qing qiu tuixing zhuxi xiaoxiang jinianzhang zhun yu fenling ge xuexiao" [On the promotion of badges bearing the chairman's portrait and their distribution to all schools], September 4, 1943, SMA, R48-H112.

71. Asahi Shimbun Co., *Media, Propaganda and Politics in 20th-Century Japan,* trans. Barak Kushner (London: Bloomsbury, 2015), 85.

72. On the INA in China, see Nirmola Sharma, "Collaborators! Aftermath of Wartime Support for the INA among Indians in China," *China Report* 54, no. 3 (2018): 325–340.

73. Mario Prayer, "Nationalist India and World War II as Seen by the Italian Fascist Press, 1938–1944," *Indian Historical Review* 23, no. 2 (July 2006): 111.

74. Anonymous, "Wang zhuxi banian qian liu dan, anran quchu" [A bullet left in Chairman Wang eight years ago is safely extracted], *Zhonghua huabao* 2, no. 1 (February 1944): 2–3.

75. Chan Cheong-Choo, *Memoirs of a Citizen of Early XXth Century China* (n.p.: 1978), 133–134.

76. Boyle, *China and Japan at War,* 323–328.
77. Harrison, *Making of the Republican Citizen,* 134.
78. Wen Shaohua, *Cong lieshi dao hanjian,* 331.
79. It can be viewed here: https://www.gettyimages.co.uk/detail/video/dignitaries-mourners-and-the-widow-chen-bijun-are-at-the-news-footage/505940049. On the Nippon Newsreel Company, see R. W. Purdy, "The Creation of the Nippon Newsreel Company: Personal Rivalry and Profit in Wartime Japan," *Historical Journal of Film, Radio and Television* 36, no. 3 (2016): 252–372.
80. Zhongyang dianxunshe, *Shishi tongxun: Jing'ai Wang zhuxi* [Topical communications: Mourning Chairman Wang] (Nanjing: Zhongyang dianxunshe, 1944), 9.
81. Such details are included in "Ge di zhi Wang zhuxi aidian weiyuanhui de dianwen" [Telegrams from various places to the committee on mourning for Chairman Wang], 1944, SHA, 2003-1-5834.
82. Ōta Unosuke, "Ji Wang zhuxi anzang dianli" [On Chairman Wang's funeral], *Zhengzhi yuekan* 8, no. 6 (1944): 15–16.
83. The claim is made in Anonymous, "Wang Jingwei si hou miwen" [Posthumous secrets about Wang Jingwei], *Hanjian choushi* (February 1945): 28–31.
84. Maps published to aid mourners in locating Wang's tomb showed its location vis-à-vis both of these sites. See, for instance, "Yi dai weiren de anzangdi: Meihuashan" [The resting place of a great man of our age: Meihuashan], *Zhong bao,* November 24, 1944, 1.
85. Cheng Jie, "Minguo shiqi Zhongshan lingyuan meihua fengjing de jianshe yu yanbian" [The construction and changes to plum blossom scenery in the Sun Yat-sen Mausoleum area during the Republican era], *Nanjing shehui kexue* 2 (2011): 151–156.
86. Though preliminary plans were made to establish a "Mr. Wang Memorial Hall" (Wang xiansheng jiniantang), these never came to fruition. See "Shanghai tebie shi jingjiju wei song jianli Wang xiansheng mubei juankuan shihan" [Correspondence to the Shanghai Municipal Government Economic Bureau regarding donations for building tombstones for Mr. Wang], 1945, SMA, R13-1-133-1.
87. Details about the dimensions of the tomb can be found in Zhou Anqing, "Wang Jingwei shi zenyang guizang Nanjing Meihuashan de."
88. Zhang Yan, *Nanjing minguo jianzhu yishu* [Republican architectural art in Nanjing] (Nanjing: Jiangsu kexue jishu chubanshe, 2000), 104–105.
89. Zhongyang dianxunshe, *Shishi tongxun: Jing'ai Wang zhuxi,* 8–10.
90. Ibid.
91. Bunker, *Peace Conspiracy,* 285.
92. This claim about the nature of Wang's resting place in Nanjing is made in Mitter, *China's War with Japan,* 357.
93. On this, see Jeremy E. Taylor, "The Production of the Chiang Kai-shek Personality Cult, 1929–1975," *China Quarterly* 185 (March 2006): 96–110.

Chapter 4: Gendered and Generational Archetypes

A number of paragraphs in this chapter are drawn and developed from Jeremy E. Taylor, "Gendered Archetypes of Wartime Occupation: 'New Women' in Occupied North China, 1937–40," *Gender and History* 28, no. 3 (2016): 660–686. They are used here with the permission of Wiley.

1. Yun Xia, *Down with Traitors: Justice and Nationalism in Wartime China* (Seattle: University of Washington Press, 2017); Liu Jiurong, *Ta de shenpan: Jindai Zhongguo guozu yu xingbie yiyi xia de zhongjian zhibian* [Her trials: Contextualizing loyalty and disloyalty in modern China from a gendered nationalist perspective] (Taipei: Zhongyang yanjiuyuan, 2013).

2. I will return to Huang's work later in this chapter.

3. Muel-Dreyfus, *Vichy and the Eternal Feminine.*

4. On this, see Nadje Al-Ali and Nicola Pratt, *What Kind of Liberation? Women and the Occupation of Iraq* (Berkeley: University of California Press, 2009), esp. 82–83.

5. Prasenjit Duara, *Sovereignty and Authenticity: Manchukuo and the East Asian Modern* (Lanham, MD: Rowman and Littlefield, 2003), 143.

6. Louise Edwards, "Policing the Modern Woman in Republican Shanghai," *Modern China* 26, no. 2 (2000): 115–147.

7. J. E. Taylor, "Gendered Archetypes." For more on the place of the "modern girl" in the prewar New Life movement, see Hsiao-pei Yen, "Body Politics, Modernity and National Salvation: The Modern Girl and the New Life Movement," *Asian Studies Review* 29, no. 2 (2005): 165–186.

8. Smith, *Resisting Manchukuo,* 32–33.

9. Ōnuma Kikuo [Da zhao Xi jiu nan], *Xinmin zhuyi zhi lilun ji qi zhankai* [The theory of the New People's ideology and its development] (Beijing: Da Dong Ya wenhua yuanjiuhui, 1944), 212–213.

10. J. E. Taylor, "Gendered Archetypes."

11. See, for example, Li Ming, "Funüjie dui guojia yingjin zhi zeren" [The responsibilities that womanhood should hold for the nation], *Xin Zhongguo* 2, no. 11–12 (December 1939): 50–52.

12. Shi Li, "Qiqi jinian funü ying you zhi renshi" [How women should view the anniversary of July 7], in *Qiqi Dong Ya minzu jiefang erzhou nian jinianji* (Commemorative collection marking the second anniversary of July 7, 1937, and the liberation of the Asian nations), ed. Daminhui (Nanjing: Daminhui, 1939), 54–57.

13. J. E. Taylor, "Gendered Archetypes," 669.

14. E. Taylor Atkins, *Primitive Selves: Koreana in the Japanese Colonial Gaze, 1910–1945* (Berkeley: University of California Press, 2010), 183.

15. "*Guniang*" and "*kūnyan*" were terms used in Japanese texts as euphemisms for "prostitute." Stefano Romagnoli, "Gendering the War: The Colonial Gaze in Hino Ashihei's *Hana to heitai,*" *Rivista degli studi orientali* 90, no. 1–4 (2016): 141–162.

16. Zhao Mengyun [Chou Muun], "Katō Minosuke to senji Shanhai *Tairiku shinpō* jidai no manga, man hanashi o chūshin ni" [Katō Minosuke's wartime Shanghai: Desultory narratives and sociopolitical cartoons from the *Tairiku shinpō*], *Chūgoku bunka kenkyū* 25 (2009): 21–46.

17. Tani E. Barlow, "Buying In: Advertising and the Sexy Modern Girl Icon in Shanghai in the 1920s and 1930s," in *The Modern Girl around the World: Consumption, Modernity, Globalization,* ed. Alys Eve Weinbaum et al. (Durham, NC: Duke University Press, 2008), 289.

18. Yen, "Body Politics," 166.

19. Ibid.

20. Madeleine Y. Dong, "Who Is Afraid of the Chinese Modern Girl?" in *The Modern Girl around the World: Consumption, Modernity, Globalization,* ed. Alys Eve Weinbaum et al. (Durham, NC: Duke University Press, 2008), 197–198.

21. One example of this was the Wuhan-based Wha Sun Cigarettes (Huasheng yancao gongsi), which filled the pages of newspapers such as the *Dachu bao* with "modern girl"–themed advertisements for its products but was also a regular sponsor of pro-regime notices in the same outlets.

22. Norman Smith, "Opiate Addiction and the Entanglements of Imperialism and Patriarchy in Manchukuo," *Social History of Alcohol and Drugs* 20 (2005): 67.

23. Chikako Nagayama, "Race as Technology and Blurred National Boundaries in Japanese Imperialism: *Nessa no chikai/Vow in the Desert,*" *Transnational Cinemas* 3 (2012): 211–230.

24. Shepherdson-Scott, "Race behind the Walls."

25. Vera C. Mackie, "Shanghai Dancers: Gender, Coloniality, and the Modern Girl," in *Shadowlines: Women and Borders in Contemporary Asia,* ed. D. Ghosh (Newcastle, UK: Cambridge Scholars, 2012), 80–95.

26. The photo shoot appears to have been conducted by a Mainichi photographer called Ono Isamu, although the material published in the *Kabun* provides only Ono's surname.

27. Anonymous, "Zhishang gongying: Riji yi ye" (Movie on paper: Page from a diary), *Huawen Daban meiri* 6, no. 1 (January 1941).

28. See, for instance, an unattributed photograph captioned as "Zhong-Ri funüjie de xiang qin xiang ai" [Mutual affection and love between Japanese and Chinese women], *Xin Zhongguo* 2, no. 11–12 (December 1939).

29. Ellen Johnston Laing, *Selling Happiness: Calendar Posters and Visual Culture in Early Twentieth-Century Shanghai* (Honolulu: University of Hawai'i Press, 2004).

30. On the origins of this story in the Northern Wei dynasty (386–534 CE) and its later adaptations, see Louise Edwards, "Transformations of the Woman Warrior Hua Mulan: From Defender of the Family to Servant of the State," *Nannü* 12, no. 2 (2010): 175–214.

31. Poshek Fu, "Projecting Ambivalence: Chinese Cinema in Semi-occupied Shanghai, 1937–41," in *Wartime Shanghai,* ed. Wen-hsin Yeh (London: Routledge, 1998), 86–110.

32. Shiamin Kwa and Wilt Idema, introduction to *Mulan: Five Versions of a Classic Chinese Legend, with Related Chinese Texts,* ed. Shiamin Kwa and Wilt Idema (Indianapolis: Hackett Publishing, 2010), xxviii.

33. Chan's role as the celebrity face of the regime has been redacted from the fan literature produced about her in more recent years. See, for example, Anonymous, *Yi dai yinghou Chen Yunshang* [Movie queen of the age, Nancy Chan] (Beijing: Xinhua shudian, 2001).

34. Yin Jian, "Chen Yunshang: Heping de zhen qin" [Nancy Chan: Chaste bird of peace], *Funü shijie* 1, no. 1 (April 1940): 13.

35. See, for example, "Dong Ya yingxing jieshao" [Introducing East Asian stars], *Nanjing xinbao,* February 18, 1940.

36. This transformation is retold in Qin Yi, "1937–1948 nian bankan zhong de Chen Yunshang" [Coverage of Nancy Chan in the press from 1937 to 1938], *Xiju yu yingshi yishu yanjiu* (April 2016): 122–127.

37. It was a print of Chan, wearing a fascinator and a Western blouse, that was chosen for the cover of *Xin Zhonghua huabao* 7, no. 4 (July 1942)—an issue in which a significant amount of copy was dedicated to the formation of the CUP. Chen, however, would appear on the cover of dozens of occupation-era film magazines.

38. I am basing such generalizations on the rich and varied collection of film magazines from this period now held in the Paul Kendel Fonoroff Collection for Chinese Film Studies, C. V. Starr East Asian Library, University of University of California, Berkeley.

39. For more on Dong Tianye and other occupation cartoonists who worked with the modern girl image, see J. E. Taylor, "Cartoons and Collaboration."

40. See, for example, Zhang Ziping, "Xin hong A zi." This story was illustrated with a series of line drawings of modern girls by Cao Hanmei.

41. J. E. Taylor, "Cartoons and Collaboration."

42. This was the main criticism in essays on cartooning, for example. See Liu Zi, "Huazhong de manhua wenti" [The problem with cartoons in central China], *Huawen Daban meiri* 7, no. 4 (August 1941): 22.

43. Ironically, photographs held in the Chu Minyi Photograph Collection (Lot 11700), Prints and Photographs Reading Room, LOC, reveal a world in which leading members of the RNG (though not, it would seem, Lin Baisheng or Wang Jingwei) and their male guests would frequently be escorted by modern girls on social occasions.

44. Zhongyang dianxunshe, *Shishi tongxun: Zhongguo funü wenti* [Topical communications: The question of Chinese women] (Nanjing: Zhongyang dianxunshe, 1945), 13.

45. Dong Tianye, "Chen Yunshang dapo kongbudang" [Nancy Chan destroys terrorists], *Zhongguo manhua* 1 (November 1942): 7–8.

46. Barlow examines the "sexy modern girl icon with her Flit gun" in "Buying In."

47. One such advertisement appears on the back cover of *Xin Zhonghua huabao* 6, no. 5 (May 1944). Tellingly, the same issue included a cover image of Burmese women in traditional dress and a photographic feature on Subhas Chandra Bose's Rani of Jhansi Regiment (an all-female regiment belonging to the Japanese-backed Indian National Army).

48. On this, see Craig Clunas, "China: Art, War, and Salvation," public lecture, Gresham College (London), February 19, 2018.

49. N. Huang, *Women, War, Domesticity,* 86.

50. Ibid., 88–89.

51. Shelley Stephenson, "A Star by Any Other Name: The (After) Lives of Li Xianglan," *Quarterly Review of Film and Radio* 19, no. 1 (2002): 1–13.

52. Gunn, *Unwelcome Muse,* 26.

53. Mark Gamsa, "Sergei Tret'iakov's *Roar, China!* Between Moscow and China," *Itinerario* 36, no. 2 (August 2012): 91–108.

54. "Nuhou ba Zhongguo!" [Roar, China!], *Zhong bao,* January 17, 1943.

55. "Gongzuo baogao" [Work report], January 1943, SHA, 2003-1-2034.

56. Zhou Yuren, *Nuhou ba Zhongguo* [Roar, China!] (Nanjing: Nanjing juyishe, 1943), script.

57. Qiu Kunliang, "Funi yu kangdi: Wang Jingwei zhengquan de xijujie" [Associating with turncoats and attacking the enemy: Drama under the Wang Jingwei regime], *Xiju yanjiu* 15 (January 2015): 117–148.

58. "Gongzuo baogao" [Work report], March 1943, SHA, 2003-1-2034.

59. The story had, after all, been invoked in *huobaoju* (living newspaper) form by resistance dramatists in 1937. Ke Fu, "Zhongguo nuhou le! Huobao juben" [Roar, China! Living newspaper script], *Shi shi leibian tekan* 4 (1937): 51–54.

60. Xiaobing Tang, "Echoes of *Roar, China!* On Vision and Voice in Modern Chinese Art," *positions* 14, no. 2 (2006): 467–494.

61. Daminhui artists such as Yan Sanyuan (whose illustrations were also featured prominently in the *Zhonghua ribao*), for example, celebrated the figure of the anonymous, pole-bearing coolie in woodcuts in 1940, in *Damin* 5, no. 3 (May 1940).

62. Wang Yingxiao, "Fa kan ci" [Remarks on the publication of the journal], *Zhongguo muke* 1 (December 1942).

63. A series of Li Hua woodcuts, including nature and village scenes, was featured in the Wuhan-based *Changjiang huakan* 4, no. 2 (March 1942).

64. X. Tang, "Echoes of *Roar, China!*" 473.

65. For example, one woodcut, published as *Matou shang* (On the docks) in *Zhongguo muke* 3 (February 1943), was attributed to an artist listed simply as "Hankei," a Japanese name.

66. Wang Yingxiao, "Yu er" [Second foreword], in *Qingxiang mukeji: Canzhan zhi ji* [Rural Pacification woodcut collection: Declaration of war edition], ed. Wang Yingxiao (Suzhou: Guomindang qingxiangqu dangwu banshichu, 1943).

67. Xia, *Down with Traitors,* 125.

68. Andrea Germer, "Adapting Russian Constructivism and Socialist Realism: The Japanese Overseas Photo Magazine *FRONT* (1942–1945)," *Studies in Contemporary History* 12 (2015): 236–263.

69. Anonymous, "Guofu huandu hou xin junren de yucheng" [The cultivation of new China's soldiers since the return of the national government], *Dong Ya Lianmeng huabao* 3, no. 3 (February 1943).

70. On the strict uniformity of dress and grooming adhered to in Manchukuo military academies, see Carter J. Eckert, *Park Chung Hee and Modern Korea: The Roots of Militarism, 1866–1945* (Cambridge, MA: Belknap Press, 2016), 111.

71. For anti–Blue Shirt literature produced under the RNG, see this book detailing Lanyishe atrocities: Chen Gongshu, *Lanyishe de neimu* [The inside story on the Blue Shirts] (Shanghai: Guomin xinwen tushu, 1942).

72. Most noticeably, the Xinminhui. "The so-called 'New People's Movement' [i.e., of the Xinminhui] is fundamentally the same as the New Citizens Movement," wrote one CNA cadre: Lu Yifeng, *Xinminhui yu xin guomin yundong* [The Xinminhui and the New Citizens Movement] (Nanjing: Zhongyang dianxunshe, 1944), 1.

73. Kristin Mulready-Stone, *CCP Internationalism, GMD Nationalism, and Japanese Collaboration* (London: Routledge, 2015), 141–163.

74. Lei Yimin, "Xin guomin yundong yu qingshaonian" [The NCM and the youth], *Beiping yuekan* 1, no. 2 (1943): 42–46.

75. MacKinnon, *War, Refugees,* 89.

76. "Xin guomin yundong wan zhong qian zhe ce" [New Citizens Movement oath to be signed by the masses], February 1942, SMA, R48-1-1445.

77. On this, see Horii Koichiro, "Ō Chōmei seiken ka sō dōin taisei no kōchiku to minshū" [The general public mobilization system under the Wang Jingwei regime:

Formation and popular participation], *Nihon Daigaku daigakuin sōgō shakai jōhō kenkyū ka kiyō* 9 (2008): 39–50.

78. The English word "gentlemen" is used in the original text.

79. Zhongyang dianxunshe, *Qingnian xunlian yu xiuyang* [The training and fostering of youth] (Nanjing: Zhongyang dianxunshe, 1942), 32–34.

80. One account details hundreds of RNG students who were in Nanjing to celebrate the third anniversary of the *huandu* listening to a public speech by the head of the RNG's Examination Yuan (Kaoshiyuan), Jiang Kanghu, who suggested that "peace is not surrender, and surrender is not peace!" See Chen Zijia [Jin Xiongbai], *Wangchao miyan lu, san* [Secret records of the Wang dynasty, volume 3] (Hong Kong: Yuzhou chubanshe, 1964), 2.

81. "Wang wei xuanchuanbu guanyu Zhong-Ri tongmeng Dong Ya lianhe gongshi zhuan an" [Bogus Ministry of Publicity files on the Sino-Japanese Pact of Alliance and the united East Asian offensive], October–December 1943, SHA, 2003-1-2168.

82. On this, see Margarita Tupitsyn, *The Soviet Photograph, 1924–1937* (New Haven, CT: Yale University Press, 1996), 106–107.

83. Lu Guowei, "Yu yi" [First foreword], in *Qingxiang mukeji: Canzhan zhi ji,* ed. Wang Yingxiao (Suzhou: Guomindang qingxiangqu dangwu banshichu, 1943).

84. This description of a "fascist aesthetic" is taken from Wendy Larson, "Zhang Yimou's *Hero:* Dismantling the Myth of Cultural Power," *Journal of Chinese Cinemas* 2, no. 3 (2008): 183.

85. Anonymous, *Dai Tōa shashin nenpō* [Photographic annual of Greater East Asia] (Tokyo: Dōmei Tsūshinsha, 1943).

86. Anonymous, "Quanguo minzhong, dadao Ying-Mei zong dongyuan" [General mobilization of the masses to overthrow Britain and America], *Zhonghua huabao* 1, no. 1 (August 1943): 8–9.

87. The episode is retold in Martin, " 'In My Heart.' "

88. Martin (ibid.) suggests that youth groups were mobilized by Lin Baisheng for strictly factional purposes.

89. On Sha Fei, see Claire Roberts, *Photography and China,* 92–94.

90. A term I borrow in this context from Jorge Dagnino, Matthew Feldman, and Paul Stoker, "Building Illiberal Subjects: The New Man in the Radical Right Universe, 1919–45," in *The "New Man" in Radical Right Ideology and Practice, 1919–45,* ed. Jorge Dagnino, Matthew Feldman, and Paul Stoker (London: Bloomsbury, 2018), 1–15.

91. Germer, "Adapting Russian Constructivism."

Chapter 5: Rivers and Mountains

1. Huang Qingshu [Wong Hing-sue], *Wang zhuxi fang Ri jinian huakan.* A person surnamed Suogeluofu (possibly Sergalov, Segalov, or Shugalov) is credited with the "artistic design" of the book.

2. On the adoption of Yue Fei as a symbol for the anti-Japanese resistance, see Huang Donglan, "Shrines of Yue Fei."

3. Stephen Daniels and Denis Cosgrove, "Introduction: Iconography and Landscape," in *The Iconography of Landscape: Essays on the Symbolic Representation, Design and Use of Past Environments,* ed. Denis Cosgrove and Stephen Daniels (Cambridge: Cambridge University Press, 1988), 1.

4. Ironically, however, much of the impetus behind the promotion of *guohua* in the prewar years had been anger about Japanese imperialism in China. On this topic, see Pedith Pui Chan, *The Making of a Modern Art World: Institutionalisation and Legitimisation of* Guohua *in Republican Shanghai* (Boston: Brill, 2017), 171–174.

5. Clunas, "China: Art, War, and Salvation."

6. Chen Xinhe, "Zhongguo huihua zhu qingxiang" [Trends in Chinese painting], *Huawen Daban meiri* 9, no. 10 (November 1942): 46.

7. Sullivan, *Art and Artists,* 107–110.

8. Claire Roberts, *Friendship in Art: Fou Lei and Huang Binhong* (Hong Kong: Hong Kong University Press, 2010), 58.

9. Fu, *Passivity, Resistance, and Collaboration,* 130–131.

10. Cao Hanmei, "Dianzhong huasheng" [Painting manual from central Yunnan], *Guoyi* 3, no. 4 (September 1941).

11. "Gongzuo baogao" [Work report], March 1943, SHA, 2003-1-2034. Lin had been associated with the resistance in Guangzhou early in the war and had relocated first to Hong Kong and then to Macao to escape the Japanese. However, her claims to an impeccably revolutionary (and Cantonese) heritage—her father was one of the "seventy-two martyrs" entombed at Huanghuagang—may have represented too much of a temptation for MoP cadres to ignore.

12. Shen Enyang, "Kang-Ri zhanzheng shiqi de Aomen meishu" [Fine art in Macao during the War of Resistance], *Nanjing yishu xueyan xuebao* (March 2009): 93–99.

13. "Wang wei xuanchuanbu niqing buzhu Riben Da Dong Ya bolanhui [Bogus Ministry of Publicity files on the invitation to subsidize Japan's Greater East Asia Exposition], October–September 1942, SHA, 2003-1-2157.

14. On *sensōga* in China, see Mark. H. Sandler, "A Painter of the 'Holy War': Fujita Tsuguji and the Japanese Military," in *War, Occupation, and Creativity: Japan and East Asia, 1920–1960,* ed. Marlene J. Mayo, J. Thomas Rimer, and E. Eleanor Kerkham (Honolulu: University of Hawai'i Press, 2001), 188–211.

15. Xuanchuanbu, *Guomin zhengfu zhi jinzhan* [The progress of the national government] (Nanjing: Xuanchuanbu, 1941), 68.

16. Hochberg, *Visual Occupations,* 5.

17. This approach contrasted with that of the Chongqing Nationalists, who fetishized the map of China in their propaganda. For an example, see Ministry of Information (China), *Introducing China* (Sydney, 1944), which has a stylized map of China on its cover.

18. Such as maps regularly included in this organization's own pictorial, *Go So shunjū: Naka Shina gurafu* [Lower Yangtze seasons: Central China graphic], copies of which are held at the Tōyō Bunko library.

19. RNG agencies accomplished this, for example, by including China within a borderless Asia. This observation is made by Torsten Weber in "Imagined Territoriality: Visual Portrayals of 'Asia' in the Age of Nationalism in East Asia," *Comparativ* 23 (2013): 37–56.

20. These are now held in the David Nelson Rowe Papers (78064), esp. Box 10, HIA, Stanford University.

21. David Nelson Rowe, "Japanese Propaganda in North China, 1937–1938," *Public Opinion Quarterly* 3, no. 4 (October 1939): 564–580.

22. "Zhongguo ming'an tu" [Map of light and darkness in China], NIDS, Chūō gunji gyōsei jōhō [Central military administration intelligence files], 69.

23. Mark Dorrian and Frédéric Pousin, introduction to *Seeing from Above: The Aerial View in Visual Culture,* ed. Mark Dorrian and Frédéric Pousin (London: I. B. Tauris, 2013), 1–10.

24. Such imagery did find its way into early propaganda published by the CNA, despite being created by Japanese agencies. An image taken from the perspective of Japanese bombers over Chongqing was reproduced in Zhongyang dianxunshe, *Guofu huandu hou de zhengzhi qingshi,* 14.

25. On this, see Parks M. Coble, "Writing about Atrocity: Wartime Accounts and Their Contemporary Uses," *Modern Asian Studies* 45, no. 2 (2011): 379–398.

26. The photo spread "Youjiu de Zhongguo" (Eternal China) was published in *Huawen Daban meiri* 4, no. 8 (April 1940). Presumably, RNG luminaries would have noticed that all but one of these sites or topographical features lay in that area of China governed by the North China Political Affairs Commission and hence beyond the realm of actual RNG control.

27. Warnke, *Political Landscape,* 53.

28. On Nanjing as it was featured in *sensōga* in 1939, see Jing Shanshan, "Nanjing lunxian shiqi, Ri-wei dui meishu, sheying, dianying de kongzhi yu liyong" [The control and use of the fine arts, photography, and cinema by the Japanese and the bogus regime in occupied Nanjing], *Shihai tanji* (July 2014): 60–64.

29. Guo Xiufeng, "Yu" [Foreword], in *E Gan shidi shichaji* [A field survey of Hubei and Jiangxi], by Xue Huizi (Nanjing: Zhongyang dianxunshe, 1940), i.

30. Xue Huizi, *E Gan shidi shichaji* [A field survey of Hubei and Jiangxi], with photographs by Xue Diwei (Nanjing: Zhongyang dianxunshe, 1940).

31. Xue Huizi, "Shinian ai le" [Ten years of sorrow and joy], *Taiping zhoubao* 1, no. 55 (1943): 1074–1076.

32. Xue Huizi, *Jinri zhi Huabei* [North China today], with photographs by He Zhang (Nanjing: Zhongyang dianxunshe, 1940).

33. Another example is Liu Longguang, "Heping de zuguo zhi xing" [Journey through a peaceful motherland], *Huawen Daban meiri* 6, no. 2 (January 1941).

34. For examples, see Wuhan tebie shi zhengfu, *Wuhan tebie shi zhengfu zhounian jinian tekan* [Special commemorative issue marking the first anniversary of the Wuhan Special Municipality] (Wuhan: Wuhan tebie shi zhengfu, 1940), which was published in April 1940. This was followed in September of the same year with the richly illustrated Anonymous, *Xin Wuhan* [New Wuhan] (Wuhan: Wuhan shi zhengfu, 1940).

35. One such account was "Shanhe posui yi Daizong" [The ruined rivers and mountains recall Mount Tai], *Zhonghua ribao,* July 13, 1939, 4.

36. On this topic, see Charles D. Musgrove, *China's Contested Capital: Architecture, Ritual, and Response in Nanjing* (Honolulu: University of Hawai'i Press, 2013).

37. On the symbolic importance of the Ming tombs to earlier Republican iconography, see Harrison, *Making of the Republican Citizen,* 209–211.

38. Ministry of Publicity, *Special Commemoration Issue.* The English term "redecorating" is used in this bilingual publication, though the images are of workmen repairing roofs, windows, and entire buildings that appear to have been damaged by war.

39. Pin Mo, "Shuodao Nanjing: Yi qi baimen lao liu" [When one talks of Nanjing, one remembers the old willow outside the white gate], *Huawen Daban meiri* 4, no. 1 (January 1940): 26–27.

40. Such as in the Daminhui-published *Xin Zhongguo* [New China] 3, no. 1 (January 1940): 60.

41. As was the case for Zhongyang dianxunshe, *Zhongyang dianxunshe disan nian.*

42. As was the case with Anonymous, *Xin Wuhan.*

43. Shaoqian Zhang, "Combat and Collaboration."

44. Mimi Hall Yiengpruksawan, "Japanese War Paint: Kawabata Ryūshi and the Emptying of the Modern," *Archives of Asian Art* 46 (1993): 76–90.

45. Smith, *Resisting Manchukuo,* 111.

46. Warnke, *Political Landscape,* 121.

47. Shepherdson-Scott, "Race behind the Walls."

48. As was the case for the front cover of *Xin Dong Ya* 1, no. 15 (October 1939).

49. A full-page cartoon, captioned "Heping jianguo" (Peace and nation-building) and attributed to an artist listed merely as "Bai" (literally, "white"), employed this motif in the Wuhan-published *E bao* 2, no. 8 (February 1942)—i.e., in the lead-up to the first anniversary of the *huandu.* The image shows rays of light shining from the city walls of Nanjing (which are themselves floating on cloud scrolls).

50. On this wider topic, see Musgrove, *China's Contested Capital.*

51. Charles D. Musgrove, "Monumentality in Nanjing's Sun Yat-sen Memorial Park," *Southeast Review of Chinese Studies* 29 (2007): 2.

52. Lai, "Searching."

53. Zhang Sheng, "Lun Wang wei dui Guomindang zhengzhi fuhao de zhengduo."

54. Photographs of ceremonial visits to the Sun Mausoleum represent a significant subset of images held in the Wang Jingwei and Lin Baisheng Photograph Collection at the East Asia Library, Stanford University (https://exhibits.stanford.edu/wangjingwei).

55. Di'er lishi dang'anguan [Second Historical Archives], ed., *Wang wei zhengfu xingzhengyuan huiyilu, diwu ce* [Record of the meetings of the Executive Yuan of the bogus Wang government, volume 5] (Beijing: Dang'an chubanshe, 1992), 429.

56. Such as Nanjing tebie shi zhengfu, *Shoudu zaolin yundong jinian kan* [Special commemorative issue on the capital forestry campaign] (Nanjing: Nanjing tebie shi zhengfu, 1941). The RNG's forestry campaign around the mausoleum was officially inaugurated on the anniversary of Sun's death in 1941.

57. "Gongzuo baogao" [Work report], March 1943, SHA, 2003-1-2034.

58. On Wang's "emotional, though ceremonial, pilgrimage" to the mausoleum, see Du, "Sun Yat-sen as *Guofu.*"

59. On that photograph, see Harrison, *Making of the Republican Citizen,* 42–43.

60. The image appeared in this vein on the front page of the *Central China Daily News* on March, 12, 1940.

61. Robert Bickers, "Moving Stories: Memorialisation and Its Legacies in Treaty Port China," *Journal of Imperial and Commonwealth History* 42, no. 5 (2014): 826–856.

62. An unattributed cartoon of the statue, and bearing this name, was produced in the RGROC-affiliated magazine *Xin Dong Ya* 1, no. 6 (January 1939).

63. This image, entitled *Wanmin huansheng* (Thousands welcome victory), was apparently submitted to the *Zhonghua ribao* by a pro–Wang Jingwei reader and published on August 6, 1939.

64. See also *Gengsheng* 2, no. 3 (July 8, 1939): 9, where the angel is presented as an anthropomorphization of *gengsheng* (regeneration).

65. This image is on the front page of the *Jiangsu ribao* for October 10, 1941.

66. The image bearing this phrase is unattributed but appears in *Dong Ya Lianmeng huabao* 1, no. 4 (June 1941).

67. Bickers, "Moving Stories."

68. Shanghai shi zhengfu mishuchu, *Guofu huandu zhounian jinian tekan* [Special commemorative issue marking the first anniversary of the return of the national government] (Shanghai: Shanghai shi zhengfu mishuchu, 1941).

69. On this film's popularity with Chinese audiences in 1943, see Michael Raine, "'You Can't Replace *Gone with the Wind* with *Chūshingura*': *China Nights* and the Problem of Japanese Film Policy in Occupied Shanghai," *Film History* 30, no. 2 (Summer 2018): 164–198. On this film more generally, see David Desser, "From the Opium War to the Pacific War: Japanese Propaganda Films of World War II," *Film History* 7, no. 1 (1995): 32–48.

70. Anonymous, "Zhong-Ri lianxi dianying: *Shanghai zhi yue*" [Sino-Japanese joint production: *Moon of Shanghai*], *Xin Zhonghua huabao* 3, no. 7 (July 1941).

71. Baskett, *Attractive Empire,* 57.

72. *Changjiang huakan* 1 (February 1942). This inaugural issue of this pictorial was entitled "Da Dong Ya zhanzheng teji hao" (Greater East Asia War special edition).

73. Germer, "Adapting Russian Constructivism."

74. Anonymous, "Fazhan zhong de Hankou" [Developing Hankou], *E bao* 1 (November 1940).

75. Zhang Renli, ed., *Wuhan tebie shi zhengfu zhounian jinian sheying ce* [Collection of commemorative photographs marking the first anniversary of the Wuhan Municipal Government's founding] (Wuhan: Wuhan tebie shi zhengfu, 1941).

76. Article 7 of the said document stated that "the Government of Japan shall abolish extraterritorial rights possessed by Japan in China and render to the latter its concessions." See "China-Japan: Treaty concerning Basic Relations and Protocol Annexed Thereto." It should be noted, of course, that there were many parts of this treaty that were never, in reality, implemented.

77. Anonymous, "Shanghai diyiqu gongsuoshu chaichu waitan dixing tongxiang" [The municipal office of the Number One District of Shanghai removes imperialist statues from the Bund], *Zhonghua huabao* 1, no. 3 (October 1943).

78. According to the Virtual Shanghai website: https://www.virtualshanghai.net/Photos/Images?ID=833.

79. A typical example of such photography is found in this photo spread: Anonymous, "Xin Shanghai de mianmao" [The appearance of new Shanghai], *Dong Ya Lianmeng huabao* 3, no. 8 (October 1943): 18.

80. Photographs of murals by MoP artists depicting *youjidui* crimes can be found in Zhonghua ribao, *Guomin zhengfu huandu huashi* [A pictorial history of the national government's return] (Shanghai: Zhonghua ribaoshe, 1942).

81. On this, see Daminhui xuanchuanbu, *Renjian diyu* [Hell on earth] (Nanjing: Daminhui, 1939). This play demonized resistance *youjidui* and presented rural Jiangsu and Zhejiang as places where insurgents raped and pillaged in local communities.

82. On this, see Shaoqian Zhang, "Combat and Collaboration."

83. See, for example, Anonymous, *Naka Shina genjō hōkoku* [Report on the recent situation in central China] (Tokyo: Sōzōsha, 1942).

84. Philip Charrier, "Fuchikami Hakuyō and the 'Manchukuo Pastoral' in 1930s Japanese Art Photography," *Japanese Studies* 34, no. 2 (2014): 169–192.

85. Kari Shepherdson-Scott, "A Legacy of Persuasion: Japanese Photography and the Artful Politics of Remembering Manchuria," *Journal of Decorative and Propaganda Arts* 27 (2015): 135.

86. The phrase is used as the title of a photo spread in *Xin Zhonghua huabao* 5, no. 11 (November 1943).

87. The phrase is used as the title of a photo spread in *Xin Zhonghua huabao* 5, no. 12 (December 1943).

88. On this, see Valérie Malenfer Ortiz, *Dreaming the Southern Song Landscape: The Power of Illusion in Chinese Painting* (Boston and Leiden: Brill, 1999).

89. Freda Freiberg, "Genre and Gender in World War II Japanese Feature Film: *China Nights* (1940)," *Historical Journal of Film, Radio and Television* 12, no. 3 (1992): 249.

90. Liu Jianhui, "Demon Capital Shanghai: The 'Modern' Experience of Japanese Intellectuals," trans. Joshua Fogel, *Sino-Japanese Studies* 16 (2009): 184–204.

91. Kushner, *Thought War,* 79–80.

92. So read the caption to an image (spread across two pages) produced in a special series of photographs in Anonymous, "Hankou de jinjiao" [The environs of Hankou], *E bao* 2 (December 1940).

93. A series of ox-themed songs and photographs is included in Anonymous, "Nongfu ge" [Farmers' songs], *Xin Zhonghua huabao* 6, no. 4 (April 1944).

94. Bo Liu, "The Multivalent Imagery of the Ox in Song Painting," *Journal of Song-Yuan Studies* 44 (2014): 33–84.

95. Bert Winther-Tamaki, "Japanese Painting during the Fifteen-Year War," *Monumenta Nipponica* 52, no. 2 (Summer 1997): 145–180.

96. On this, see Andrew Shih-ming Pai, "Modernity in Agony: Contemporaneity, Landscape, and the Representation of Modern Life in Colonial Taiwanese Art," *Southeast Review of Asian Studies* 33 (2011): 4–33.

97. Wen-Chien Chen, "Paintings of Traveling Bullock Carts (*Panche Tu*) in the Song Dynasty (960–1279)," *Archives of Asian Art* 66, no. 2 (2016): 239–269.

98. Wang Zhenghua, "Wanshan wanli qing."

99. Xuanchuanbu, ed., *Xuanchuanbu diyi jie quanguo xuanchuan huiyi shilu* [Record of the first national publicity conference of the Ministry of Publicity] (Nanjing: Xuanchuanbu, 1941), frontispiece.

100. Anonymous, "Dong Lian xiangcun gongzuotuan hongzhao" [Traces of the East Asia League village work teams], *Dong Ya Lianmeng huabao* 2, no. 8 (September 1942).

101. Lei (perhaps wisely) qualified such statements by suggesting that this had all been the result of Chiang Kai-shek's use of scorched-earth tactics. Lei Yimin, "Jiaogong yu qingxiang" [Communist extermination campaigns and Rural Pacification], *Beiping yuekan* 1, no. 2 (1943): 14–20.

102. A typical example of such an illustrated account can be found in Zhengzhi gongzuotuan, *Zhenggong baogaoshu* [Report on political work] (Shanghai: Jiangsu sheng Zhenjiang qingxiang diqu zhengzhi gongzuotuan, 1943).

103. *Lai ri fangchang* [The days to come] (Shanghai: Hua ying, ca. 1943), film pamphlet, Paul Kendel Fonoroff Collection for Chinese Film Studies, C. V. Starr East Asian Library, University of California, Berkeley.

104. David C. Earhart, *Certain Victory: Images of World War II in the Japanese Media* (Armonk, NY: M. E. Sharpe, 2008), 286–291.

105. Anonymous, *Dai Tōa shashin nenpō,* includes a specific section on Rural Pacification in its chapter on RNG China.

106. I am thinking here of the sorts of imagery that were reproduced in pro-occupation propaganda pictorials in Indonesia, such as *Djawa Baroe* (New Java). On this publication, see Aiko Kurasawa, "Propaganda Media on Java under the Japanese, 1942–1945," *Indonesia* 44 (October 1987): 59–116.

107. The account I am drawing from here can be found in Charles D. Musgrove, "Cheering the Traitor: The Post-war Trial of Chen Bijun, April 1946," *Twentieth-Century China* 30, no. 2 (2005): 3–27.

108. FitzGerald, *Fragmenting Modernisms,* 22.

Conclusion

1. Hannah Beech, "The World's Next Superpower Announces Itself with an Epic Parade," *Time,* September 3, 2015.

2. For the full text of this speech (in English translation), see http://www.scmp.com/news/china/policies-politics/article/1854943/full-text-xi-jinping-military-parade-speech-vows-china.

3. Chang Jui-te, "The Politics of Commemoration: A Comparative Analysis of the Fiftieth-Anniversary Commemoration in Mainland China and Taiwan of the Victory in the Anti-Japanese War," in *Scars of War: The Impact of Warfare on Modern China,* ed. Diana Lary and Stephen MacKinnon (Vancouver: UBC Press, 2001), 136–160. As Chang notes, Li Peng made reference to wartime collaboration in September 1995 as a means of attacking the Taiwan independence movement: "History repeatedly demonstrates that anyone who tries to lean on foreigners to divide and betray the mother country will be thoroughly discredited" (139).

4. Ironically, the PRC's former leader Jiang Zemin was in attendance, however. In the years leading up to 2015, Jiang had been the subject of a number of theories circulating in China, some of which posited that his father had served as a high-ranking member of the RNG bureaucracy. On such theories, see John Garnaut, "High Stakes in China's Game of Thrones," *Sydney Morning Herald,* November 17, 2012.

5. Frederic Wakeman Jr., "A Revisionist View of the Nanjing Decade: Confucian Fascism," *China Quarterly* 150 (June 1997): 432.

6. FitzGerald, *Fragmenting Modernisms.*

7. See, for example, Hwang, "Wartime Collaboration."

8. Zanasi, "Globalizing *Hanjian.*"

9. The newsreel is now held by Getty and can be viewed online: https://www.gettyimages.co.nz/detail/video/nationalist-government-president-wang-and-imperial-news-footage/505525795.

10. The story is retold in Sullivan, *Art and Artists,* 108–110.

11. See, for example, Mirzoeff, "Invisible Empire."

12. Hochberg, *Visual Occupations,* 3.

Bibliography

Akami, Tomoko. "Japan's New Empire and the Dōmei News Agency in Occupied Southeast Asia, 1942–45." *Japan Focus* 13, issue 1, no. 3 (2015): 1–28.

Al-Ali, Nadje, and Nicola Pratt. *What Kind of Liberation? Women and the Occupation of Iraq*. Berkeley: University of California Press, 2009.

American Information Committee. *Japan's Cultural Aggression in Asia: A General Study of Methods and Results*. Shanghai: American Information Committee, 1939.

Anonymous. "Ben kan zhu Hua banshichu zai Nanjing chengli" [The establishment of this magazine's China Office in Nanjing]. *Huawen Daban meiri* 7, no. 7 (October 1941): 29.

———. *Dai Tōa shashin nenpō* [Photographic annual of Greater East Asia]. Tokyo: Dōmei Tsūshinsha, 1943.

———. "De Yi deng ba guo chengren guomin zhengfu" [Eight countries, including Germany and Italy, recognize the national government]. *Huawen Daban meiri* 7, no. 2 (July 1941).

———. "Diyi ci huiyi jingguo" [Record of the first meeting]. In *Xuanchuanbu diyi jie xuanchuan huiyi shilu* [Record of the first national publicity conference of the Ministry of Publicity], ed. Xuanchuanbu, 57–60. Nanjing: Xuanchuanbu, 1941.

———. "Dong Lian xiangcun gongzuotuan hongzhao" [Traces of the East Asia League village work teams]. *Dong Ya Lianmeng huabao* 2, no. 8 (September 1942).

———. "Fa kan ci" [Remarks on the publication of the journal]. *Zhonghua huabao* 1, no. 1 (August 1943).

———. "Fang Junbi nüshi ji hua chuban" [A collection of paintings by Ms. Fan Tchunpi has been published]. *Nanhua pinglun* 3, no. 17 (December 1932): 8.

———. "Fang Junbi youhua zhan jinri juxing yuzhan" [Preview of Fan Tchunpi's exhibition of oil paintings starts today]. *Zhonghua ribao,* May 4, 1945, 2.

———. "Fazhan zhong de Hankou" [Developing Hankou]. *E bao* 1 (November 1940).

———. "Guangdong sheng Da Dong Ya qingnian dahui" [The Greater East Asia Youth Convention in Guangdong]. *Dong Ya Lianmeng huabao* 3, no. 11 (December 1943).

———. "Guanyu xuanchuan de zuotanhui" [On a roundtable about propaganda]. *Huawen Daban meiri* 6, no. 2 (January 1941): 6–9.

———. "Guofu huandu hou xin junren de yucheng" [The cultivation of new China's soldiers since the return of the national government]. *Dong Ya Lianmeng huabao* 3, no. 3 (February 1943).

———. "Hankou de jinjiao" [The environs of Hankou]. *E bao* 2 (December 1940).

———. "Madame Chen Pi-chun." *Xin Zhonghua huabao* 5, no. 9 (September 1943).

———. "Manhua dipan" [Cartoon base]. *Dong Ya Lianmeng huabao* 4, no. 2 (April 1944).

———. *Naka Shina genjō hōkoku* [Report on the recent situation in central China]. Tokyo: Sōzōsha, 1942.

———. "Nongfu ge" [Farmers' songs]. *Xin Zhonghua huabao* 6, no. 4 (April 1944).

———. "President Wang Ching-wei Celebrates His 62nd Birthday." *Xin Zhonghua huabao* 6, no. 6 (June 1944).

———. "President Wang Ching-wei in Uniform." *Xin Zhonghua huabao* 3, no. 10 (October 1941).

———. *Qingshao xunlian yu xiuyang* [The training and fostering of youth]. Nanjing: Zhongyang dianxunshe, 1942.

———. "Quanguo minzhong, dadao Ying-Mei zong dongyuan" [General mobilization of the masses to overthrow Britain and America]. *Zhonghua huabao* 1, no. 1 (August 1943): 8–9.

———. "Renwu jieshao: Yan Wenliang" [Introducing Yan Wenliang]. *Zhonghua huabao* 1, no. 4 (November 1943): 14.

———. "Shanghai diyiqu gongsuoshu chaichu waitan dixing tongxiang" [The municipal office of the Number One District of Shanghai removes imperialist statues from the Bund]. *Zhonghua huabao* 1, no. 3 (October 1943).

———. "Wang Jingwei si hou miwen" [Posthumous secrets about Wang Jingwei]. *Hanjian choushi* (February 1945): 28–31.

———. "Wang weiyuanzhang san ci xunshi qingxiangqu ji" [An account of Chairman Wang's third tour of the Rural Pacification areas]. *Zhongyang daobao zhoukan* 2, no. 39 (April 1942): 19.

———. "Wang zhuxi banian qian liu dan, anran quchu" [A bullet left in Chairman Wang eight years ago is safely extracted]. *Zhonghua huabao* 2, no. 1 (February 1944): 2–3.

———. "Wang zhuxi fang Ri zuo fan jing" [Chairman Wang returned to Nanjing yesterday after a visit to Japan]. *Zhong bao,* September 24, 1943, 1.

———. *Xin guomin yundong yanlunji, shangce* [Collection of NCM speeches, volume 1]. Nanjing: Nanjing tebie shi xuanchuanchu, 1942.

———. "Xin Shanghai de mianmao" [The appearance of new Shanghai]. *Dong Ya Lianmeng huabao* 3, no. 8 (October 1943): 18.

———. *Xin Wuhan* [New Wuhan]. Wuhan: Wuhan shi zhengfu, 1940.

———. "Xuanchuan huiyi qunxiang" [Group images of publicity conference attendees]. *Taiping* 3, no. 1 (1944).

———. *Yi dai yinghou Chen Yunshang* [Movie queen of the age, Nancy Chan]. Beijing: Xinhua shudian, 2001.

———. "Zhishang gongying: Riji yi ye" [Movie on paper: Page from a diary]. *Huawen Daban meiri* 6, no. 1 (January 1941).

———. "Zhong-Ri funüjie de xiang qin xiang ai" [Mutual affection and love between Japanese and Chinese women]. *Xin Zhongguo* 2, no. 11–12 (December 1939).

———. "Zhong-Ri lianxi dianying: *Shanghai zhi yue*" [Sino-Japanese joint production: *Moon of Shanghai*]. *Xin Zhonghua huabao* 3, no. 7 (July 1941).

———. "Zhong-Ri wenhua jiaoliu: Lingnan meizhan diwu jie" [Sino-Japanese cultural exchange: The fifth exhibition of Lingnan painting]. *Dong Ya Lianmeng huabao* 1, no. 4 (June 1941).

Arendt, Hannah. *Men in Dark Times*. New York: Harcourt, Brace and World, 1968.

Asahi Shimbun Co. *Media, Propaganda and Politics in 20th-Century Japan*. Translated by Barak Kushner. London: Bloomsbury, 2015.

Atkins, E. Taylor. *Primitive Selves: Koreana in the Japanese Colonial Gaze, 1910–1945*. Berkeley: University of California Press, 2010.

Bader, A. L. "China's New Weapon—Caricature." *American Scholar* 10, no. 2 (Spring 1941): 228–240.

Barlow, Tani E. "Buying In: Advertising and the Sexy Modern Girl Icon in Shanghai in the 1920s and 1930s." In *The Modern Girl around the World: Consumption, Modernity, Globalization,* edited by Alys Eve Weinbaum et al., 222–318. Durham, NC: Duke University Press, 2008.

Barrett, David P. Introduction to *Chinese Collaboration with Japan, 1932–1945: The Limits of Accommodation,* edited by David P. Barrett and Larry N. Shyu, 1–17. Stanford, CA: Stanford University Press, 2001.

———. "The Wang Jingwei Regime, 1940–1945: Continuities and Disjunctures with Nationalist China." In *Chinese Collaboration with Japan, 1932–1945: The Limits of Accommodation,* edited by David P. Barrett and Larry N. Shyu, 102–115. Stanford, CA: Stanford University Press, 2001.

Baruch, Marc Olivier. "Charisma and Hybrid Legitimacy in Pétain's *État français* (1940–44)." *Totalitarian Movements and Political Religions* 7, no. 2 (2006): 215–224.

Baskett, Michael. *The Attractive Empire: Transnational Film Culture in Imperial Japan*. Honolulu: University of Hawai'i Press, 2008.

Bate, Don. *Wang Ching Wei: Puppet or Patriot*. Chicago: Ralph Fletcher Seymour, 1941.

Beech, Hannah. "The World's Next Superpower Announces Itself with an Epic Parade." *Time,* September 3, 2015.

Beijingshi dang'anguan, ed. *Ri-wei Beijing Xinminhui* [The Japanese-bogus regimes' Xinminhui in occupied Beijing]. Beijing: Guangming ribao chubanshe, 1989.

Benton, Gregor. *New Fourth Army: Communist Resistance along the Yangtze and the Huai, 1938–1941*. Berkeley: University of California Press, 1999.

Berger, John. *Ways of Seeing*. London: Penguin, 1973.

Bertrand Dorléac, Laurence. *Art of the Defeat: France 1940–1944*. Translated by Jane Marie Todd. Los Angeles: Getty Research Institute, 2008.

Bickers, Robert. "Moving Stories: Memorialisation and Its Legacies in Treaty Port China." *Journal of Imperial and Commonwealth History* 42, no. 5 (2014): 826–856.

Bonnell, Victoria E. *Iconography of Power: Soviet Political Posters under Lenin and Stalin*. Berkeley: University of California Press, 1997.

Boorman, Howard L. "Wang Ching-wei: China's Romantic Radical." *Political Science Quarterly* 79, no. 4 (1964): 504–525.

Boyle, John Hunter. *China and Japan at War, 1937–1945: The Politics of Collaboration*. Stanford, CA: Stanford University Press, 1972.

Bredekamp, Horst. *Image Acts: A Systematic Approach to Visual Agency*. Translated by Elizabeth Clegg. Berlin: De Gruyter, 2017.

———. "A Neglected Tradition? Art History as *Bildwissenschaft*." *Critical Inquiry* 29, no. 3 (Spring 2003): 418–428.

Brook, Timothy. *Collaboration: Japanese Agents and Local Chinese Elites in Wartime China*. Cambridge, MA: Harvard University Press, 2005.

———. "Collaborationist Nationalism in Occupied Wartime China." In *Nation Work: Asian Elites and National Identities*, edited by Timothy Brook and Andrew Schmid, 159–190. Ann Arbor: University of Michigan Press, 2000.

———. "The Creation of the Reformed Government in Central China, 1938." In *Chinese Collaboration with Japan, 1932–1945: The Limits of Accommodation*, edited by David P. Barrett and Larry N. Shyu, 79–101. Stanford, CA: Stanford University Press, 2001.

———. "Occupation State Building." In *China at War: Regions of China, 1937–1945*, edited by Stephen R. MacKinnon, Diana Lary, and Ezra F. Vogel, 22–43. Stanford, CA: Stanford University Press, 2007.

Brose, Benjamin. "Resurrecting Xuan Zang: The Modern Travels of a Medieval Monk." In *Recovering Buddhism in Modern China*, edited by Jan Kiely and J. Brooks Jessup, 143–176. New York: Columbia University Press, 2016.

Bruhn, Matthias. "The Warburg Electronic Library in Hamburg: A Digital Index of Political Iconography." *Visual Resources* 15, no. 4 (2000): 405–423.

Buchanan, Andrew. " 'I Felt like a Tourist instead of a Soldier': The Occupying Gaze—War and Tourism in Italy, 1943–1945." *American Quarterly* 68, no. 3 (September 2016): 593–615.

Bunker, Gerald E. *The Peace Conspiracy: Wang Ching-wei and the China War, 1937–1941*. Cambridge, MA: Harvard University Press, 1972.

Cai Dejin. *Lishi de guaitai: Wang wei guomin zhengfu shimo* [Freak of history: The beginning and end of the bogus Wang national government]. Beijing: Tuanjie chubanshe, 2008.

———, ed. *Zhou Fohai riji quanbian, shangbian* [The complete, edited diaries of Zhou Fohai, part 1]. Beijing: Zhongguo wenlian chubanshe, 1998.

Cao Hanmei. "Dianzhong huasheng" [Painting manual from central Yunnan]. *Guoyi* 3, no. 4 (September 1941).

Carruthers, Susan L. "Why Can't We See Insurgents? Enmity, Invisibility and Counterinsurgency in Iraq and Afghanistan." *Photography and Culture* 8, no. 2 (2015): 191–211.

Chan Cheong-Choo. *Memoirs of a Citizen of Early XXth Century China*. N.p.: 1978.

Chan, Pedith. "The Discourse of *Guohua* in Occupied Shanghai." Paper presented at the Cultural and Intellectual Histories of Japanese-Occupied China Workshop, Asia House (London), September 16, 2019.

———. "The Institutionalization and Legitimatization of *Guohua:* Art Societies in Republican Shanghai." *Modern China* 39, no. 5 (2013): 541–570.

Chan, Pedith Pui. *The Making of a Modern Art World: Institutionalisation and Legitimisation of* Guohua *in Republican Shanghai*. Boston: Brill, 2017.

Chang Jui-te. "The Politics of Commemoration: A Comparative Analysis of the Fiftieth-Anniversary Commemoration in Mainland China and Taiwan of the Victory in the Anti-Japanese War." In *Scars of War: The Impact of Warfare on Modern China,* edited by Diana Lary and Stephen MacKinnon, 136–160. Vancouver: UBC Press, 2001.

Charrier, Philip. "Fuchikami Hakuyō and the 'Manchukuo Pastoral' in 1930s Japanese Art Photography." *Japanese Studies* 34, no. 2 (2014): 169–192.

Cheah Boon Kheng. "Memory as History and Moral Judgement: Oral and Written Accounts of the Japanese Occupation of Malaya." In *War and Memory in Malaysia and Singapore,* edited by Lim Pui Huen and Diana Wong, 23–41. Singapore: ISEAS, 2000.

Chen Gongshu. *Lanyishe de neimu* [The inside story on the Blue Shirts]. Shanghai: Guomin xinwen tushu, 1942.

Chen, Jianyue. "Chen Gongbo: A National Traitor or a Collaborationist Nationalist? A Case Study of Chinese Wartime Collaborationism." *Chinese Historical Review* 13, no. 2 (2006): 292–312.

Chen, Wen-Chien. "Paintings of Traveling Bullock Carts (*Panche Tu*) in the Song Dynasty (960–1279)." *Archives of Asian Art* 66, no. 2 (2016): 239–269.

Chen Xinhe. "Zhongguo huihua zhu qingxiang" [Trends in Chinese painting]. *Huawen Daban meiri* 9, no. 10 (November 1942): 46.

Chen Xuesheng. *Xunhui shiluo de minguo sheying* [Searching for the lost photography of the Republican era]. Taipei: Fukai yishu, 2015.

Chen Yanqiao. *Kangzhan xuanchuanhua* [Propaganda pictures for the War of Resistance]. Guangzhou: Liming shudian, 1938.

Chen Zijia [Jin Xiongbai]. *Wangchao miyan lu, san* [Secret records of the Wang dynasty, volume 3]. Hong Kong: Yuzhou chubanshe, 1964.

Cheng Jie. "Minguo shiqi Zhongshan lingyuan meihua fengjing de jianshe yu yanbian" [The construction and changes to plum blossom scenery in the Sun Yat-sen Mausoleum area during the Republican era]. *Nanjing shehui kexue* 2 (2011): 151–156.

Cheung, Andrew. "Slogans, Symbols, and Legitimacy: The Case of Wang Jingwei's Nanjing Regime." Indiana East Asia Working Paper Series, 6 (July 1995).

"China-Japan: Treaty concerning Basic Relations and Protocol Annexed Thereto." *American Journal of International Law* 35, no. 3 (1941): 125–128.

Chiu, Lawrence M. W. "The *South China Daily News* and Wang Jingwei's Peace Movement, 1939–1941." *Journal of the Royal Asiatic Society of Hong Kong* 50 (2010): 343–370.

Clinton, Maggie. *Revolutionary Nativism: Fascism and Culture in China, 1925–1937.* Durham, NC: Duke University Press, 2017.

Clunas, Craig. "China: Art, War, and Salvation." Public lecture, Gresham College (London), February 19, 2018.

———. "Chinese Art and Chinese Artists in France (1924–1925)." *Arts asiatiques* 44 (1989): 100–106.

Coble, Parks. "China's New Remembering of the Anti-Japanese War of Resistance, 1937–1945." *China Quarterly* 190 (2007): 394–410.

———. "Writing about Atrocity: Wartime Accounts and Their Contemporary Uses." *Modern Asian Studies* 45, no. 2 (2011): 379–398.

Cochran, Sherman. *Chinese Medicine Men: Consumer Culture in China and Southeast Asia.* Cambridge, MA: Harvard University Press, 2006.

Cody, Jeffrey W., and Frances Terpak, eds. *Brush and Shutter: Early Photography in China.* Hong Kong: Hong Kong University Press, in association with the Getty Research Institute, 2011.

Cook, James A., Joshua Goldstein, Matthew D. Johnson, and Sigrid Schmalzer. Introduction to *Visualizing Modern China: Image, History and Memory, 1750–Present,* edited by James A. Cook, Joshua Goldstein, Matthew D. Johnson, and Sigrid Schmalzer, 1–24. Lanham, MD: Lexington Books, 2014.

Croizier, Ralph. *Art and Revolution in Modern China: The Lingnan (Cantonese) School of Painting, 1906–1951.* Berkeley: University of California Press, 1988.

Culp, Robert. "Rethinking Governmentality: Training, Cultivation, and Cultural Citizenship in Nationalist China." *Journal of Asian Studies* 65, no. 3 (2006): 529–554.

Dagnino, Jorge, Matthew Feldman, and Paul Stoker. "Building Illiberal Subjects: The New Man in the Radical Right Universe, 1919–45." In *The "New Man" in Radical Right Ideology and Practice, 1919–45,* edited by Jorge Dagnino, Matthew Feldman, and Paul Stoker, 1–15. London: Bloomsbury, 2018.

Daminhui xuanchuanbu. *Renjian diyu* [Hell on earth]. Nanjing: Daminhui, 1939.

———. *Wang Jingwei xiansheng yu xin zhongyang zhengfu* [Mr. Wang Jingwei and the new central government]. Nanjing: Daminhui, 1940.

Daniels, Stephen, and Denis Cosgrove. "Introduction: Iconography and Landscape." In *The Iconography of Landscape: Essays on the Symbolic Representation, Design and Use of Past Environments,* edited by Denis Cosgrove and Stephen Daniels, 1–10. Cambridge: Cambridge University Press, 1988.

Delury, John, Sheila A. Smith, Maria Repnikova, and Srinath Raghavan. "Looking Back on the Seventieth Anniversary of Japan's Surrender." *Journal of Asian Studies* 74, no. 4 (November 2015): 797–820.

Desser, David. "From the Opium War to the Pacific War: Japanese Propaganda Films of World War II." *Film History* 7, no. 1 (1995): 32–48.

Di'er lishi dang'anguan, ed. *Wang wei zhengfu xingzhengyuan huiyilu, diwu ce* [Record of the meetings of the Executive Yuan of the bogus Wang government, volume 5]. Beijing: Dang'an chubanshe, 1992.

Donald, Stephanie Hemelryk. "Tang Wei: Sex, the City, and the Scapegoat in *Lust, Caution*." *Theory, Culture and Society* 27, no. 4 (2010): 46–68.

Dong, Madeleine Y. "Who Is Afraid of the Chinese Modern Girl?" In *The Modern Girl around the World: Consumption, Modernity, Globalization*, edited by Alys Eve Weinbaum et al., 194–219. Durham, NC: Duke University Press, 2008.

Dong Tianye. "Chen Yunshang dapo kongbudang" [Nancy Chan destroys terrorists]. Series of cartoons. *Zhongguo manhua* 1 (November 1942): 7–8.

Dorrian, Mark, and Frédéric Pousin. Introduction to *Seeing from Above: The Aerial View in Visual Culture*, edited by Mark Dorrian and Frédéric Pousin, 1–10. London: I. B. Tauris, 2013.

Du, Yue. "Sun Yat-sen as *Guofu*: Competition over Nationalist Party Orthodoxy in the Second Sino-Japanese War." *Modern China* 45, no. 2 (2019): 201–235.

Duara, Prasenjit. *Sovereignty and Authenticity: Manchukuo and the East Asian Modern*. Lanham, MD: Rowman and Littlefield, 2003.

Dunand, Frank, ed. *The Pavilion of Marital Harmony: Chinese Painting and Calligraphy between Tradition and Modernity*. Geneva: Collections Baur, 2002.

Duus, Peter. "Imperialism without Colonies: The Vision of a Greater East Asia Co-Prosperity Sphere." *Diplomacy and Statecraft* 7, no. 1 (1996): 54–72.

Earhart, David C. *Certain Victory: Images of World War II in the Japanese Media*. Armonk, NY: M. E. Sharpe, 2008.

Eckert, Carter J. *Park Chung Hee and Modern Korea: The Roots of Militarism, 1866–1945*. Cambridge, MA: Belknap Press, 2016.

Edwards, Louise. "Policing the Modern Woman in Republican Shanghai." *Modern China* 26, no. 2 (2000): 115–147.

———. "Transformations of the Woman Warrior Hua Mulan: From Defender of the Family to Servant of the State." *Nannü* 12, no. 2 (2010): 175–214.

Eykholt, Mark S. "Living the Limits of Occupation in Nanjing, China, 1937–1945." PhD diss., University of California–San Diego, 1998.

Fang Junbi. *Fang Junbi huaji yice* [A collection of paintings by Fan Tchunpi]. Changsha: Shangwu yinshuguan, 1938.

Finnane, Antonia. *Changing Clothes in China: Fashion, History, Nation*. New York: Columbia University Press, 2008.

FitzGerald, Carolyn. *Fragmenting Modernisms: Chinese Wartime Literature, Art, and Film, 1937–49*. Boston and Leiden: Brill, 2013.

Fogel, Joshua A. *The Literature of Travel in the Japanese Rediscovery of China: 1862–1945*. Stanford, CA: Stanford University Press, 1996.

Freiberg, Freda. "Genre and Gender in World War II Japanese Feature Film: *China Nights* (1940)." *Historical Journal of Film, Radio and Television* 12, no. 3 (1992): 245–252.

Fu, Poshek. "The Ambiguity of Entertainment: Chinese Cinema in Japanese-Occupied Shanghai, 1941 to 1945." *Cinema Journal* 37, no. 1 (Autumn 1997): 66–84.

———. *Passivity, Resistance, and Collaboration: Intellectual Choices in Occupied Shanghai, 1937–1945*. Stanford, CA: Stanford University Press, 1993.

———. "Projecting Ambivalence: Chinese Cinema in Semi-occupied Shanghai, 1937–41," in *Wartime Shanghai,* edited by Wen-hsin Yeh, 86–110. London: Routledge, 1998.

Gamsa, Mark. "Sergei Tret'iakov's *Roar, China!* Between Moscow and China." *Itinerario* 36, no. 2 (August 2012): 91–108.

Gao Danyu and Xu Shaohong. "Nanjing wei weixin zhengfu ji qi Daminhui" [The bogus Nanjing RGROC and its Daminhui]. *Minguo dang'an* 2 (2000): 89–94.

Gao, Yingying. "A Survey of Twenty-First-Century Studies of the Japanese-Occupied Areas in China." Translated by Tian Xiansheng. *Journal of Modern Chinese History* 9, no. 1 (2015): 130–151.

Garnaut, John. "High Stakes in China's Game of Thrones." *Sydney Morning Herald,* November 17, 2012.

Geertz, Clifford. Negara: *The Theatre State in Nineteenth-Century Bali.* Princeton, NJ: Princeton University Press, 1980.

Germer, Andrea. "Adapting Russian Constructivism and Socialist Realism: The Japanese Overseas Photo Magazine *FRONT* (1942–1945)." *Studies in Contemporary History* 12 (2015): 236–263.

———. "Artists and Wartime Politics: Natori Yōnosuke—a Japanese Riefenstahl?" *Contemporary Japan* 24 (2012): 21–50.

———. "Visible Cultures, Invisible Politics: Propaganda in the Magazine *Nippon Fujin,* 1942–1945." *Japan Forum* 25, no. 4 (2013): 505–539.

———. "Visual Propaganda in Wartime East Asia: The Case of Natori Yōnosuke." *Japan Focus* 20, no. 3 (2011): 1–35.

Gunn, Edward M., Jr. *Unwelcome Muse: Chinese Literature in Shanghai and Peking, 1937–1945.* New York: Columbia University Press, 1980.

Guo Xiufeng. "Yu" [Foreword]. In *E Gan shidi shichaji* [A field survey of Hubei and Jiangxi], by Xue Huizi, i. Nanjing: Zhongyang dianxunshe, 1940.

Guomindang qingxiangqu dangwu banshichu. *Qingxiangqu dangwu baogaoshu* [Report on party services in the Rural Pacification areas]. Suzhou: Guomindang qingxiangqu dangwu banshichu, 1942.

Harrison, Henrietta. *The Making of the Republican Citizen: Political Ceremonies and Symbols in China, 1911–1929.* Oxford: Oxford University Press, 2000.

He Peng. "Yi wei sheyingshi yanli de Wang Jingwei" [Wang Jingwei in the eyes of a photographer]. *Shijixing* (May 1995): 34–36.

Henriot, Christian, and Wen-hsin Yeh. "Introduction. China Visualised: What Stories Do Pictures Tell?" In *Visualising China, 1845–1965: Life/Still Images in Historical Narratives,* edited by Christian Henriot and Wen-hsin Yeh, vii–xxv. Leiden: Brill, 2013.

Herren, Madeleine. "Fascist Internationalism." In *Internationalisms: A Twentieth-Century History,* edited by Glenda Sluga and Patricia Clavin, 191–212. Cambridge: Cambridge University Press, 2016.

Ho, Virgil Kit-yin. "Martyrs or Ghosts? A Short Cultural History of a Tomb in Revolutionary Canton, 1911–1970." *East Asian History* 27 (June 2004): 99–138.

Hochberg, Gil Z. *Visual Occupations: Violence and Visibility in a Conflict Zone.* Durham, NC: Duke University Press, 2015.

Horii Koichiro. "Ō Chōmei seiken ka sō dōin taisei no kōchiku to minshū" [The general public mobilization system under the Wang Jingwei regime: Formation and popular participation]. *Nihon Daigaku daigakuin sōgō shakai jōhō kenkyū ka kiyō* 9 (2008): 39–50.

Hotta, Eri. *Pan-Asianism and Japan's War, 1931–1945.* Basingstoke, UK: Palgrave Macmillan, 2007.

Hu Shua. "Zheng gong shouji" [Notes on political work]. *Qingxiang qianxian* 2, no. 4 (June 1943): 26–28.

Huang Donglan. "Shrines of Yue Fei: Spaces for Creation of Public Memory." *Chinese Sociology and Anthropology* 37, no. 23 (2005): 74–112.

Huang Meizhen. *Ri-wei dui Huazhong lunxianqu jingji de lüeduo yu tongzhi* [The economic pillage and control of the occupied areas of central China under the Japanese and the bogus regime]. Beijing: Shehui kexue wenxian, 2005.

Huang, Nicole. "Fashioning Public Intellectuals: Women's Print Culture in Occupied Shanghai (1941–1945)." In *In the Shadow of the Rising Sun: Shanghai under Japanese Occupation,* edited by Christian Henriot and Wen-hsin Yeh, 325–345. Cambridge: Cambridge University Press, 2004.

———. *Women, War, Domesticity: Shanghai Literature and Popular Culture of the 1940s.* Boston and Leiden: Brill, 2005.

Huang Qingshu [Wong Hing-sue], ed. *Wang zhuxi fang Ri jinian huakan* [Special pictorial in commemoration of Chairman Wang's visit to Japan]. Nanjing: Xuanchuanbu, 1941.

Huang Renyuan, ed. *Wang Jingwei yu Wang wei zhengfu, shang* [Wang Jingwei and the bogus Wang government, part 1]. Taipei: Taiwan shangwu yinshuguan, 1994.

———, ed. *Wang Jingwei yu Wang wei zhengfu, xia* [Wang Jingwei and the bogus Wang government, part 2]. Taipei: Taiwan shangwu yinshuguan, 1994.

Hung, Chang-tai. *Mao's New World: Popular Culture in the Early People's Republic.* Ithaca, NY: Cornell University Press, 2010.

———. *War and Popular Culture: Resistance in Modern China.* Berkeley: University of California Press, 1994.

Hwang, Dongyoun. "Wartime Collaboration in Question: An Examination of the Postwar Trials of the Chinese Collaborators." *Inter-Asia Cultural Studies* 6, no. 1 (2005): 75–97.

Ikeda Katsumi. *Shinsei Chūgoku no kao* [The face of a newborn China]. Tokyo: ARS, 1944.

Jackson, Julia. *France: The Dark Years, 1940–1944.* Oxford: Oxford University Press, 2001.

Jenner, W. J. F. "Race and History in China." *New Left Review* 11 (September–October 2001): 55–77.

Jennings, Eric. "Reinventing Jeanne: The Iconology of Joan of Arc in Vichy Schoolbooks, 1940–1944." *Journal of Contemporary History* 29 (1994): 711–734.

Jian Qing. "Heping de husheng" [Cry for peace]. Illustration. *Dong Ya Lianmeng huabao* 2, no. 7 (August 1942).

Jiang Fan. "Qi shi" [Begging for food]. Woodcut. *Zhonghua huabao* 1, no. 5 (December 1943): 28.

Jiang Hao. "The KMT Reorganization Faction and Its Activities in Shanghai." *Chinese Studies in History* 27, no. 1–2 (1993): 123–130.

Jiang Yingjing. "Hu Shi and Wang Jingwei: Discussions on Sino-Japanese Issues before and after the War of Resistance against Japan." *Chinese Studies in History* 42, no. 1 (2008): 3–46.

Jiangsu sheng xuanchuanchu. "Xuanchuan" [Propaganda]. In *Wang wei zhengquan ziliao xuanbian: Wang Jingwei guomin zhengfu "qingxiang" yundong* [Collection of material relating to the bogus Wang regime: The Wang national government's "Rural Pacification" campaign], edited by Yu Zidao, Liu Qikui, and Cao Zhenwei, 399–403. Shanghai: Xinhua shuju, 1985.

Jiaoyubu, ed. *Guomin li* [Citizens' calendar]. Nanjing: Xingzhengyuan jiaoyubu, 1941.

Jing bao. "Guofu mingling: Zi wu ri qi, chuqu guoqi huangse biaozhi" [The national government decrees that from [February] 5, the yellow pennant shall be removed from the national flag]. February 3, 1943.

———. "Zhongyang xuanchuan jiangxisuo gaikuang" [The current state of affairs at the Central Propaganda Institute]. December 12, 1940.

Jing Shanshan. "Nanjing lunxian shiqi, Ri-wei dui meishu, sheying, dianying de kongzhi yu liyong" [The control and use of the fine arts, photography, and cinema by the Japanese and the bogus regime in occupied Nanjing]. *Shihai tanji* (July 2014): 60–64.

Jing Shenghong. *Nanjing lunxian banian shi (xia)* [The eight-year history of Nanjing's occupation, part 2]. Beijing: Shehui kexue wenxian chubanshe, 2013.

Johnstone, William C. "Japan's 'New' China Policy." *Far Eastern Survey* 12, no. 19 (September 1943): 185–191.

Jowett, Philip. *Rays of the Rising Sun*. Vol. 1, *Japan's Asian Allies 1931–45, China and Manchukuo*. Trowbridge, UK: Helion and Co., 2004.

Ke Fu. "Zhongguo nuhou le! Huobao juben" [Roar, China! Living newspaper script]. *Shi leibian tekan* 4 (1937): 51–54.

Kovner, Sarah. *Occupying Power: Sex Workers and Servicemen in Postwar Japan*. Stanford, CA: Stanford University Press, 2012.

Kurasawa, Aiko. "Propaganda Media on Java under the Japanese, 1942–1945." *Indonesia* 44 (October 1987): 59–116.

Kushner, Barak. *The Thought War: Japanese Imperial Propaganda*. Honolulu: University of Hawai'i Press, 2006.

Kwa, Shiamin, and Wilt Idema. Introduction to *Mulan: Five Versions of a Classic Chinese Legend, with Related Chinese Texts,* edited by Shiamin Kwa and Wilt Idema, xi–xxxii. Indianapolis: Hackett Publishing, 2010.

Kwon, Heonik, and Byung-Ho Chung. *North Korea: Beyond Charismatic Politics.* Lanham, MD: Rowman and Littlefield, 2012.

Lai, Delin. "Searching for a Modern Chinese Monument: The Design of the Sun Yat-sen Mausoleum in Nanjing." *Journal of the Society of Architectural Historians* 64, no. 1 (March 2005): 22–55.

Lai ri fangchang [The days to come]. Film pamphlet. Shanghai: Hua ying, ca. 1943.

Laing, Ellen Johnston. *Selling Happiness: Calendar Posters and Visual Culture in Early Twentieth-Century Shanghai.* Honolulu: University of Hawai'i Press, 2004.

Larson, Wendy. "Zhang Yimou's *Hero:* Dismantling the Myth of Cultural Power." *Journal of Chinese Cinemas* 2, no. 3 (2008): 181–196.

Lei Yimin. "Jiaogong yu qingxiang" [Communist extermination campaigns and Rural Pacification]. *Beiping yuekan* 1, no. 2 (1943): 14–20.

———. "Xin guomin yundong yu qingshaonian" [The New Citizens Movement and the youth]. *Beiping yuekan* 1, no. 2 (1943): 42–46.

Lent, John A., and Xu Ying. *Comics Art in China.* Jackson: University Press of Mississippi, 2017.

Li, Jie. "Phantasmagoric Manchukuo: Documentaries Produced by the South Manchuria Railway Company, 1932–1940." *positions* 22, no. 2 (2014): 329–369.

Li Ming. "Funüjie dui guojia yingjin zhi zeren" [The responsibilities that womanhood should hold for the nation]. *Xin Zhongguo* 2, no. 11–12 (December 1939): 50–52.

Li Shiqun. "Nuli shengchan xuanchuan wancheng gaodu qingxiang" [Strive to produce propaganda and finalize a high level of Rural Pacification]. *Qingxiang qianxian* 1, no. 11 (March 1943): 5.

Li Zhongming. *Kang-Ri zhanzheng shiqi de Zhongguo wenhua* [Chinese culture during the War of Resistance]. Beijing: Tuanjie chubanshe, 2015.

Lin Baisheng. "Wang xiansheng zhi zhongyao jianyi" [The important suggestions of Mr. Wang]. In *Wang Jingwei xiansheng zhongyao jianyi* [Important suggestions from Mr. Wang Jingwei], edited by *Nanhua ribao,* 11. Hong Kong: Nanhua ribao she, 1939.

———. "Xian jieduan xuanchuan de fendou" [The struggle in the current stage of propaganda]. In *Xuanchuanbu diyi jie quanguo xuanchuan huiyi shilu* [Record of the first national publicity conference of the Ministry of Publicity], edited by Xuanchuanbu, 22–30. Nanjing: Xuanchuanbu, 1941.

———. "Zhengzhi baogao" [Political report]. In *Xuanchuanbu diyi jie quanguo xuanchuan huiyi shilu* [Record of the first national publicity conference of the Ministry of Publicity], edited by Xuanchuanbu, 5–22. Nanjing: Xuanchuanbu, 1941.

Lin Chang. *Yanmo de beihuan: Zhong lian, Hua ying dianying chutan* [The decline of tragedy and happiness: A preliminary study of the CUP and the CUMP]. Hong Kong: Zhonghua shuju, 2014.

Lincoln, Toby. "The Rural and Urban at War: Invasion and Reconstruction in China during the Anti-Japanese War of Resistance." *Journal of Urban History* 20, no. 10 (2012): 1–19.

Linebarger, Paul. *The China of Chiang Kai-shek: A Political Study*. Boston: World Peace Foundation, 1943.

Liu, Bo. "The Multivalent Imagery of the Ox in Song Painting." *Journal of Song-Yuan Studies* 44 (2014): 33–84.

Liu Jianhui. "Demon Capital Shanghai: The 'Modern' Experience of Japanese Intellectuals." Translated by Joshua Fogel. *Sino-Japanese Studies* 16 (2009): 184–204.

Liu Jie. "Kangzhan chuqi Huadong lunxianqu qin-Ri qunti yanjiu: Yi Daminhui Zhenjiang lianhe zhibu wei zhongxin de tantao" [A study of pro-Japanese groups in occupied areas of east China in the early stages of the War of Resistance: A discussion of the Daminhui's branch office in Zhenjiang]. *Zhongyang yanjiuyuan jindaishi yanjiusuo jikan* 98 (2017): 89–114.

———. "Wang Jingwei and the 'Nanjing Nationalist Government': Between Collaboration and Resistance." Translated by Konrad Lawson. In *Toward a History beyond Borders: Contentious Issues in Sino-Japanese Relations,* edited by Daqing Yang, Jie Liu, Hiroshi Mitani, and Andrew Gordon, 205–239. Cambridge, MA: Harvard University Asia Center, 2012.

Liu Jiurong. *Ta de shenpan: Jindai Zhongguo guozu yu xingbie yiyi xia de zhongjian zhibian* [Her trials: Contextualizing loyalty and disloyalty in modern China from a gendered nationalist perspective]. Taipei: Zhongyang yanjiuyuan, 2013.

Liu Longguang. "Heping de zuguo zhi xing" [Journey through a peaceful motherland]. *Huawen Daban meiri* 6, no. 2 (January 1941).

———. "Heping yu zuguo" [Peace and the motherland]. *Huawen Daban meiri* 5, no. 5 (March 1941): 19–23.

Liu Zi. "Cong Shanghai manhua xiehui tan dao Huazhong manhuajie" [From the Shanghai Cartoonists Association to the cartooning field in central China]. *Huawen Daban meiri* 9, no. 5 (September 1942): 43–45.

———. "Huazhong de manhua wenti" [The problem with cartoons in central China]. *Huawen Daban meiri* 7, no. 4 (August 1941): 22–23.

Lloyd, Christopher. *Collaboration and Resistance in Occupied France: Representing Treason and Sacrifice*. London: Palgrave Macmillan, 2003.

Lu Guowei. "Yu yi" [First foreword]. In *Qingxiang mukeji: Canzhan zhi ji,* edited by Wang Yingxiao. Suzhou: Guomindang qingxiangqu dangwu banshichu, 1943.

Lu Yifeng. *Xinminhui yu xin guomin yundong* [The Xinminhui and the New Citizens Movement]. Nanjing: Zhongyang dianxunshe, 1944.

Luo Junqiang. "Weiting youying lu: Dui Wang wei zhengfu de huiyi jishi" [Secret records of the puppet government: My memoirs of the bogus Wang government]. In *Wei ting youying lu: Dui Wang wei zhengquan de huiyi* [A secret record of the puppet government: Memoirs of the bogus Wang regime], edited by Huang Meizhen, 1–66. Beijing: Dongfang chubanshe, 1986.

Ma Wu. "Bing ding si tong" [Pondering one's pain after being cured]. Cartoon. *Nanjing xinbao,* January 11, 1939.

Mabuchi Itsuo. *Hōdō sensen* [Reporting on the front]. Tokyo: Kaizōsha, 1941.

Mackie, Vera C. "Shanghai Dancers: Gender, Coloniality, and the Modern Girl." In *Shadowlines: Women and Borders in Contemporary Asia,* edited by D. Ghosh, 80–95. Newcastle, UK: Cambridge Scholars, 2012.

MacKinnon, Stephen R. "Conclusion: Wartime China." In *China at War: Regions of China, 1937–1945,* edited by Stephen R. MacKinnon, Diana Lary, and Ezra F. Vogel, 335–351. Stanford, CA: Stanford University Press, 2007.

———. *War, Refugees, and the Making of Modern China: Wuhan, 1938.* Berkeley: University of California Press, 2008.

Mark, Ethan. *Japan's Occupation of Java in the Second World War: A Transnational History.* London: Bloomsbury, 2018.

Martin, Brian G. "'In My Heart I Opposed Opium': Opium and the Politics of the Wang Jingwei Government, 1940–45." *European Journal of East Asian Studies* 2, no. 2 (2003): 365–410.

———. "Patriotic Collaboration? Zhou Fohai and the Wang Jingwei Government during the Second Sino-Japanese War." In *Japan as the Occupier and the Occupied,* edited by Christine de Matos and Mark E. Caprio, 152–171. London: Palgrave Macmillan, 2015.

———. "Shield of Collaboration: The Wang Jingwei Regime's Security Service, 1939–1945." *Intelligence and National Security* 16, no. 4 (2001): 89–148.

Mayo, Marlene J., J. Thomas Rimer, and E. Eleanor Kerkham, eds. *War, Occupation, and Creativity: Japan and East Asia, 1920–1960.* Honolulu: University of Hawai'i Press, 2001.

Ministry of Information (China). *Introducing China.* Sydney, 1944.

Ministry of Publicity. *Special Commemoration Issue: Return of the National Government of the Republic of China to Its Capital.* Nanjing: Ministry of Publicity, 1940.

Mirzoeff, Nicholas. "Introduction: For Critical Visuality Studies." In *The Visual Culture Reader,* edited by Nicholas Mirzoeff, xxix–xxxviii. London: Routledge, 2013.

———. "Invisible Empire: Visual Culture, Embodied Spectacle, and Abu Ghraib." *Radical History Review* 95 (Spring 2006): 21–44.

———. *Watching Babylon: The War in Iraq and Global Visual Culture.* London: Routledge, 2004.

Mitter, Rana. *China's War with Japan, 1937–45: The Struggle for Survival.* London: Allen Lane, 2013.

———. "Contention and Redemption: Ideologies of National Salvation in Republican China." *Totalitarian Movements and Political Religions* 3, no. 3 (2002): 44–74.

———. "The Visual Imaginary of the War of Resistance, 1937–1947." *European Journal of East Asian Studies* 7, no. 2 (2008): 167–192.

Mittler, Barbara. *A Continuous Revolution: Making Sense of Cultural Revolution Culture.* Cambridge, MA: Harvard University Press, 2013.

Mote, Frederick W. *Japanese-Sponsored Governments in China: An Annotated Bibliography Compiled from Materials in the Chinese Collection of the Hoover Library.* Stanford, CA: Stanford University Press, 1954.

Muel-Dreyfus, Francine. *Vichy and the Eternal Feminine: A Contribution to a Political Sociology of Gender.* Translated by Kathleen A. Johnson. Durham, NC: Duke University Press, 2001.

Müller, Marion G. "Iconography." In *The International Encyclopedia of Communication,* edited by Wolfgang Donsbach, 1–3. Malden, MA: Blackwell, 2008.

Mulready-Stone, Kristin. *CCP Internationalism, GMD Nationalism, and Japanese Collaboration.* London: Routledge, 2015.

Musgrove, Charles D. "Cheering the Traitor: The Post-war Trial of Chen Bijun, April 1946." *Twentieth-Century China* 30, no. 2 (2005): 3–27.

———. *China's Contested Capital: Architecture, Ritual, and Response in Nanjing.* Honolulu: University of Hawai'i Press, 2013.

———. "Monumentality in Nanjing's Sun Yat-sen Memorial Park." *Southeast Review of Chinese Studies* 29 (2007): 1–19.

Nagayama, Chikako. "Race as Technology and Blurred National Boundaries in Japanese Imperialism: *Nessa no chikai/Vow in the Desert.*" *Transnational Cinemas* 3 (2012): 211–230.

Naikaku Jōhōbu. *Senden jihō (Shina kankei)* [Propaganda times (China relations)]. March 10, 1940.

Nanhua ribaoshe, ed. *Nanhua Ribao gaikuang* [The current status of the *South China Daily News*]. Hong Kong: Nanhua ribaoshe, 1941.

Nanjing tebie shi zhengfu. *Shoudu zaolin yundong jinian kan* [Special commemorative issue on the capital forestry campaign]. Nanjing: Nanjing tebie shi zhengfu, 1941.

Nanjing xinbao. "Dong Ya yingxing jieshao" [Introducing East Asian stars]. February 18, 1940.

Narangoa, Li. "Japanese Imperialism and Mongolian Buddhism, 1932–1945." *Critical Asian Studies* 35, no. 4 (2003): 492–510.

Nedostup, Rebecca. *Superstitious Regimes: Religion and the Politics of Chinese Modernity.* Cambridge, MA: Harvard University Asia Center, 2009.

Nornes, Markus. *Japanese Documentary Film: The Meiji Era through Hiroshima.* Minneapolis: University of Minnesota Press, 2003.

North China Daily News. *Five Months of War.* Shanghai: North China Daily News and Herald, 1938.

Ōnuma Kikuo [Da zhao Xi jiu nan]. *Xinmin zhuyi zhi lilun ji qi zhankai* [The theory of the New People's ideology and its development]. Beijing: Da Dong Ya wenhua yuanjiuhui, 1944.

Ortiz, Valérie Malenfer. *Dreaming the Southern Song Landscape: The Power of Illusion in Chinese Painting.* Boston and Leiden: Brill, 1999.

Ōta Unosuke [Tai tian Yu zhi zhu]. "Ji Wang zhuxi anzang dianli" [On Chairman Wang's funeral]. *Zhengzhi yuekan* 8, no. 6 (1944): 15–16.

Pai, Andrew Shih-ming. "Modernity in Agony: Contemporaneity, Landscape, and the Representation of Modern Life in Colonial Taiwanese Art." *Southeast Review of Asian Studies* 33 (2011): 4–33.

Pan Min. *Jiangsu Ri-wei jiceng zhengquan yanjiu (1937–1945)* [A study of Japanese-bogus regime rule at the local level in Jiangsu (1937–1945)]. Shanghai: Shanghai renmin chubanshe, 2006.

Paul, Gerhard. "Visual History" (English version). *Docupedia-Zeitgeschichte,* July 11, 2011. http://docupedia.de/zg/paul_visual_history_v1_en_2011.

Pearson, Chris. *Scarred Landscapes: War and Nature in Vichy France.* London: Palgrave, 2008.

Pepper, Suzanne. "The Political Odyssey of an Intellectual Construct: Peasant Nationalism and the Study of China's Revolutionary History—a Review Essay." *Journal of Asian Studies* 63, no. 1 (2004): 105–125.

Perry, Elizabeth J. "Reclaiming the Chinese Revolution." *Journal of Asian Studies* 67, no. 4 (November 2008): 1147–1164.

Phillips, R. T. "The Japanese Occupation of Hainan." *Modern Asian Studies* 14, no. 1 (1980): 93–109.

Pin Mo. "Shuodao Nanjing: Yi qi baimen lao liu" [When one talks of Nanjing, one remembers the old willow outside the white gate]. *Huawen Daban meiri* 4, no. 1 (January 1940): 26–27.

Plamper, Jan. *The Stalin Cult: A Study in the Alchemy of Power.* New Haven, CT: Yale University Press, 2012.

Poon, Shuk-wah. *Negotiating Religion in Modern China: State and Common People in Guangzhou.* Hong Kong: Chinese University Press, 2011.

Prayer, Mario. "Nationalist India and World War II as Seen by the Italian Fascist Press, 1938–1944." *Indian Historical Review* 23, no. 2 (July 2006): 89–111.

Purdy, R. W. "The Creation of the *Nippon Newsreel* Company: Personal Rivalry and Profit in Wartime Japan." *Historical Journal of Film, Radio and Television* 36, no. 3 (2016): 252–372.

Qin Yi. "1937–1948 nian bankan zhong de Chen Yunshang" [Coverage of Nancy Chan in the press from 1937 to 1938]. *Xiju yu yingshi yishu yanjiu* (April 2016): 122–127.

Qiu Kunliang. "Funi yu kangdi: Wang Jingwei zhengquan de xijujie" [Associating with turncoats and attacking the enemy: Drama under the Wang Jingwei regime]. *Xiju yanjiu* 15 (January 2015): 117–148.

Raine, Michael. "'You Can't Replace *Gone with the Wind* with *Chūshingura*': *China Nights* and the Problem of Japanese Film Policy in Occupied Shanghai." *Film History* 30, no. 2 (Summer 2018): 164–198.

Ramaswamy, Sumathi. *The Goddess and the Nation: Mapping Mother India.* Durham, NC: Duke University Press, 2010.

Rees, E. A. "Leader Cults: Varieties, Preconditions and Functions." In *The Leader Cult in Communist Dictatorships: Stalin and the Eastern Bloc,* edited by Balázs Apor et al., 3–26. London: Palgrave Macmillan, 2004.

Rimer, J. Thomas. "Paris in Nanjing: Kishida Kunio Follows the Troops." In *War, Occupation, and Creativity: Japan and East Asia, 1920–1960,* edited by Marlene J. Mayo, J. Thomas Rimer, and E. Eleanor Kerkham, 176–187. Honolulu: University of Hawai'i Press, 2001.

Roberts, Claire. *Friendship in Art: Fou Lei and Huang Binhong.* Hong Kong: Hong Kong University Press, 2010.

———. *Photography and China.* Hong Kong: Hong Kong University Press, 2013.

Romagnoli, Stefano. "Gendering the War: The Colonial Gaze in Hino Ashihei's *Hana to heitai.*" *Rivista degli studi orientali* 90, no. 1–4 (2016): 141–162.

Rowe, David Nelson. "Japanese Propaganda in North China, 1937–1938." *Public Opinion Quarterly* 3, no. 4 (October 1939): 564–580.

Ruoff, Kenneth. "Japanese Tourism to Mukden, Nanjing, and Qufu, 1938–1943." *Japan Review* 27 (2014): 171–200.

Sandler, Mark H. "A Painter of the 'Holy War': Fujita Tsuguji and the Japanese Military." In *War, Occupation, and Creativity: Japan and East Asia, 1920–1960,* edited by Marlene J. Mayo, J. Thomas Rimer, and E. Eleanor Kerkham, 188–211. Honolulu: University of Hawai'i Press, 2001.

Schneider, Pablo. "Political Iconography and the Picture Act: The Execution of Charles I in 1649." In *Pictorial Cultures and Political Iconographies: Approaches, Perspectives, Case Studies from Europe and America,* edited by Udo J. Hebel and Christoph Wagner, 63–83. Berlin: De Gruyter, 2011.

Schoppa, R. Keith. *In a Sea of Bitterness: Refugees during the Sino-Japanese War.* Cambridge, MA: Harvard University Press, 2012.

Serfass, David. "Le dilemme de Nankin: Tergiversations autour de la reconnaissance du gouvernement de collaboration chinois (1940–1945)" [The Nanjing dilemma: Procrastinations over the recognition of the Chinese collaborationist government (1940–1945)]. *Vingtième siècle* 133 (January–March 2017): 99–111.

———. "Le gouvernement collaborateur de Wang Jingwei: Aspects de l'État d'occupation durant la guerre sino-japonaise, 1940–1945 [Wang Jingwei's collaborationist government: Aspects of the occupation state during the Sino-Japanese War, 1940–1945]. PhD diss., École des hautes études en sciences sociales, Paris, 2017.

———. "L'occupation japonaise comme objet pour l'histoire de l'État chinois: L'exemple de la campagne de pacification rurale du gouvernement de Wang Jingwei, 1941–45" [The Japanese occupation as an object for the history of the Chinese state: The example of the Rural Pacification campaigns of the Wang Jingwei government, 1941–45]. *Études chinoises* 35, no. 2 (2016): 123–137.

———. "Occupation japonaise et collaboration chinoise: Tendances historiographiques récentes" [The Japanese occupation and Chinese collaboration: Recent historiographical tendencies]. *Revue historique* 680 (April 2016): 941–966.

———. "Résister ou négocier face au Japon: La genèse du gouvernement de collaboration de Nankin (janvier 1938–avril 1939)" [Resistance against or negotiation with Japan: The origins of the Nanjing collaborationist government (January 1938–April 1939)]. *Vingtième siècle: Revue d'histoire* 125 (January–March 2015): 121–132.

Shanghai shi zhengfu mishuchu. *Guofu huandu zhounian jinian tekan* [Special commemorative issue marking the first anniversary of the return of the national government]. Shanghai: Shanghai shi zhengfu mishuchu, 1941.

Shao Hou, ed. *Wang Jingwei wenxuan* [Collected writings of Wang Jingwei]. Shanghai: Fanggu shuju, 1937.

Sharma, Nirmola. "Collaborators! Aftermath of Wartime Support for the INA among Indians in China." *China Report* 54, no. 3 (2018): 325–340.

Shen Enyang. "Kang-Ri zhanzheng shiqi de Aomen meishu" [Fine art in Macao during the War of Resistance]. *Nanjing yishu xueyan xuebao* (March 2009): 93–99.

Shepherdson-Scott, Kari. "A Legacy of Persuasion: Japanese Photography and the Artful Politics of Remembering Manchuria." *Journal of Decorative and Propaganda Arts* 27 (2015): 124–147.

———. "Race behind the Walls: Contact and Containment in Japanese Images of Urban Manchuria." In *The Affect of Difference: Representations of Race in East Asian Empires,* edited by Christopher Hanscom and Dennis Washburn, 180–206. Honolulu: University of Hawai'i Press, 2016.

Shi Li. "Qiqi jinian funü ying you zhi renshi" [How women should view the anniversary of July 7]. In *Qiqi Dong Ya minzu jiefang erzhou nian jinianji* [Commemorative collection marking the second anniversary of July 7, 1937, and the liberation of the Asian nations], edited by Daminhui, 54–57. Nanjing: Daminhui, 1939.

Shu, Seyuan, ed. *Poems of Wang Ching-wei.* London: George Allen and Unwin, 1938.

Smith, Norman. *Intoxicating Manchuria: Alcohol, Opium and Culture in China's Northeast.* Vancouver: UBC Press, 2012.

———. "Opiate Addiction and the Entanglements of Imperialism and Patriarchy in Manchukuo, 1932–45." *Social History of Alcohol and Drugs* 20 (2005): 66–104.

———. *Resisting Manchukuo: Chinese Women Writers and the Japanese Occupation.* Vancouver: UBC Press, 2007.

So, Wai Chor. "Race, Culture, and the Anglo-American Powers: The Views of Chinese Collaborators." *Modern China* 37, no. 1 (2001): 69–103.

Song Yuwu. "Meiguo guohui tushuguan cang Zhong-Ri zhanzheng (1937–1945) Zhongwen qikan wenxian" [Chinese-language periodicals and documents from the era of the Sino-Japanese War (1937–1945) held in the Library of Congress]. *Guoshiguan yanjiu tongxun* 13 (December 2017): 124–131.

Stengs, Irene. "The Commodification of King Chulalongkorn: His Portraits, Their Cultural Biographies, and the Enduring Aura of a Great King of Siam." In

Commodification: Things, Agency, and Identities, edited by Wim M. J. van Binsbergen and Peter L. Geschiere, 301–318. Münster: Lit Verlag, 2005.

Stephenson, Shelley. "A Star by Any Other Name: The (After) Lives of Li Xianglan." *Quarterly Review of Film and Radio* 19, no. 1 (2002): 1–13.

Sullivan, Michael. *Art and Artists of Twentieth-Century China.* Berkeley: California University Press, 1996.

Tai Shi Gong. "Tingshen fenqi heping jiuguo" [Lifting himself upright to save the nation through peace]. *Huawen Daban meiri* 3, no. 5 (September 1939): 4.

Tan Qixu. *Wang zhuxi fang Ri tekan* [Special supplement on Chairman Wang's visit to Japan]. Tokyo: Yuandong yuebaoshe, 1941.

T'ang Leang-li, ed. *China and Japan: Natural Friends—Unnatural Enemies; A Guide for China's Foreign Policy by Dr. Sun Yat-sen.* Shanghai: China United Press, 1941.

———. *Wang Ching-wei: A Political Biography.* Tianjin: China United Press, 1931.

Tang, Xiaobing. "Echoes of *Roar, China!* On Vision and Voice in Modern Chinese Art." *positions* 14, no. 2 (2006): 467–494.

Tao Kangde and Qiu Shimu. *Shenbao nianjian* [The *Shenbao* almanac]. Shanghai: Shenbaoshe, 1944.

Taylor, George E. *The Struggle for North China.* New York: Institute of Pacific Relations, 1940.

Taylor, Jeremy E. "The Bund: Littoral Space of Empire in the Treaty Ports of East Asia." *Social History* 27, no. 2 (2002): 125–142.

———. "Cartoons and Collaboration in Wartime China: The Mobilization of Chinese Cartoonists under Japanese Occupation." *Modern China* 41, no. 4 (2015): 406–435.

———. "Chinese Film Exhibition in Occupied Manila (1942–1945)." *Modern Asian Studies* 47, no. 5 (2013): 1588–1621.

———. "Discovering a Nationalist Heritage in Present-Day Taiwan." *China Heritage Quarterly* 17 (March 2009). http://www.chinaheritagequarterly.org/articles.php?searchterm=017_taiwan.inc&issue=017.

———. "From Traitor to Martyr: Drawing Lessons from the Death and Burial of Wang Jingwei, 1944." *Journal of Chinese History* 3, no. 1 (2019): 137–158.

———. "Gendered Archetypes of Wartime Occupation: 'New Women' in Occupied North China, 1937–40." *Gender and History* 28, no. 3 (2016): 660–686.

———. "The Production of the Chiang Kai-shek Personality Cult, 1929–1975." *China Quarterly* 185 (March 2006): 96–110.

———. "Republican Personality Cults in Wartime China: Contradistinction and Collaboration." *Comparative Studies in Society and History* 57, no. 3 (2015): 665–693.

———. "The Sinification of Soviet Agitational Theatre: 'Living Newspapers' in Mao's China." *Journal of the British Association of Chinese Studies* 2 (2013): 27–50.

Tong Bingxue. *Zhongguo zhaoxiangguan shi, 1859–1956* [A history of Chinese photographic studios, 1859–1956]. Hong Kong: Shangwu yinshuguan, 2017.

Treat, John Whittier. "Seoul and Nanking, Baghdad and Kabul: A Response to Timothy Brook and Michael Shin." *Journal of Asian Studies* 71, no. 1 (2012): 121–125.

Tsuruya, Mayu. "*Sensō Sakusen Kirokuga:* Seeing Japan's War Documentary Painting as a Public Monument." In *Since Meiji: Perspectives on the Japanese Visual Arts, 1868–2000,* edited by J. Thomas Rimer, 99–119. Honolulu: University of Hawai'i Press, 2011.

Tupitsyn, Margarita. *The Soviet Photograph, 1924–1937.* New Haven, CT: Yale University Press, 1996.

Tworek, Heidi. "Magic Connections: German News Agencies and Global News Networks, 1905–1945." *Enterprise and Society* 15, no. 4 (December 2014): 672–686.

Uchiyama Kanzō [Nei shan Wan zao]. "Muke zhi fuxing" [The renaissance of woodcuts]. *Zhongguo muke* 2 (January 1943): 1.

Wagner, Rudolf G. "Ritual, Architecture, Politics, and Publicity during the Republic: Enshrining Sun Yat-sen." In *Chinese Architecture and the Beaux-Arts,* edited by Jeffrey Cody, Nancy S. Steinhardt, and Tony Atkin, 223–278. Honolulu: University of Hawai'i Press, 2011.

Wakeman, Frederic, Jr. "'*Hanjian*' (Traitor)! Collaboration and Retribution in Wartime Shanghai." In *Becoming Chinese: Passages to Modernity and Beyond,* edited by Wen-hsin Yeh, 298–341. Berkeley: University of California Press, 2000.

———. "A Revisionist View of the Nanjing Decade: Confucian Fascism." *China Quarterly* 150 (June 1997): 395–432.

———. "The Struggle between Western and Chinese Medicine." In *China at War: Regions of China, 1937–1945,* edited by Stephen R. MacKinnon, Diana Lary, and Ezra F. Vogel, 265–287. Stanford, CA: Stanford University Press, 2007.

Wang, David Der-wei. *The Lyrical in Epic Time: Modern Chinese Intellectuals and Artists through the 1949 Crisis.* New York: Columbia University Press, 2015.

Wang, Grace. "The Color of Our Emotions, or *Se, jie.*" *RogerEbert.com* (blog). February 1, 2013. https://www.rogerebert.com/far-flung-correspondents/the-color-of-our-emotions-or-.

Wang Jingwei. "Wang zhuxi dui quanguo guangbo" [Chairman Wang broadcasts to the people of the nation]. *Changjiang huakan* 1 (February 1942).

———. *Zufu huandu yanlunji* [Collection of speeches on the return of the reorganized national government]. Guangzhou: Guomindang Guangdong sheng zhixing weiyuanhui, 1940.

Wang Kewen. "Wang Jingwei zuihou zhi xinqing" [Wang Jingwei's last sentiments]. *Dangdai* 155 (July 2000): 50.

Wang Ke-wen. "Irreversible Verdict? Historical Assessments of Wang Jingwei in the People's Republic and Taiwan." *Twentieth-Century China* 28, no. 1 (November 2002): 57–81.

———. "Wang Jingwei and the Policy Origins of the 'Peace Movement,' 1932–1937." In *Chinese Collaboration with Japan: The Limits of Accommodation,* edited by David P. Barrett and Larry N. Shyu, 21–37. Stanford, CA: Stanford University Press, 2001.

Wang Qingfang. "Muke jiangzuo" [Lectures on woodcuts]. *Huawen Daban meiri* 8, no. 5 (March 1942): 44–45.

Wang Yingxiao. "Fa kan ci" [Remarks on the publication of the journal]. *Zhongguo muke* 1 (December 1942).

———. "Yu er" [Second foreword]. In *Qingxiang mukeji: Canzhan zhi ji* [Rural Pacification woodcut collection: Declaration of war edition], edited by Wang Yingxiao. Suzhou: Guomindang qingxiangqu dangwu banshichu, 1943.

Wang Zhenghua. "Wanshan wanli qing: Jiashu zhong de zhanshi shenghuo" [Far apart but close at heart: Wartime life through private letters]. *Guoshiguan xueshu jikan* 17 (September 2008): 86–128.

Wang Zihe. "Ruhe tuijin xin guomin yundong" [How to promote the New Citizens Movement]. In *Ruhe tuijin xin guomin yundong* [How to promote the New Citizens Movement], edited by Minguo ribao she, 1–7. Nanjing: Minguo ribao she, 1942.

Ward, Jared. "Zhou Fohai: Nationalism of Collaboration." *Quarterly Journal of Chinese Studies* 2, no. 3 (2012): 35–47.

Warnke, Martin. *Political Landscape: The Art History of Nature*. London: Reaktion Books, 1994.

Wasserstrom, Jeffrey N., ed. *Oxford Illustrated History of Modern China*. Oxford: Oxford University Press, 2016.

———. *Student Protests in Twentieth-Century China: The View from Shanghai*. Stanford, CA: Stanford University Press, 1991.

Weber, Torsten. *Embracing "Asia" in China and Japan: Asianism Discourse and the Contest for Hegemony*. Basingstoke, UK: Palgrave Macmillan, 2018.

———. "Imagined Territoriality: Visual Portrayals of 'Asia' in the Age of Nationalism in East Asia." *Comparativ* 23 (2013): 37–56.

Wei Jianxin. "Qingxiangqu de huigu yu qianzhan" [A retrospective view of and the prospects for Rural Pacification areas]. *Huawen Daban meiri* 9, no. 3 (August 1942): 15–17.

Wei, Shuge. "News as a Weapon: Hollington Tong and the Formation of the Guomindang Centralized Foreign Propaganda System, 1937–1938." *Twentieth-Century China* 39, no. 2 (2014): 118–143.

Weiss, Ruth. *China's War Art Front*. Chungking: China Information Committee, 1940.

Weitz, Margaret Collins. "Art in the Service of Propaganda: The Poster War in France during World War II." *Religion and the Arts* 4, no. 1 (2000): 43–75.

Wen Shaohua. *Cong lieshi dao hanjian: Wang Jingwei zhuan* [From martyr to traitor: A biography of Wang Jingwei]. Hong Kong: Zhonghua shuju, 2013.

Wen Zongyao. "Daminhui Wen huizhang gao minzhong shu" [Letter from Director Wen of the Daminhui to the people]. *Xin Zhongguo* 2, no. 11–12 (December 1939): 2–3.

Winther-Tamaki, Bert. "Japanese Painting during the Fifteen-Year War." *Monumenta Nipponica* 52, no. 2 (Summer 1997): 145–180.

Wirth Brentini, Sophie. "Fan Tchunpi (1898–1986): Between East and West." In *The Pavilion of Marital Harmony: Chinese Painting and Calligraphy between Tradition and Modernity,* edited by Frank Dunand, 70. Geneva: Collections Baur, 2002.

Wu, T'ien-wei. "Contending Political Forces during the War of Resistance." In *China's Bitter Victory: The War with Japan, 1937–1945,* edited by James C. Hsiung and Steven I. Levine, 51–78. Armonk, NY: East Gate, 1992.

Wu Xuebin. "Xuerou zuocheng de changcheng: Yijiu sansan nian de xin tuxiang yu xin guannian" [A Great Wall of flesh and blood: The new imagery and new opinions of 1933]. *Wenyi yanjiu* 1 (2015): 134–143.

Wu Zhuoliu. *Nanjing zagan* [Nanjing sketches]. Taipei: Yuanxing, 1977.

Wuhan tebie shi zhengfu. *Wuhan tebie shi zhengfu zhounian jinian tekan* [Special commemorative issue marking the first anniversary of the Wuhan Special Municipality]. Wuhan: Wuhan tebie shi zhengfu, 1940.

Xia, Yun. *Down with Traitors: Justice and Nationalism in Wartime China.* Seattle: University of Washington Press, 2017.

Xiao Mi [Li Lihua]. "Xin Nanjing sumiao" [Descriptions of new Nanjing]. *Huawen Daban meiri* 6, no. 1 (January 1941): 30–31.

———. "Yingxing zai Nanjing" [Movie stars in Nanjing]. *Huawen Daban meiri* 8, no. 2 (June 1942): 34–35.

Xu Daren, ed. *Wang Jingwei ma Wang Zhaoming* [Wang Jingwei curses Wang Zhaoming]. Cunjinqiao: Lingnan chubanshe, 1939.

Xu Jinsheng. "Qin Hua Rijun de xuanchuan zhan: Yi Rijun di shiyi jun zhizhi xuanchuanpin wei zhongxin" [The Japanese propaganda war during the invasion of China: A study of Japan's Eleventh Army's printed propaganda materials]. *Minguo dang'an* (March 2017): 112–119.

Xu Xuehai. "Wang wei haijun jianli jingwei yu xiachang" [The complex process of the establishment of Wang's bogus navy and its aftermath]. *Zhuanji wenxue* 112, no. 6 (June 2018): 30–37.

Xuanchuanbu. *Guomin zhengfu zhi jinzhan* [The progress of the national government]. Nanjing: Xuanchuanbu, 1941.

———. *Wang zhuxi heping jianguo yanlunji* [Collection of Chairman Wang's speeches on peace and nation building]. Nanjing: Xuanchuanbu, 1941.

———, ed. *Xuanchuanbu diyi jie quanguo xuanchuan huiyi shilu* [Record of the first national publicity conference of the Ministry of Publicity]. Nanjing: Xuanchuanbu, 1941.

Xue Huizi. *E Gan shidi shichaji* [A field survey of Hubei and Jiangxi]. With photographs by Xue Diwei. Nanjing: Zhongyang dianxunshe, 1940.

———. *Jinri zhi Huabei* [North China today]. With photographs by He Zhang. Nanjing: Zhongyang dianxunshe, 1940.

———. "Shinian ai le" [Ten years of sorrow and joy]. *Taiping zhoubao* 1, no. 55 (1943): 1074–1076.

Xue Huizi and Xue Feng. *Women de lingxiu, Wang zhuxi* [Our leader, Chairman Wang]. Nanjing: Nanjing tebie shi zhengfu xuanchuanchu, 1942.

Yan Keding. "Xuanchuan fangfa lun (shang)" [On the theory of propaganda, part 1]. *Zhongyang daobao zhoukan* 1, no. 46 (June 15, 1941): 3–6.

Yang, Zhiyi. "The Road to Lyric Martyrdom: Reading the Poetry of Wang Zhaoming (1883–1944)." *Chinese Literature* 37 (2015): 135–164.

Yeh, Wen-hsin. "Prologue: Shanghai Besieged, 1937–45." In *Wartime Shanghai,* edited by Wen-hsin Yeh, 1–17. London: Routledge, 2004.

Yen, Hsiao-pei. "Body Politics, Modernity and National Salvation: The Modern Girl and the New Life Movement." *Asian Studies Review* 29, no. 2 (2005): 165–186.

Yi Junzuo. *Shengli yu huandu* [Victory and return to the capital]. Taipei: Sanmin shuju, 1970.

Yick, Joseph K. S. "Communist-Puppet Collaboration in Japanese-Occupied China: Pan Hannian and Li Shiqun, 1939–43." *Intelligence and National Security* 16, no. 4 (2001): 61–88.

———. " 'Pre-Collaboration': The Political Activity and Influence of Chen Bijun in Wartime China, January 1938–May 1940." *Southeast Review of Asian Studies* 36 (2014): 58–74.

Yiengpruksawan, Mimi Hall. "Japanese War Paint: Kawabata Ryūshi and the Emptying of the Modern." *Archives of Asian Art* 46 (1993): 76–90.

Yin Jian. "Chen Yunshang: Heping de zhen qin" [Nancy Chan: Chaste bird of peace]. *Funü shijie* 1, no. 1 (April 1940): 13.

Yong Zhou, Vincent K. L. Chang, and Xiaohui Gong. "Recalling the War in China: The *Dahoufang* Project in Chongqing and the Restoration of a Legacy." *Frontiers of History in China* 9, no. 4 (December 2014): 611–627.

Young, Louise. *Japan's Total Empire: Manchuria and the Culture of Wartime Imperialism.* Berkeley: University of California Press, 1998.

———. "When Fascism Met Empire in Japanese-Occupied Manchuria." *Journal of Global History* 12 (2017): 274–296.

Yu Zidao, Liu Qikui, and Cao Zhenwei, eds. *Wang wei zhengquan ziliao xuanbian: Wang Jingwei guomin zhengfu "qingxiang" yundong* [Selected materials from the bogus Wang regime: The Wang national government's "Rural Pacification" campaign] (Shanghai: Xinhua shuju, 1985).

Zanasi, Margherita. "Globalizing *Hanjian:* The Suzhou Trials and the Post–World War II Discourse on Collaboration." *American Historical Review* 113, no. 3 (2008): 731–751.

———. *Saving the Nation: Economic Modernity in Republican China.* Chicago: Chicago University Press, 2006.

Zhang Dianxing. *Wang Jingwei funi yanjiu* [Research on the traitor Wang Jingwei]. Beijing: Renmin chubanshe, 2008.

Zhang Jiangcai. *Wang Jingwei xiansheng gengxu mengnan shi lu* [The true record of Mr. Wang Jingwei's tribulations in 1910]. Nanjing, 1940.

———. *Wang Jingwei xiansheng xingshilu* [A true record of Mr. Wang Jingwei's activities]. Dongguan: Baiyuantang, 1943.

Zhang Renli, ed. *Wuhan tebie shi zhengfu zhounian jinian sheying ce* [Collection of commemorative photographs marking the first anniversary of the Wuhan Municipal Government's founding]. Wuhan: Wuhan tebie shi zhengfu, 1941.

Zhang Shaofu. "Wo suo zhidao de Wang wei haijun" [The bogus Wang navy that I knew]. In *Wei ting youying lu: Dui Wang wei zhengquan de huiyi* [A secret record of the puppet government: Memoirs of the bogus Wang regime], edited by Huang Meizhen, 186–230. Beijing: Dongfang chubanshe, 1986.

Zhang, Shaoqian. "Combat and Collaboration: The Clash of Propaganda Prints between the Chinese Guomindang and the Japanese Empire in the 1930s–1940s." *Transcultural Studies* 1 (January 2014): 95–133.

Zhang Sheng. "Lun Wang wei dui Guomindang zhengzhi fuhao de zhengduo" [On the RNG's struggle over Kuomintang political symbols]. *Kang-Ri zhanzheng yanjiu* 2 (2005): 1–33.

Zhang Tongle. *Huabei lunxianqu Ri-wei zhengquan yanjiu* [A study of the Japanese-bogus regime in occupied north China]. Shanghai: Sanlian shudian, 2012.

Zhang Xianwen. *Zhonghua minguo shi (disan juan): Riben quanmian qin Hua* [A history of the Republic of China, volume 3: The complete invasion of China by Japan]. Nanjing: Nanjing daxue chubanshe, 2006.

Zhang Yan. *Nanjing minguo jianzhu yishu* [Republican architectural art in Nanjing]. Nanjing: Jiangsu kexue jishu chubanshe, 2000.

Zhang Ziping. "Xin hong A zi" [New red A train]. *Huawen Daban meiri* 7, no. 5 (September 1941): 19–23.

Zhao Mengyun [Chou Muun]. "Katō Minosuke to senji Shanhai Tairiku shinpō jidai no manga, man hanashi o chūshin ni" [Katō Minosuke's wartime Shanghai: Desultory narratives and sociopolitical cartoons from the *Tairiku shinpō*]. *Chūgoku bunka kenkyū* 25 (2009): 21–46.

Zheng Chuangu. *Zhanshi tuhua shouce* [Handbook of wartime pictures]. Chongqing: Shanghai zazhi gongsi, 1942.

Zhengzhi gongzuotuan. *Zhenggong baogaoshu* [Report on political work]. Shanghai: Jiangsu sheng Zhenjiang qingxiang diqu zhengzhi gongzuotuan, 1943.

Zhong bao. "Nuhou ba Zhongguo!" [Roar, China!]. January 17, 1943.

———. "Qingzhu guomin zhengfu huandu tekan" [Special edition to commemorate the return of the national government]. March 30, 1940.

———. "Wang zhuxi fang Ri zuo fan jing" [Chairman Wang returned to Nanjing yesterday after a visit to Japan]. September 24, 1943.

———. "Xuangua guoqi ying zhuyi gedian" [Take note of the following points when flying the national flag]. March 31, 1940.

———. "Yi dai weiren de anzangdi: Meihuashan" [The resting place of a great man of our age: Meihuashan]. November 24, 1944.

Zhongguo geming bowuguan. *Kang-Ri zhanzheng shiqi xuanchuanhua* [Propaganda images from the period of the War of Resistance]. Beijing: Wenwu chubanshe, 1990.

Zhongguo Guomindang Jin-Pu tielu tebie dangbu, ed. *Er zhounian huandu tekan* [Special issue commemorating the second anniversary of the return to the capital]. Nanjing: Zhongguo Guomindang Jin-Pu tielu tebie dangbu, 1942.

Zhongguo tongxinshe. *Shin Chūgoku no keizai dōkō* [Economic trends in new China]. Tokyo: Zhongguo tongxinshe Dongjing shiju, 1943.

Zhonghua manhua xiehui. "Huandu san zhounian shoudu fengguang: Zhongshan ling xiexiang ji" [The scenery of the capital on the third anniversary of the *huandu:* A sketch record of the Sun Mausoleum]. *Zhongguo manhua* 6 (May 1943): 14.

Zhonghua ribao. *Guomin zhengfu huandu huashi* [A pictorial history of the national government's return]. Shanghai: Zhonghua ribaoshe, 1942.

Zhonghua ribao. *Shanhe posui yi Daizong* [The ruined rivers and mountains recall Mount Tai]. July 13, 1939, 4.

Zhong-Ri wenhua xiehui. *Zhong-Ri wenhua xiehui Wuhan fenhui erzhounian jinian tekan* [Special commemorative edition celebrating the second anniversary of the founding of the Wuhan chapter of the Sino-Japanese Cultural Association]. Wuhan: Zhong-Ri wenhua xiehui, 1943.

Zhongyang dang'anguan and Zhongguo di'er lishi dang'anguan. *Ri-Wang de qingxiang* [Japan and the Wang government's Rural Pacification campaign]. Beijing: Xinhua shudian, 1995.

Zhongyang dianxunshe. *Guofu huandu hou de zhengzhi qingshi* [Political trends since the return of the national government]. Nanjing: Zhongyang dianxunshe, 1941.

———. *Qingnian xunlian yu xiuyang* [The training and fostering of youth]. Nanjing: Zhongyang dianxunshe, 1942.

———. *Shishi tongxun: Jing'ai Wang zhuxi* [Topical communications: Mourning Chairman Wang]. Nanjing: Zhongyang dianxunshe, 1944.

———. *Shishi tongxun: Zhongguo funü wenti* [Topical communications: The question of Chinese women]. Nanjing: Zhongyang dianxunshe, 1945.

———, ed. *Zhongguo canzhan yi lai dashi xiezhen zhuanji* [An album of photographs of major events in China since the declaration of war on the Allies]. Nanjing: Zhongyang dianxunshe, 1944.

———. *Zhongyang dianxunshe disan nian* [The third year of the Central News Agency]. Nanjing: Zhongyang dianxunshe, 1943.

Zhou Aimin. *Yan'an muke yishu yanjiu* [A study of Yan'an woodcut art]. Shijiazhuang: Hebei jiaoyu chubanshe, 2009.

Zhou Anqing. "Wang Jingwei shi zenyang guizang Nanjing Meihuashan de" [How Wang Jingwei was buried on Plum Blossom Mount]. *Dongfang shoucang* 1 (2012): 116–118.

Zhou Yuren. *Nuhou ba Zhongguo* [Roar, China!]. Script. Nanjing: Nanjing juyishe, 1943.

Zhu Jiayu. "Dai wu zi de Suzhou lao baozhi" [The old newspapers of Suzhou that carried the character "wu" in their titles]. *Zhongguo difangzhi* 8 (2007): 43–45.

Zhu, Pingchao. *Wartime Culture in Guilin, 1938–1944: A City at War.* Lanham, MD: Lexington Books, 2015.

Zhu Shuirong. "Gu wei jin yong: *Jin ping mei* quantu lianhuanhua quanban" [Using the past for present purposes: The complete publication of the comic version of the *Golden Lotus*]. *Meishu zhi you* 1 (2003): 27.

Zhu Yayun. "Nanking: Chronology." *China Heritage Annual 2017.* http://chinaheritage.net/annual/2017/chronology/?lang=zh.

Zhu Zijia [Jin Xiongbai]. *Wang zhengquan de kaichang yu shouchang shang* [The beginning and end of the Wang regime, part 1]. Taipei: Fengyun shidai, 2012.

Zuigao guofang huiyi [Supreme Council for National Defense]. "Zhanshi wenhua xuanchuan zhengce jiben gangyao" [Basic outline on policy for wartime culture and propaganda]. In *Wang wei zhengquan ziliao xuanbian: Wang Jingwei guomin zhengfu "qingxiang" yundong* [Selected materials from the bogus Wang regime: The Wang national government's "Rural Pacification" campaign], edited by Yu Zidao, Liu Qikui, and Cao Zhenwei, 392–398. Shanghai: Xinhua shuju, 1985.

Index

About the Author

Jeremy E. Taylor is associate professor in modern Asian history at the University of Nottingham. He is the author of *Rethinking Transnational Chinese Cinemas: The Amoy-Dialect Film Industry in Cold War Asia* (2011) and is the founder of a number of digital humanities initiatives, including the "Enemy of the People" Database (https://www.dhi.ac.uk/chiangkaishek/) and the COTCA Digital Archive (www.cotca.org). He has published articles in *Gender and History, Comparative Studies in Society and History,* and the *Journal of Asian Studies,* as well as various other articles on a range of topics relating to the modern cultural history of the Chinese-speaking world.